$4.95x

# ECONOMIC INSTABILITY
# AND GROWTH

# ECONOMIC INSTABILITY AND GROWTH:
## THE AMERICAN RECORD

**Robert Aaron Gordon**
University of California, Berkeley

**Harper & Row, Publishers**
New York   Evanston   San Francisco   London

To Peg and Bob and Dave

Sponsoring Editor: John Greenman
Project Editor: William B. Monroe
Production Supervisor: Robert A. Pirrung

ECONOMIC INSTABILITY AND GROWTH: The American Record

Library of Congress Cataloging in Publication Data

Gordon, Robert Aaron.
  Economic instability and growth.

  1. United States—Economic conditions.
2. United States—Economic policy. I. Title
HC106.G655      330.9'73      73-10196
ISBN 0-06-042408-7

# Contents

## 7. Retrospect and Prospect                                          195

A Look at the Record—The Changed Role of Government—
Evolution of the Macroeconomic Goals—The Instruments of
Policy—A Final Comment

# Preface

I hope this book will serve several purposes. First of all, it is intended to stand on its own feet as a historical survey of the dynamic behavior of the American economy since World War I and of the evolution of macroeconomic policy in the United States. As such, I trust that it will be useful to economists generally. The book is also intended as a possible supplementary text in courses dealing with macroeconomic theory and policy. Too often such courses are taught in a historical vacuum, with perhaps a few casual references to very recent experience. And finally, courses in American economic history may find useful material here on the evolution of the American economy during the twentieth century.

Chapters 2–5 represent a revision and updating of the historical chapters in the second edition of my *Business Fluctuations*. Chapter 5 has been extended through the 1960–1961 downswing, and more important, new material on the evolution of macroeconomic policy has been added to all of these earlier chapters. Chapter 6 is entirely new, carrying the story through the 1960s and into the opening months of President Nixon's second term. Not surprisingly, the relative space devoted to policy developments in this chapter is greater than in those covering the earlier decades. Chapter 1 is almost entirely new, and the concluding chapter was written after President Nixon began his second term.

My debts to those who have helped in the preparation of this volume are numerous. Chapter 1 owes a great deal to Robert J. Gordon, who also was good enough to read and comment on Chapter 6. Arthur Okun read and offered suggestions for the improvement of Chapter 6. Throughout the preparation of this volume, I leaned heavily on the staff of the Institute of Industrial Relations at Berkeley. The Institute's librarian, Gwendolyn Lloyd, could be counted on to find the sources of information that I needed and to uncover new sources of which I was previously unaware. Barbara Porter patiently typed the various drafts of the manuscript with speed and accuracy. And Dennis Roth was the perfect research assistant, helping me in more ways than I can list here to prepare the manuscript and to see it through the press.

Finally, I want to express my continued debt to my wife, who encouraged me to write this book, read and criticized large parts of the manuscript, and otherwise shared with me her excellent judgment and critical faculties.

R. A. Gordon

# The Overall Record

American economic history records a gratifying story of technological progress, rapid increases in productive capacity, and a rising standard of living that has long been the envy of other peoples. Table 1.1 compares the rate of American economic growth with that of a number of other industrial nations over the last century and during the more recent past. Since 1870 the growth of output in the United States has, on the average, been more rapid than in any of the other countries listed except Japan—and of course Japan began in 1870 with a far lower level of output per capita than did the United States.

## THE KINDS OF ECONOMIC CHANGE

This is the record if we look at the past century as a whole. But even apart from the ups and downs of the business cycle, growth does not proceed evenly at an ever-constant rate. This is dramatically illustrated by a comparison of the two columns in Table 1.1. For Japan and all of the European countries listed, economic growth during 1955–1970 was *much* more rapid than over the century as a whole. Indeed, one of the most striking aspects of recent economic history is the acceleration of economic growth in Western Europe and Japan after World War II.

But this has not been true of the United States. During the decade-and-a-half ending in 1970, the total output of the American economy grew no faster than it has during the last century as a whole. (The figure of 3.4 percent shown in the second column of Table 1.1 for the United States gives a slightly misleading impression because 1970 was a recession year in which real gross national product actually declined a bit. The average growth rate for 1955–1969 was 3.7 percent.) As we shall see later on, a pronounced retardation in growth occurred in the United States in the second half of the 1950s and the early 1960s. While the expansion of output accelerated again during 1964–1968 in response first to federal tax reductions and then to expanded military expenditures during the Vietnam buildup, retardation in growth set in again at the end of the 1960s as the economy first began to press

**Table 1.1**  Annual Rates of Growth of Total Output, Selected Countries, 1870–1970 (Countries ranked by growth rate during 1870–1964)

|  | 1870–1964 | 1955–1970 |
|---|---|---|
| Japan | 3.8%[a] | 10.3% |
| United States | 3.7[b] | 3.4 |
| Canada | 3.5 | 4.8 |
| Germany | 2.8 | 5.8 |
| Italy | 2.0 | 5.7[c] |
| United Kingdom | 1.9 | 2.8 |
| France | 1.7 | 5.6 |

[a]Initial year is 1879.

[b]Initial year is 1871.

[c]Period is 1958–1970.

Sources: Data for 1870–1964 are from U.S. Department of Commerce, *Long Term Economic Growth*, 1860–1965 (Washington, D.C., GPO, 1966), pp. 101, 248, 251; figures for 1955–1970 are from Federal Reserve Bank of St. Louis, *Rates of Change in Economic Data for Ten Industrial Countries*, August, 1971.

against a capacity ceiling and then moved into the business recession of 1969–1970.

The notion of economic progress implies a persistent and significant increase in the output of goods and services—and particularly in output per capita—although this growth may occur at average rates that vary from decade to decade. But growth is not the only kind of economic change that we have experienced. In fact, the economic progress enjoyed by the Western world over the last two centuries or so—and this is true particularly for the United States—has involved not only long-term growth but also short-term instability. Progress has come in fits and starts, and periods of rapid growth and increasing prosperity have alternated with periods of declining output, rising unemployment, falling profits, and general economic distress.

These ups and downs in economic activity—these booms and depressions (or recessions)—are what we call business cycles. Since 1914, in a little over two generations, the United States has experienced the catastrophic depression of the 1930s, the great inflationary booms of the two world wars, and most recently the boom and inflation set off by the Vietnam war. There have been other disturbances as well—the violent deflation of 1920–1921, the sharp recession of 1937–1938, and mild but still disturbing recessions during the 1920s and in the years since Warld War II, most recently in 1969–1970. Thus the

American economy has been characterized by both *growth* (more rapid during some decades than others) and *instability;* on the whole, this has been true of other industrialized nations also.

As we are all too aware, this instability extends to the prices of the things we buy. The great increase in prices since the 1930s is one of the outstanding characteristics of recent economic history, not only in the United States but in every country. Prices tend to show the same kind of short-run fluctuations as business generally, but they have also moved through longer periods of rise and fall. Today's college students have lived their entire lives during a period of secularly (i.e., long-run) rising prices, and the belief is widely held that "creeping inflation" (which sometimes breaks into a gallop) has become a permanent ingredient of American economic life. If anything, this belief is held even more strongly in other countries. It is generally assumed that in the foreseeable future we shall not experience protracted declines in prices such as occurred in the closing decades of the nineteenth century or again between 1920 and 1933. Indeed, a major concern today is to hold inflation within tolerable bounds.

## THE GOAL OF FULL EMPLOYMENT

Most of us have short memories, and the inflationary years since Pearl Harbor have helped blur our impression of the 1930s. In mid-1929, there was little unemployment in the United States; production was setting new records; business generally was prosperous; the stock market was booming. Three years later, a quarter or more of our working force could not find jobs, and a substantial number of those employed were working part time; industrial production had fallen by more than 50 percent; the national income had been cut in half; thousands of farm mortgages were being foreclosed; and our banking system was on the brink of complete collapse. The depression was worldwide, and the tensions it created helped bring on the catastrophe of World War II.

It was a shock to all Americans that our recovery after the low point of the Great Depression of the 1930s seemed so weak. Even at the peak of the boom, in 1937, there were still seven or eight million men and women who could not find jobs. When Hitler marched his armies into Poland in 1939, there were still some nine million unemployed in the United States. It was not until after Pearl Harbor, when the productive machine was straining to meet the insatiable demands of total war, that the American economy was again able to provide jobs for all who wanted work.

World War II brought not only full employment but also the firm resolve, both in the United States and abroad, that the human suffering and waste of resources of another Great Depression must be avoided at all costs. It was agreed that we must never again have a Great Depression and that even less overwhelming catastrophies can and must be avoided. Virtually all governments in the world have now put the maintenance of a high and stable level of employment close to the top of their list of domestic objectives. The American Employment Act of 1946 stated that "it is the continuing policy and responsibility of the Federal Government to use all practical means. . .to promote maximum employment, production, and purchasing power." Similiarly, under the United Nations Charter the subscribing governments pledged themselves to take action to promote "higher standards of living, full employment, and conditions of economic and social progress and development."[1]

## THE CONCEPT OF POTENTIAL OUTPUT

As a means of promoting "maximum employment, production, and purchasing power," the Employment Act of 1946 requires that the President submit to Congress each year an *Economic Report* that, among other things, states ". . . the levels of employment, production, and purchasing power obtaining in the United States and such levels needed to carry out the policy" of the Act. In different words, the President was requested to estimate each year the *potential output* of the American economy—what it is capable of producing at maximum or full employment. Then a comparison of the *actual* performance of the economy with its *potential* will indicate the direction and magnitude of the policy measures required to achieve the objective of the Employment Act.[2]

This concept of potential output is an important one, and with it we can conveniently describe our most important domestic macroeconomic goals. These are *rapid growth, full employment,* and *price stability.* Before doing so, however, we should take a moment to elaborate on the notion of potential output, a concept that we shall encounter again in this and subsequent chapters.

[1] Articles 55 and 56 of the United Nations Charter.
[2] Actually, only since the beginning of the Kennedy administration have formal estimates of potential output and of the "full-employment gap" been regularly presented. See *Economic Report of the President,* January, 1962, pp. 49–53; January, 1963, pp. 26–28. Estimates of potential GNP and of the "gap" are now presented on a quarterly basis in *Business Conditions Digest,* published monthly by the U.S. Department of Commerce. See, for example, Figure 6.3, p. 148.

There is no single number that precisely defines a nation's potential output at any given time. What we consider the potential output of the economy may vary over a considerable range, depending on the portion of the population that chooses to be in the labor force, the minimum unemployment rate that we take to correspond to full employment, the average number of hours worked per week, and the productivity per man-hour of the labor force. If, as in wartime, the total demand for goods is at such a high level that unemployment is forced down to abnormally low rates—if, in short, aggregate demand considerably exceeds potential output at the existing price level—prices and wages will be bid up relatively rapidly (in the absence of wage and price controls) and an inflationary situation will exist. If, on the other hand, aggregate demand is below the level of potential output at existing levels of wages and prices, we have a situation of excessive unemployment, and we say that the economy is operating below the level of full employment. Our definition of potential output—which, of course, increases with a growing labor force and rising productivity—represents a compromise between, on the one hand, too intensive a use of resources, so that an unacceptable degree of inflation results, P. O. and on the other, too low a rate of resource use, so that we have excessive unemployment. The compromise adopted by the President's Council of Economic Advisers in recent years has been to define potential output as the level of output that the nation can produce when the unemployment rate is about 4 percent.

## THE GOALS OF MACROECONOMIC POLICY

What determines the rate of growth of potential output? What causes the level of actual output and the level of prices to behave as they do in fact, with the resulting record of economic instability? What can be done to stimulate growth and to make the economy more stable? These are the kinds of questions with which the field of macroeconomics is concerned. It analyzes the behavior of the economy in its "macro" aspects—as such behavior is reflected in total income and spending, total output, the levels of employment and unemployment, and the general level of prices—and it considers how society can more effectively achieve the three chief goals of macroeconomic policy—rapid growth, full employment, and price stability—to which we need to add maintaining equilibrium in our balance of international payments.

As the historical material in the chapters that follow makes clear, we have not always pursued all of these macroeconomic goals. Indeed, not until after the Great Depression had brought the economy to a state of near paralysis did maintaining employment become a deliberate government policy, and the embodiment of the full-employment goal in legislation did not come until 1946. Rapid economic growth did not become a conscious goal of policy until after World War II, and then it was adopted as a goal sooner and much more strongly in most of the countries of Western Europe than in the United States. In the 1920s, it is not much of an exaggeration to say, the goals of American macroeconomic policy (insofar as there was a conscious policy) were balance-of-payments equilibrium and prevention of inflation—and keeping the role of the federal government in economic affairs at a minimum.

The purpose of the chapters that follow is to trace the evolution of these policy goals in the United States during the last half-century and, in particular, to see how well or (all too frequently) how poorly we have achieved them. But before turning to the detailed record, let us look at these policy targets in a little more detail.

1. *Rapid growth*   We rely on a rising trend in total production not only to feed, clothe, and house a growing population but also to provide an ever-expanding standard of living for everyone. This means not only growth in *total* output but also in output *per capita*. The standard of living that today's college students will enjoy in their later lives will depend on the rate of increase in per capita income (in constant prices). Thus per capita disposable income in the United States in 1972 was about $3,800 per year.[3] In the year 2000, when today's college students will be middle-aged, this figure will be about $5,000 if real per capita disposable income rises at an annual rate of 1 percent; it will be about $6,600 if per capita income increases at an annual rate of 2 percent. After allowing for price changes, the rise in real per capita disposable income between 1929 and 1972 occurred at a rate of about 1.9 percent per year. The rate of growth of output (and income) in the United States will not only determine the standard of private consumption of the nation's population but also set a limit on the resources available to assist newly developing nations, to carry the burden of military expenditures, and to finance the ever-growing need for better education, medical care, adequate urban transportation, recreation facilities, and other public services.

Achieving a given rate of growth involves a twofold challenge: ensuring first that *potential* output grows at the desired rate and second that *actual* output is maintained at the level of potential output. If actual output is not equal to potential output, employment is below

---

3 *Economic Report of the President,* January, 1973, p. 213. Disposable income is personal income after taxes.

the desired level, and unemployment exceeds the necessary minimum. This has all too often been the case in the United States, most recently in the early years of the 1970s.

2. *Full employment* A rapidly growing potential output will provide neither goods nor jobs if there is not a demand for that output. In an economy operating below its potential, there are not enough jobs for all who want to work. Unemployment is an evil not only because it deprives men and women of the opportunity to earn an income but also because it forces them against their will to be idle. In the United States unemployment bears most heavily on the less privileged—blacks, other minority groups, teenagers out of school, and unskilled people in general. Inadequate aggregate demand also limits freedom of choice and the efficient allocation of labor by restricting the opportunities that workers have to change jobs. And by creating the fear of unemployment, the fact or threat of slack demand leads many labor unions to resist technological progress.

As we have already noted, the United States and other economically advanced countries emerged from World War II committed to the goal of full employment. Some have been more successful than others in adhering to that goal. (The United States has not been one of the more successful in this respect.) But protracted periods of low unemployment have brought with them a steadily rising price level, and creeping inflation has become a steady source of concern on both sides of the Atlantic (and of the Pacific also).

3. *Price stability* A more or less stable price level is to be desired for a number of reasons. Rising prices reduce the real income of pensioners and others on fixed incomes, and penalizes savers whose funds are in bonds and savings accounts. If prices rise too rapidly, speculative excesses may eventually cause a boom to collapse and, if the rise in prices continues to accelerate, loss of confidence in the currency may result. A problem that many countries have had to face in recent years is that of a price level at home that rises faster than the price levels of other countries. This situation can help bring on a crisis in a nation's international balance of payments. For all these reasons price stability is an important goal of economic policy. The conflict between this goal and the inflationary pressure unleashed by the Vietnam war eventually led the Nixon Administration to impose direct wage and price controls in 1971.

4. *Balance-of-payments equilibrium* In our interdependent world, each country makes payments to other countries (for its imports of goods and services, to pay interest and dividends to foreign investors, to finance foreign aid and to invest in other countries, and so on).

It receives payments from other countries in exchange for its exports and in the form of interest and dividends from its investments abroad and from new investments made by foreigners in the country in question. Receipts from foreigners represent a demand for a country's currency—say, the dollar; payments made to other countries by the United States represent a supply of dollars and simultaneously a demand for foreign currencies. This demand and supply come together in foreign-exchange markets and, if those markets operate freely, determine the value of each country's currency with respect to that of every other country.

Nearly every country desires to keep the value of its currency fixed in terms of other currencies. Thus most countries have a "parity" for their currencies; they seek to maintain the quoted value within a narrow range around this fixed value. This requires that the demand for and supply of the country's currency be approximately in balance, or that there be an equilibrium in the country's balance of payments at the parity value. If there is not—if, say, the country has a deficit in its balance of payments and its demand for foreign currencies exceeds the supply available from the payments it receives from other countries—it must make up the discrepancy by selling gold or any stock of foreign currencies it might have on hand, by borrowing foreign currencies, or by inducing foreign governments and central banks to hold off the market the excess supply of the deficit country's currency.

This, in fact, has been the situation of the United States in recent years. Our balance of payments has been continuously in deficit, and the deficit has been worsening. The climax came in August, 1971, when the American government gave up trying to support the dollar and allowed it to depreciate in foreign-exchange markets, which meant that the values of other currencies appreciated. A new set of parities between the dollar and other currencies was fixed in December, 1971; however, this did not last very long. The dollar was devalued again in February, 1973, and it depreciated further in the months following. Thus it is clear that the United States had failed to achieve this particular macroeconomic goal in the early 1970s.

## A BRIEF PREVIEW OF THE RECORD

Leaving aside the balance-of-payments problem, the American economy has thus far not been able simultaneously and continuously to achieve rapid growth, full employment, and price stability. Figure 1.1 shows several aspects of the American performance during the twentieth century. The instability of actual output stands out in the series in the upper part, which compares the record of actual output with estimates of potential output. During the years of World War II, when overtime was common and equipment was operated around the clock, the actual output of the economy significantly exceeded the normal peacetime potential. Indeed, during 1943–1945 unemployment averaged less than 2 percent compared to the 4 percent rate that is most often taken to correspond to full employment. Output also exceeded potential in World War I and, to a modest degree, during the Vietnam boom of 1966–1969.

But for much of the period since 1909 the actual output of the American economy has fallen significantly below potential output, resulting in a gap of wasted resources. The gap was most severe during the 1930s, but substantial gaps also occurred at the time of the severe deflation of 1921, during 1957–1965, and again during 1970–1972. The gap between actual and potential output between 1957 and 1965 represents about $300 billion of lost output (in 1971 prices) that we could have produced with the available resources. This enormous sum is equal to almost one-third of the entire GNP in 1971. A further significant loss was suffered during 1970–1972.

The series at the bottom of Figure 1.1 shows the percentage of the civilian labor force unemployed in each year. By comparing the top and bottom series, we can see that the fluctuations in unemployment correspond to fluctuations in the gap between potential and actual output. The unemployment rate is highest during the years of greatest relative deficiency in actual output. The succession of very high unemployment rates from 1930 to 1941 is a dramatic reminder of the human suffering caused by the gap between actual and potential output during the Great Depression and inadequate recovery of the 1930s. Other periods of substantial unemployment were the years immediately before and after World War I, the period after 1957, and again beginning in 1970. The employment-creating power of World War II is shown by the steep reduction in the unemployment rate from 14.6 percent in 1940 to 1.2 percent in 1944. Less dramatically, the chart also brings out the significant decline in unemployment during the 1960s.

The middle series of Figure 1.1 traces the changing trends in the Consumer Price Index. Obviously, the goal of price stability has been met only rarely during the period covered. Prices rose most rapidly in the World War I period (1916–1920) and during the early years of World War II and the several years after, demonstrating the inflationary pressures of wartime and immediate postwar demand. (The rate of

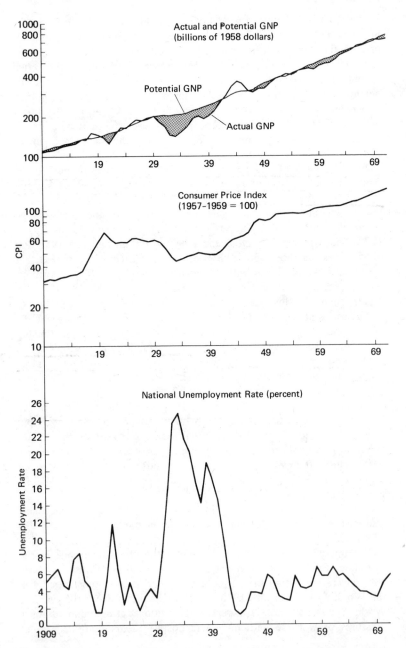

Actual and Potential GNP
(billions of 1958 dollars)

Potential GNP

Actual GNP

Consumer Price Index
(1957–1959 = 100)

CPI

National Unemployment Rate (percent)

Unemployment Rate

price change during the wartime years 1943–1945 was relatively low despite the strain of demand pressure because of strict price controls). The significant declines in prices occurred in years of depression or recession, such as 1921, 1930–1932, 1938, and 1949. There was, however, a slight downward trend in prices during the prosperous 1920s. The accelerated rise in prices at the beginning of the Korean war and again during the expanded American involvement in Vietnam can also be seen in Figure 1.1.

By comparing the three series in Figure 1.1, we can see that the price declines tend to coincide with relatively high rates of unemployment and large gaps between actual and potential output. This was particularly true until the 1950s. The years of price increase, on the other hand, tend to be periods when unemployment is relatively low and actual output is close to potential. Thus Figure 1.1 suggests a fundamental dilemma for policymakers: *To eliminate excessive unemployment we may have to risk some degree of inflation, and the complete avoidance of inflation may necessitate more unemployment than we can tolerate.* Indeed, during 1970–1972 we experienced both excessive unemployment and an unacceptable rate of price increase, leading to the institution of wage and price controls in 1971. A number of European countries also instituted price controls at about the same time as the problem of inflation seemed to become more and more intractable.

## SOME HISTORICAL PERSPECTIVE

Our detailed story begins with the decade following World War I. But it is not wise to try to study the behavior of the economy during a given period without some longer historical perspective. So let us begin by looking very briefly at the several decades that preceded the American entry into World War I.

The American economy grew more rapidly through the first decade

**Figure 1.1** Actual and Potential Output, Consumer Prices, and Unemployment, 1909–1971

(Source: U.S. Department of Commerce, *Long Term Economic Growth, 1860–1965,* and *Economic Report of the President,* January, 1972. In the case of potential output, figures for some years have been arbitrarily adjusted to make them more consistent with actual GNP and estimated unemployment. In the case of all series in the chart, estimates for different subperiods from different original sources have been put on a common base and spliced together as required.)

**Table 1.2**  Annual Rates of Change in Real Gross National Product and in Consumer Prices in Successive Decades, 1889–1969

| Decade | Annual Rate of Increase (percent) | | Unemployment Rate (first and last years of decade) (percent) |
| --- | --- | --- | --- |
| | GNP (constant prices) | Consumer Price Index | |
| 1889–1899 | 4.3 | −1.0[a] | 4.0[a]— 6.5 |
| 1899–1909 | 4.2 | 0.9 | 6.5 — 5.1 |
| 1909–1919 | 2.3 | 6.6 | 5.1 — 1.4 |
| 1919–1929 | 3.4 | −0.05 | 1.4 — 3.2 |
| 1929–1939 | 0.3 | −2.1 | 3.2 —17.2 |
| 1939–1949 | 4.5 | 5.5 | 17.2 — 5.9 |
| 1949–1959 | 3.9 | 2.0 | 5.9 — 5.5 |
| 1959–1969 | 4.3 | 2.3 | 5.5 — 3.5 |

[a]Initial year is 1890.

Source: U.S. Department of Commerce, *Long Term Economic Growth, 1860–1965* (Washington, D.C., GPO, 1966), and *Economic Report of the President*, January, 1972.

of the twentieth century than it did during the several decades that followed—including the boom period of the 1920s. This is suggested by the figures in Table 1.2, which presents rates of *actually realized* growth in real GNP by decade since 1889. The two italicized words are significant, as the unemployment figures in the last column of the table make clear. Over a period as short as a decade, the average annual rate of growth *actually* achieved may differ significantly from the rate of growth in *potential* output, depending on how close the economy is to full employment in the initial and terminal years of the decade.

Thus between 1889 and 1909 real GNP grew at an annual rate of a bit more than 4.2 percent, although as Table 1.2 indicates, unemployment was somewhat higher at the end than at the beginning of this 20-year period. Growth was much slower in the decade covering World War I, despite the war boom and the sharp decline in the unemployment rate. The prosperity of the 1920s did not involve a particularly rapid rate of growth, even if we allow for the moderate increase in the unemployment rate from its abnormally low level in 1919.[4]

[4] The growth rate between 1923 and 1929 was about the same as for 1919–1929.

Despite the fact that *potential* output continued to increase during the 1930s (although at a retarded rate) in response to growth in the labor force and in productivity, *actual* GNP (in constant prices) was not much greater in 1939 than in 1929. The average rate of increase was a minuscule 0.3 percent per year. The reason for this is bluntly given by the unemployment figures in Table 1.2. The unemployment rate in 1939 was about 17 percent, a figure that would be politically intolerable today. (As we shall see, the figure was still higher in 1933, at the bottom of the Great Depression.)

As we have already noted, full employment was not an official goal of government policy before World War II. Before 1914 as well as after, the American economy moved through the ups and downs of the business cycle, with mild recessions or occasional severe depressions (and sometimes financial crises) following periods of business expansion and falling unemployment. Because of the long and severe depression that began in 1893, unemployment was above 10 percent during more than half the decade of the nineties.[5] Unemployment averaged only a bit over 4 percent in the first decade of this century, the only really high unemployment (about 8 percent) coming in the severe but brief depression following the panic of 1907. But the unemployment record worsened thereafter. Unemployment fell below 5 percent in only two years between 1909 and 1917, and averaged about 8 percent during 1914–1915 (see Figure 1.1). The abnormal boom following our entry into World War I finally brought the unemployment rate down below 2 percent, to about the very same low level achieved in World War II.

At this point a word of warning is in order. The unemployment figures that have been cited are unofficial estimates based on fragmentary data and are less reliable than the official estimates after World War II. Perhaps, more important, they apply to a period when agricultural employment was a far greater fraction of the total labor force than it is today. Unemployment in agriculture tends to be relatively low. Thus although unemployment averaged only about 4.4 percent of the entire civilian labor force during 1900–1909, this represented no less than 9.8 percent of total *nonfarm* employment. (About one-third of total employment was in agriculture in 1909). This contrast becomes

---

[5] There are no official unemployment figures for the years before 1929. The figures cited here are the unofficial estimates of Stanley Lebergott, which go back to 1890. They are reproduced in U.S. Department of Commerce, *Long Term Economic Growth, 1860–1965* (Washington, D.C., GPO, 1966), pp. 190–191. See also Stanley Lebergott, *Manpower in Economic Growth: The United States Record Since 1800* (New York, McGraw-Hill, 1964), p. 512.

steadily less pronounced as agriculture declines in importance. Thus in the 1950s, when unemployment averaged about 4.5 percent of the total civilian labor force, this constituted less than 6 percent of nonfarm employment.[6]

Let us turn now to price trends. As Table 1.2 brings out, the interwar period followed approximately two decades of rising prices. But in the last third of the nineteenth century the trend in prices had been downward, as it was to be again during the interwar period. The shift from a declining to a rising trend in prices came at the end of the 1890s and was a worldwide development. This new secular rise in prices in the United States between the nineties and the beginning of World War I was of the same order of magnitude as that which occurred between about 1950 and 1965 (see Figure 1.1, page 10), but the factors responsible were quite different in the two periods. The worldwide shift from a declining to a rising price trend at the end of the nineteenth century was brought on by "the tremendous outpouring of gold after 1890 that resulted from discoveries in South Africa, Alaska, and Colorado and from the development of improved methods of mining and refining."[7] It did not result from expansionary policies on the part of the monetary and fiscal authorities or from strong cost-push factors originating in labor and commodity markets. And there was no official full-employment policy, in this or any other country, to bolster demands for rapid wage increases. In all of these respects the inflationary period after World War II was quite different.

The moderate inflation of the first decade of this century accelerated rapidly during World War I—how rapidly can be seen in a quick reference to Figure 1.1. As a result the average rate of inflation during 1909–1919 was the highest of any decade in this century, although it was nearly matched by the average price increase during 1939–1949, the decade including World War II (Table 2.1). Indeed, our story of the interwar period begins with the final inflationary upsurge that followed the armistice in November, 1918. Two decades of rising prices were coming to an end. As Table 1.2 and Figure 1.1 indicate, the trend in prices was downward during the next 20 years, even during the boom of the 1920s.

6 See Lebergott, *op. cit.*, p. 512. Other trends are also relevant here, including the decline in the relative importance of self-employment in the nonfarm sector, the increased participation of women in the labor force, the growing ability of workers to endure periods of unemployment, structural changes affecting the volume of seasonal unemployment, etc. Cf. Lebergott, *op. cit.*, pp. 165 ff.

7 Milton Friedman and Anna J. Schwartz, *A Monetary History of the United States, 1867–1960* (Princeton, N. J., Princeton University Press, 1963), p. 137.

## THE STATE OF MACROECONOMIC POLICY AFTER WORLD WAR I

The United States emerged from World War I with little more in the way of a set of macroeconomic goals than it had had before 1914. On the side of policy, however, at least two significant changes did occur between 1914 and 1918. First, in 1914 the Federal Reserve System was established (the Federal Reserve Act was passed in 1913), giving this country for the first time a reasonable approximation of a central bank equipped to use the instruments of monetary policy. Second, World War I created a large federal debt, held by banks and the nonbanking public.[8] This posed a problem of debt management for the Treasury and the Federal Reserve System, but it also provided a large supply of government securities as a basis for future open-market operations by the Federal Reserve.

The Federal Reserve Act provided the authorities with little guidance in the exercise of their new powers. Essentially the Federal Reserve System was to "furnish an elastic currency" under conditions that would maintain the dollar on the gold standard at a fixed parity and would also meet the needs of business as these needs changed with the growth and cyclical fluctuations of the economy. In the words of one authority, the Federal Reserve Act gave the new monetary authorities "no direct guidance on what is now considered to be monetary policy. The development of monetary policy as a conscious device for regulating the stock of money and the cost and availability of credit did not appear until the 1920s."[9]

Fiscal policy was in an even more embryonic state at the time our story begins. Keynesian economics as a justification for a stabilizing fiscal policy did not yet exist; the federal government sought to minimize its role in a private-enterprise economy; and a desirable fiscal policy was one that always kept the federal budget balanced or, better, provided some surplus with which to retire the public debt. The notion of using public works to stimulate the economy in a depression already existed, however, and gained further adherents during the twenties. But at the beginning of the decade the federal government was content merely to encourage state and local governments—and private busi-

[8] The interest-bearing federal debt jumped from less than a billion dollars in mid-1916 to $25.2 billion in June, 1919. It then declined by nearly $10 billion during the following decade.

[9] G. L. Bach, *Making Monetary and Fiscal Policy* (Washington, D.C., Brookings, 1971), p. 64. On the beginnings of the Federal Reserve System, see also Clay J. Anderson, *A Half-Century of Federal Reserve Policymaking, 1914–1964* (Philadelphia, Federal Reserve Bank of Philadelphia, 1965), chap. 1, and Friedman and Schwartz, *op. cit.*, chap. 5.

ness—to provide job-creating projects. We shall see an example of this attitude when we look at the depression of 1920–1921.[10]

In short, macroeconomic policy was in a most embryonic state as the interwar period began. There was no full-employment goal. The desirability of some measure of price stability was not ignored, but it was not an explicit target. Economic growth in the form of a rising standard of living was, of course, desirable, but it could be achieved through a minimum of government interference, a sound and elastic credit system (which had supposedly been provided by the Federal Reserve Act), and low federal taxes and a balanced budget. On the international side, the government, chiefly through the Federal Reserve System, had the obligation to maintain the gold parity of the dollar—and, as we moved into the twenties, to help European countries return to the gold standard.

Against this background let us go on to consider in the next two chapters the American record of growth and stability (or rather instability) between the two world wars. It is a record that culminated in the catastrophe of the Great Depression and the frantic efforts of the New Deal to cope with the resulting wreckage. Out of the wreckage, on both sides of the Atlantic, emerged the resolve of national governments to maintain employment at a high level—to pursue the goal of full employment.

In subsequent chapters we shall carry the story up to the 1970s.

10 The standard work on the evolution of fiscal policy in the United States is Herbert Stein, *The Fiscal Revolution in America* (Chicago, University of Chicago Press, 1969). See particularly pp. 6–16.

# 2

# The Boom of the Twenties

In this chapter we shall examine the American record during the decade 1919–1929, from the inflationary boom that immediately followed World War I, through the severe but brief depression of 1920–1921 and the prolonged boom that followed, to the stock market crash and the beginning of the Great Depression in 1929. In the next chapter we shall look at the decade of the thirties—at the calamitous decline in economic activity during 1929–1933 and this country's painful efforts to restore prosperity between 1933 and the outbreak of World War II.[1]

## POSTWAR BOOM AND DEPRESSION, 1919–1921

When World War I ended in November, 1918, the United States was just beginning to achieve all-out production of war goods. The economy had been through a strong cumulative expansion of four years' duration. Following the armistice a minor recession in business occurred, not unlike the one that followed the end of World War II. In both cases resources had to be shifted from war to peacetime production, businessmen were uncertain about future prospects, and unemployment temporarily increased.[2] But, as in 1945–1946, the lull was short-lived.

---

[1] The most useful studies of American business cycles during the interwar period are Thomas Wilson, *Fluctuations in Income and Employment*, 3d ed. (New York, Pitman, 1948), part 2; S. H. Slichter, "The Period 1919–1936 in the United States: Its Significance for Business Cycle Theory," *Review of Economic Statistics 19* (February, 1937): 1–19; and J. A. Schumpeter, *Business Cycles* (New York, McGraw-Hill, 1939), vol. 2, chaps. 14–15. See also R. A. Gordon, "Cyclical Experience in the Interwar Period: The Investment Boom of the 'Twenties," in Universities-National Bureau Committee, *Conference on Business Cycles* (New York, National Bureau of Economic Research, 1951). For the experience of other countries, see particularly W. A. Lewis, *Economic Survey, 1919–1939* (London, Allen & Unwin, 1949) and Erick Lundberg, *Instability and Economic Growth* (New Haven, Conn., Yale University Press, 1968), chap. 2.

[2] The chief difference between the two periods lies in the sphere of prices. Price control in World War I was much less stringent and less extensive than in World War II, and as a consequence the rise in prices was greater. After the 1918

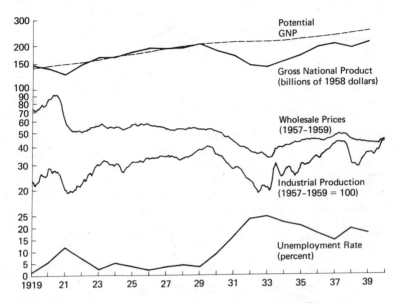

**Figure 2.1**  Selected Indicators of Economic Activity, 1919–1939

(Source: For actual and potential GNP, U.S. Department of Commerce, *Long Term Economic Growth, 1860–1965*, and *Economic Report of the President*, January, 1972. Other series are from U.S. Department of Labor, Bureau of Labor Statistics, and Board of Governors of the Federal Reserve System.)

The postarmistice recession reached a low point in the spring of 1919; thereafter aggregate demand began to rise. There ensued a speculative boom and a sharp reaction, which together mark off the first full cycle of the interwar period. The expansion phase lasted from March, 1919 to January, 1920; the downswing that followed reached a low point in July, 1921 (see Figure 2.1).

The causes of the boom of 1919–1920 bear a marked likeness to those responsible for the expansion immediately after World War II. The great difference is that after World War II the boom was not immediately followed by a severe decline in prices, a significant reduc-

---

armistice businessmen generally expected that the then-high level of prices could not be maintained and that prices would fall to "more normal" levels. This led to caution in buying.

tion in wages, and a sharp increase in unemployment. The following were the most important factors operating early in 1919 to generate a rise in total demand:

1. A strong pent-up demand by business for capital goods for replacement and expansion, after a year-and-a-half in which such goods had not been available.
2. Similar pent-up demands by consumers for housing, automobiles, and other items not freely available during the war.
3. The existence of a large volume of liquid assets and a high level of money incomes to make these pent-up demands effective.
4. Maintenance of an abnormally high level of foreign demand for American goods.
5. Continuation of government expenditures on a large scale.

Indeed, federal expenditures in the fiscal year ending June 30, 1919 were nearly 50 percent higher than in the preceding 12 months. Because of this the monetary authorities were compelled to maintain an easy-money policy during most of 1919.

Thus in the spring of 1919 businessmen saw that aggregate demand was being well maintained and in fact was rising. Previous expectations that prices would decline, which had led to caution in placing orders, now gave way to optimism. There was a rush to expand output and accumulate inventories; consumers, with their accumulated savings and rising incomes, bought freely; foreign nations competed with Americans for goods, and the value of exports rose above even the wartime peak. Prices increased sharply as money demand expanded more rapidly than output. Because of limitations of capacity, labor shortages and strikes, and transportation difficulties, total output expanded only moderately from the postarmistice low; indeed, for the year 1919 as a whole it was little if any greater than in 1918. This was a "demand-pull" type of inflationary process, with aggregate demand rising faster than aggregate supply.

The rise in prices inspired expectations of further price increases—an outstanding feature of the expansion was the extent of speculative buying in commodities, securities, and real estate. (There was considerably less speculative activity after World War II.) A good deal of this speculation was done with borrowed money, and loans and deposits of commercial banks rose rapidly. Wages followed prices upward, and there were widespread complaints of labor inefficiency.

By the early months of 1920, the American economy was in a vulnerable position. Business inventories were high; firms and speculators were heavily in debt to the banks, and the banks had rediscounted heavily at the Federal Reserve Banks; consumers were showing resistance to the high levels retail prices had reached; construction was beginning to decline because of high building costs and the unavailability of mortgage credit; there were increasing fears that Europe could not long continue to finance the abnormally high level of American exports; and costs were high, with numerous bottlenecks.

Two additional factors had also begun to exert a significant deflationary force. First, government spending was steadily decreasing. By the fourth quarter of 1919 the budget had been balanced, and a small excess of receipts over disbursements had emerged. Thus by the beginning of 1920 government finance had come to exercise a strong deflationary force on the economy.

Second, monetary forces now began to work in the same direction. Through most of 1919 the Federal Reserve authorities had rediscounted liberally for the banks in order to help the Treasury sell the securities necessary to finance the federal deficit. Toward the end of the year, the improvement in federal finances and a deteriorating gold reserve spurred authorities to tighten credit. Rediscount rates were raised several times between November, 1919 and May, 1920, and informal pressure was placed on member banks to curb the expansion of credit, particularly for speculative purposes. Parallel with these developments, interest rates rose markedly. Although the volume of loans did not decline until well after the turning point had come, the rate of credit expansion was retarded and various types of speculative ventures undoubtedly were hampered.[3]

In these circumstances a sharp downswing was inevitable. A combination of factors seems to have been responsible for the beginning of the downswing early in 1920. In the industries in which raw-material prices had risen most, businessmen began to fear price declines and curtailed their purchases accordingly. In textiles the curtailment began as early as January, 1920 and was accelerated by growing consumer resistance to high prices. The existence of heavy inventories permitted retailers, wholesalers, and manufacturers to curtail their purchases sharply once they began to anticipate a decline.

Also beginning early in 1920, exports showed a tendency to fall,

[3] The contrast here with monetary policy after World War II is striking. Under pressure from the U.S. Treasury to keep interest rates low and to support government bond prices, the Fed was compelled after World War II to maintain a very easy monetary policy until it finally regained freedom of action in 1951. By then the boom generated by the Korean war was well under way. Monetary policy after World War II is discussed in subsequent chapters.

and there were growing indications that foreign countries could not maintain much longer the existing level of export demand. (There was no Marshall Plan after World War I.) This again reacted directly on business expectations and production. The peak in wholesale prices in a number of countries seems to have come in April; in this country the peak was in May. By then, production had already been declining for several months in a number of industries; construction had been falling since the beginning of the year; and reduced ordering and even cancellation of orders were beginning to be widespread.

The downswing that now occurred was severe but relatively short (see Figure 2.1.) Its outstanding feature was the extreme decline in prices. Unemployment rose sharply from an annual average of 1.4 percent in 1919 to 5.2 percent in 1920 and 11.7 percent in 1921. The depression was worldwide, though it was complicated by financial difficulties and continued efforts toward reconstruction and monetary stabilization in various European countries.

Government policy to moderate the depression and speed recovery was minimal. The Federal Reserve authorities were largely passive. The Federal Reserve Banks did not begin to lower their discount rates until the downswing had virtually ended, and the system had not yet learned how to use open-market operations as a stabilizing instrument of monetary policy. Federal Reserve policy was aimed at "orderly liquidation" and limiting new credit to nonspeculative, productive uses. The economy had to purge itself, but not too drastically, of its previous speculative excesses.[4]

Nor was any use made of fiscal policy. Government expenditures, which had dropped by nearly two-thirds between fiscal 1919 and fiscal 1920, declined further in fiscal 1921.[5] The modest budgetary surplus that emerged in fiscal 1920 increased in fiscal 1921. In short, the federal budget was deflationary while the downswing was in progress.

The federal government was not oblivious to the depression. In 1921 a Conference on Unemployment was held under the chairmanship of Herbert Hoover, then Secretary of Commerce. The attitude of the federal government was expressed by President Harding in his welcoming speech at the conference: "There has been vast unemployment before and there will be again. There will be depression and inflation

---

[4] For an account of Federal Reserve policy during 1920–1921, see Clay J. Anderson, *A Half-Century of Federal Reserve Policy Making, 1914–1964* (Philadelphia, Federal Reserve Bank of Philadelphia, 1965), pp. 25–30, and Milton Friedman and Anna J. Schwartz, *A Monetary History of the United States, 1867–1960* (Princeton, N. J., Princeton University Press, 1963), pp. 231 ff.

[5] The federal government's fiscal year ends on June 30.

just as surely as the tides ebb and flow. I would have little enthusiasm for any proposed remedy which seeks either palliation or tonic from the Public Treasury." Secretary Hoover called for cooperative action by business and state and local governments, which would demonstrate "that independence and ability of action amongst our own people that saves our Government from that ultimate paternalism that will undermine our whole political life."[6]

Despite the absence of a stimulative government policy, however, recovery was not long delayed. Production declined much more sharply than retail sales, resulting in rapid liquidation of inventories at all stages of production and distribution. Building costs came down promptly, and the volume of construction improved steadily after the close of 1920. Wage decreases were both general and substantial, and there was apparently a widespread improvement in labor efficiency with a consequent decline in production costs. Credit conditions gradually eased as business liquidated its bank borrowings and banks reduced their indebtedness to the Federal Reserve System.

By the middle of 1921 the worst of the price decline was over, and some prices were advancing. Exports continued at a high level, though not in so large a volume as in 1920. Gradually confidence returned. The process was helped by the fact that the decline in prices had been fairly well balanced: Prices of finished products fell nearly as much as those of raw materials, and the decline in agricultural prices was not so much greater than that in industrial prices as to lead to serious distortions of the price structure. In this respect 1920–1921 presents a much better picture than 1929–1932.

Most important of all, the long-term investment opportunities that had existed in 1919–1920 were still present in 1921. The need for commercial and residential buildings of all types was very great. In particular, there was a heavy pent-up demand for housing. The automobile industry was still in a stage of rapid growth and hence required further expansion in an array of auxiliary industries, in road building, and in other directions. There was an increasing demand for electric power and electrical equipment. Public construction, especially by local government bodies, also provided a strong stimulus. In short, the downswing in 1920–1921 was associated chiefly with short-run factors—overaccumulation of inventories, speculative excesses, some horizontal maladjustments, tightening credit, the rapid elimination of the large federal deficit, and a change in *short-term* expectations. As

---

6 This episode is described in R. A. Gordon, *The Goal of Full Employment* (New York, Wiley, 1967), pp. 43–44.

soon as the short-term factors had been corrected, the favorable long-term investment situation again made itself felt, and recovery set in. In this respect the 1921 depression, though severe during the short period it lasted, differed markedly from that of the 1930s or, for example, the protracted depressions of the 1870s or the 1890s.

## THE PROSPERITY OF THE 1920S

### The Nature of the Expansion in Output and Employment

The economy recovered rapidly from the depression of 1921, and by 1923 total output substantially exceeded the peak reached in 1919–1920. From 1923 through 1929 economic activity remained at a high level and tended to increase still further, with minor interruptions in 1924 and 1927. The period culminated with a particularly large increase in industrial output and total GNP in 1929 (see Figure 2.1 and Table 2.1). Then came the deluge, and the Great Depression began.

The components of gross national product in the 1920s, as estimated by Simon Kuznets, are given in Table 2.1. These are not the official figures of the Department of Commerce, which begin only in 1929. In particular, these figures do not separate out government expenditures, which are concealed in the data on the flow of consumer goods and on gross capital formation.[7]

The middle years of the 1920s were marked by a steady increase in GNP, but the rate of expansion was much less than in either 1921–1923 or 1928–1929. More than four-fifths of the increase in GNP between 1919 and 1929 (which averaged about 3.4 percent per year) was in the flow of consumer goods (see Table 2.1). The expansion in services was particularly marked, in both absolute and relative terms. The increase in output of consumer durables, dominated by the rapid expansion in the automobile industry, was even greater in percentage terms, though not in absolute amount.

The outstanding fact about the movement of total capital formation in this decade is the high level reached by 1923 and the maintenance of this level for seven years. We have here a prolonged period of high-level investment in producer durable goods and construction. Inventory accumulation and the excess of exports over imports did not play the same important role they had played in 1919–1920. It is significant that both producer and consumer durables formed a larger

[7] Estimates using the Department of Commerce definitions and showing government expenditures have been made, but the figures shown in Table 2.1 seem to be more reliable. For the other estimates, see U.S. Department of Commerce, *Long Term Economic Growth* (Washington, D.C., GPO, 1966), pp. 167, 171.

**Table 2.1** Gross National Product and its Chief Components, 1919-1929 (In billions of dollars; in 1929 prices)

| | 1919 | 1920 | 1921 | 1922 | 1923 | 1924 | 1925 | 1926 | 1927 | 1928 | 1929 |
|---|---|---|---|---|---|---|---|---|---|---|---|
| Gross national product | 67.8 | 68.5 | 65.5 | 70.4 | 80.0 | 81.6 | 84.3 | 89.8 | 90.6 | 91.9 | 98.0 |
| Flow to consumers | 49.7 | 51.3 | 54.1 | 56.5 | 61.2 | 65.3 | 64.0 | 68.9 | 70.7 | 72.5 | 76.9 |
| Perishable | 19.9 | 21.0 | 21.8 | 22.6 | 23.5 | 25.3 | 25.1 | 26.3 | 26.8 | 26.7 | 28.0 |
| Semidurable | 7.5 | 6.5 | 7.8 | 8.9 | 9.8 | 9.0 | 10.0 | 10.0 | 11.2 | 11.2 | 11.8 |
| Durable | 5.0 | 4.9 | 4.0 | 5.1 | 6.6 | 6.9 | 7.8 | 8.6 | 8.2 | 8.4 | 8.8 |
| Services | 17.3 | 18.9 | 20.4 | 19.9 | 21.3 | 24.1 | 21.2 | 24.0 | 24.5 | 26.2 | 28.4 |
| Gross capital formation | 18.1 | 17.2 | 11.4 | 13.9 | 18.7 | 16.2 | 20.3 | 20.9 | 19.9 | 19.4 | 21.1 |
| Producer durables | 5.5 | 5.3 | 3.6 | 4.2 | 5.8 | 5.4 | 6.0 | 6.5 | 6.1 | 6.5 | 7.5 |
| Construction | 6.3 | 5.4 | 6.3 | 8.8 | 9.7 | 10.8 | 12.1 | 12.8 | 12.7 | 12.3 | 11.2 |
| Residential nonfarm | 1.5 | 1.0 | 2.1 | 3.6 | 4.2 | 5.0 | 5.4 | 5.4 | 5.1 | 4.7 | 3.4 |
| Nonresidential | 4.8 | 4.4 | 4.2 | 5.2 | 5.5 | 5.8 | 6.7 | 7.4 | 7.6 | 7.6 | 7.8 |
| Change in inventories | 2.8 | 4.2 | 0.0 | 0.3 | 2.8 | -0.9 | 1.6 | 1.2 | 0.4 | -0.4 | 1.7 |
| Foreign investment | 3.5 | 2.3 | 1.5 | 0.7 | 0.5 | 1.0 | 0.7 | 0.4 | 0.7 | 1.0 | 0.8 |

Source: Simon Kuznets, *Capital in the American Economy: Its Formation and Financing* (New York, National Bureau of Economic Research, 1961), Appendix A. We have used his "Variant I." Kuznets presents estimates of total construction only. We have reproduced his calculations to obtain separate estimates of residential and nonresidential construction.

fraction of the GNP during the 1920s than during any period before World War I. We thus have a picture of a prolonged investment boom, which supported a steady expansion in incomes and consumer demand, and at the same time provided the enlarged capacity necessary to meet the rising demand for goods and services.

This sustained boom, from 1923 to 1929, supported a high level of employment. If we can believe the unofficial estimates available for this period, unemployment averaged as low as 3.3 percent of the civilian labor force during these seven years.[8] It is important to remember that this record was achieved without a high and rising level of military expenditures. We have not been able to do as well since then. Sustained periods of less than 4 percent unemployment after 1929 occurred only during World War II and the immediate postwar boom, during the Korean war, and during the Vietnam period, 1966–1969.

Despite the low level of unemployment, prices were stable during the 1920s. The Consumer Price Index was virtually the same in 1929 as in 1923, while the Wholesale Price Index declined slightly. The rate of increase in labor productivity was quite rapid during the twenties, more so than during the preceding three decades, and wages did not rise as fast, with the result that unit labor costs fell.[9] American labor was relatively unorganized: There was no Wagner Act to guarantee the right of collective bargaining, and the federal government had made no commitment, explicit or implied, to maintain full employment. In addition, after the price and wage deflation of 1921–1922, both employers and workers assumed that prices would remain stable, and there were no inflationary expectations to bolster wage demands and weaken employer resistance. In all these respects the situation was quite different after World War II.

Table 2.2 throws further light on the nature of the sustained pros-

---

[8] The unemployment rate for the *nonfarm* labor force was higher. See Stanley Lebergott, *Manpower in Economic Growth: The United States Record Since 1800* (New York, McGraw-Hill, 1964), p. 512; also p. 13 of this book. Agriculture, with its very low level of recorded unemployment, still accounted for more than one-fifth of total employment during the 1920s compared to less than 5 percent in the early 1970s.

[9] Between 1923 and 1929 average hourly earnings in manufacturing increased about 8 percent, while output per man-hour increased by some 30 percent. (Bureau of Labor Statistics data as published in *Historical Statistics of the United States, 1789–1945*.) For evidence that the upward trend in labor productivity accelerated after World War I, see the authoritative study by John W. Kendrick, *Productivity Trends in the United States* (Princeton, N. J., Princeton University Press, 1961), chap. 3.

**Table 2.2** Income and Employment by Major Industries, 1919–1929 ($Y$ = income originating in each industry; $E$ = employees, excluding self-employed; income in billions of dollars, employees in millions)

| | 1919 | | 1921 | | 1923 | | 1928 | | 1929 | |
|---|---|---|---|---|---|---|---|---|---|---|
| Industry | $Y$ | $E$ | $Y$ | $E$ | $Y$ | $E$ | $Y$ | $E$ | $Y$ | $E$ |
| Manufacturing | 16.2 | 9.9 | 12.6 | 7.6 | 16.8 | 9.5 | 17.9 | 9.2 | 19.8 | 9.9 |
| Mining | 1.8 | 1.1 | 1.7 | 0.9 | 2.0 | 1.1 | 1.6 | 1.0 | 1.8 | 1.0 |
| Construction | 2.0 | 1.0 | 2.0 | 1.1 | 3.3 | 1.6 | 4.0 | 1.8 | 4.1 | 1.8 |
| Transportation and public utilities | 6.0 | 3.3 | 6.3 | 3.0 | 7.1 | 3.3 | 8.0 | 3.2 | 8.5 | 3.3 |
| Trade | 10.2 | 3.9 | 9.5 | 3.8 | 10.1 | 4.4 | 11.0 | 4.9 | 11.4 | 5.2 |
| Finance | 6.8 | 0.9 | 7.8 | 1.0 | 8.8 | 1.0 | 10.9 | 1.4 | 10.9 | 1.5 |
| Service | 6.1 | 3.6 | 6.7 | 3.8 | 8.3 | 4.4 | 10.7 | 5.2 | 11.3 | 5.5 |
| Government | 3.8[a] | 3.5 | 6.2 | 2.8 | 7.0 | 2.7 | 8.3 | 3.1 | 8.9 | 3.2 |
| Miscellaneous | 2.2 | 1.2 | 2.0 | 1.1 | 2.7 | 1.3 | 3.7 | 1.6 | 3.5 | 1.7 |
| Agriculture | 10.9 | 2.1 | 5.5 | 2.0 | 6.7 | 2.0 | 7.3 | 2.0 | 7.7 | 2.0 |
| Total | 65.9 | 30.4 | 60.3 | 27.1 | 72.9 | 31.4 | 83.4 | 33.4 | 87.8 | 35.1 |

[a]This item, from some points of view, is not fully comparable with the figures for income originating in government for later years. In 1919 the large government deficit not matched by productive capital formation resulted in a large figure for government dissaving, which reduced the figure for income generated by government shown in the table.

Source: Simon Kuznets, *National Income and Its Composition, 1919–1938* (New York, National Bureau of Economic Research, 1941), pp. 310, 314. The income figures are not adjusted for price changes.

perity of the 1920s. The two columns for each year show, respectively, the total net income originating in each major industry and the amount of employment in that industry. Between 1919 and 1929 net income rose by about $22 billion. Manufacturing accounted for only about one-sixth of the increase. The service industries and finance each contributed a larger share to the increase in national income than did manufacturing; the increase in construction and public utilities was also substantial. Manufacturing employed no more people in 1929 than in 1919; the increase in factory output was achieved entirely through greater productivity per worker, largely with the help of more and better equipment. The main increases in employment during the decade were in trade, service, finance, and construction, which together accounted for virtually all of the expansion in employment between 1919 and 1929. Expansion in manufacturing output and employment bulk large in the rapid increase between 1921 and 1923, and again in the final upsurge between 1928 and 1929, but the expansion between 1923 and 1928 was primarily in other sectors of the economy.

The investment boom and the rise in consumption during the 1920s were accompanied by a steady expansion in bank credit, the flotation of an enormous volume of new security issues, and a mounting tide of speculative fever reflected particularly in the promotion of new enterprises, a boom in real estate, the development of a variety of unsound financial practices, and an upsurge in stock prices that culminated in the stock market crash of 1929.

## Nonmonetary Stimuli to Investment

The main underlying factors responsible for the high level of investment in the 1920s were (1) pent-up demand for plant and equipment created by the war; (2) the direct and indirect effects of the automobile; (3) the rapid expansion of other relatively new industries such as electric power, electrical equipment, radio and telephone, air transportation, motion pictures, and rayon; (4) the rapid pace of technological change, leading to great increases in labor productivity; and (5) the rise to a peak of a long building cycle. Superimposed on these was a wave of optimism (which must be treated in part as an independent factor), a fairly high propensity to consume, and an elastic credit supply.[10]

It is impossible to say precisely how important World War I was in creating a demand for plant and equipment. It is clear, however, that

[10] For a stimulating and more detailed discussion of many of the topics considered in this subsection, see Schumpeter, *op. cit.,* vol. 2, pp. 767 ff.

the pent-up demand that existed after the armistice was not satisfied during 1919–1920; a substantial amount of investment in the early 1920s must have represented replacement and expansion programs deferred from the war years and investment to capitalize on technological changes occurring during the war.

The most important stimulus to investment and to the expansion of total output in the 1920s was the automobile. No single innovation provided a stimulus of comparable relative magnitude after World War II. Like electric power, this was a prewar innovation, but its full impact on the American economy was not felt until the 1920s. Production of motor vehicles had already risen from 485,000 in 1913 to 1,934,000 in 1919. It jumped to 4,180,000 by 1923 and then rose further to a peak of 5,622,000 in 1929, or nearly three times the number produced a decade earlier.

The effect of the automobile on aggregate demand came from two sources: expanded *production* of cars and trucks, and enormously increased *use* of motor vehicles. The increase in production created a demand for new plant and equipment in both the automobile industry and the industries serving it—parts and accessories, rubber, steel, plate glass, lead, and so on. Here we have an example of the working of the acceleration principle. Even more important was the growing use of automobiles, again with acceleration effects. Motor vehicle production nearly trebled between 1919 and 1929, but the increase in the number of cars and trucks on the road was even larger. Moreover, steadily greater use was made of each vehicle. The result was an enormous expansion in employment in oil refining, filling stations and garages, truck and bus driving, selling of supplies and accessories, and construction and repair of roads. Expansion in these activities meant new investment—in buildings, equipment, and roads. And as the automobile changed methods of living, still further investment was required—in the development of suburban communities, for example.

Another prewar innovation, electric power, was a highly important stimulus to investment. Electric-power production, which requires a high ratio of capital to output, more than doubled between 1920 and 1929, and generating capacity increased in proportion. Use of this power in turn required electrical equipment and opened up methods of reducing costs, which involved other types of new machinery. Value added by the electrical-machinery industry also more than doubled between 1919 and 1929 compared to an increase of about 30 percent for manufacturing as a whole. Along with the growth of electric-power production and the use of electrically driven machinery and material-handling equipment in industry went rapid expansion in the telephone industry (again a prewar innovation), the growth of radio (entirely a postwar development), and the rapid electrification of the home.

Other new industries and products helped maintain investment and expand production—various chemical products (particularly rayon), oil and rubber products other than gasoline and tires, natural gas, production and distribution of motion pictures, the airplane, and so on. Most of these represented prewar innovations that added more to output in the postwar than in the prewar period.

In addition to the introduction of new products, the increased tempo of technological change stimulated investment in new production techniques. Productivity per man-hour in manufacturing rose some 70 percent between 1919 and 1929. Mass-production techniques were extended, greater use was made of automatic and special-purpose machinery, and radical improvements occurred in material-handling methods. These developments made a major contribution to the demand for producer durable goods. And as we have already noted, labor costs fell steadily during the 1920s as wages failed to rise as rapidly as productivity (in marked contrast to the situation after World War II). As a result stable or falling prices went together with expanded profit margins. The latter bolstered expectations and encouraged further investment; the former led to illusions, in the midst of the speculative boom of the late 1920s, that "conditions were fundamentally sound" because commodity prices were not rising.

As would be expected, corporate profits were high during most of the 1920s. Profit per unit in manufacturing was stable at a high level during 1923–1926, declined in 1927, and rose above the 1923–1926 level in 1929. The rate of profit on invested capital of manufacturing corporations remained at a high level, with no marked trend either upward or downward between 1923 and 1929.

We have already mentioned the importance of construction in maintaining investment in the 1920s. The sources of demand for building are shown in Table 2.3. The most important single component of new construction was residential building, which comprised 40 percent or more of the total through 1926, when a decline set in that lasted until 1933. In the nonresidential field, public-utility, government, and "other" construction (i.e., stores, office buildings, etc.) were all more important than strictly industrial (i.e., factory) building. About half the government figure represented road building. Some of the large volume of building reflected accumulated demand from the war years and the needs of an expanding population, part was in response to speculative

**Table 2.3**   New Construction Activity in the United States, 1919–1939 (In billions of dollars)

| Year | Total | Residen-tial (non-farm) | Private Nonresidential | | | | Govern-ment |
| | | | Indus-trial | Farm | Public Utility | Other[a] | |
|---|---|---|---|---|---|---|---|
| 1920 | 6.7 | 2.0 | 1.1 | 0.6 | 0.8 | 0.9 | 1.4 |
| 1921 | 6.0 | 2.1 | 0.6 | 0.2 | 0.6 | 0.9 | 1.6 |
| — | | | | | | | |
| 1923 | 9.3 | 4.4 | 0.5 | 0.3 | 1.2 | 1.3 | 1.6 |
| 1924 | 10.4 | 5.1 | 0.5 | 0.3 | 1.4 | 1.3 | 1.9 |
| 1925 | 11.4 | 5.5 | 0.5 | 0.3 | 1.3 | 1.7 | 2.1 |
| 1926 | 12.1 | 5.6 | 0.7 | 0.3 | 1.4 | 1.9 | 2.1 |
| 1927 | 12.0 | 5.2 | 0.7 | 0.4 | 1.5 | 2.0 | 2.4 |
| 1928 | 11.6 | 4.8 | 0.8 | 0.3 | 1.4 | 1.9 | 2.5 |
| 1929 | 10.8 | 3.6 | 0.9 | 0.3 | 1.6 | 1.8 | 2.5 |
| — | | | | | | | |
| 1933 | 2.9 | 0.5 | 0.2 | 0.0 | 0.3 | 0.3 | 1.6 |
| — | | | | | | | |
| 1936 | 6.5 | 1.6 | 0.3 | 0.2 | 0.5 | 0.5 | 3.5 |
| 1937 | 7.0 | 1.9 | 0.5 | 0.2 | 0.7 | 0.6 | 3.1 |
| 1938 | 7.0 | 2.0 | 0.2 | 0.2 | 0.6 | 0.6 | 3.4 |
| 1939 | 8.2 | 2.7 | 0.3 | 0.2 | 0.7 | 0.6 | 3.8 |

[a]Includes warehouses, offices, stores, restaurants, and garages, and religious, educational, social, recreational, hospital, and institutional building.

Source:   From U.S. Departments of Labor and Commerce, *Construction Volume and Costs, 1915–1954,* statistical supplement to vol. I of *Construction Review,* (1955): 1–6.

enthusiasm and the ease with which mortgage credit could be obtained, and part was the direct result of the automobile and the changes in living habits that it inspired. The large volume of commercial building reflected the great expansion in the trade, service, and finance industries that occurred during the 1920s, a trend that was renewed after World War II. Only a minor part of total construction was required by expanding industrial production. Table 2.3 also reveals how completely these various stimuli disappeared in the 1930s.

Particular attention should be given to the behavior of residential building in the 1920s. The peak of the housing boom was reached as early as 1926, and by 1929 residential construction had declined by $2 billion, or more than one-third. This decline was not fully offset by other forms of private investment (nonresidential construction, producer durables, and inventory accumulation). GNP continued to expand in the late twenties because of a rapid increase in consumer expenditures (reflecting a rising ratio of consumption to GNP), increased expenditures by state and local governments, and a rise in net exports.[11]

The decline in residential building after 1926 reflected a number of factors. The high level of construction in the early and midtwenties eventually permitted the supply of housing to catch up with demand;[12] the rate of population increase began to decline after the early 1920s and eventually the housing stock became excessive. The satisfaction of pent-up demand would by itself have called for some decline in building, and overbuilding made the situation worse.[13] Thus 1926 marked the peak of another long building cycle.

## Monetary Factors

There is a difference of opinion as to the precise role of monetary developments in the boom of the 1920s and the depression that followed. It is fairly clear that the supply of bank credit was fully adequate for the needs of business. It is also obvious that credit expansion helped finance the speculative boom in securities and real estate. It is not clear, however, that the boom was due primarily to easy credit conditions or that a different monetary policy in 1927–1929 or earlier could have prevented the depression, although it almost certainly could have helped make it less severe.

The American economy began the 1920s with a money supply about double that of 1914. Between 1921 and 1929 total loans and investments of commercial banks, as well as deposits, increased still further, as is indicated in Table 2.4. The expansion in loans after 1921 took the form primarily of loans on securities, and there was also a significant increase in real-estate loans. A substantial part of the

[11] There was also a modest increase in federal government expenditures between fiscal 1926 and fiscal 1929 and some decline in the budgetary surplus. The federal budget was in substantial surplus throughout the 1920s.

[12] There was a large pent-up demand for housing after World War I, just as after World War II.

[13] See R. A. Gordon, "Population Growth, Housing, and the Capital Coefficient," *American Economic Review 46* (June, 1956): 307–332. For a review of the evidence as to whether a housing surplus developed in the 1920s and some new material on the subject, see Ben Bolch, Rendigs Fels, and Marshall McMahon, "Housing Surplus in the 1920's?," *Explorations in Economic History 8* (Spring, 1971): 259–283.

**Table 2.4** Loans, Investments, and Deposits of Commercial Banks, 1914–1939 (In billions of dollars)

| Year (June 30) | Loans and Investments | | | Adjusted Demand Deposits and Currency Outside Banks[a] | Time Deposits of Commercial Banks |
|---|---|---|---|---|---|
| | Total | Loans | Investments | | |
| 1914 | 16.9 | 13.2 | 3.7 | 11.6 | 4.4 |
| 1921 | 34.2 | 26.1 | 8.1 | 20.8 | 10.9 |
| 1923 | 37.1 | 26.9 | 10.2 | 22.7 | 13.4 |
| 1929 | 49.4 | 35.7 | 13.7 | 26.2 | 19.6 |
| 1933 | 30.4 | 16.3 | 14.0 | 19.2 | 10.8 |
| 1937 | 39.5 | 17.4 | 22.0 | 30.7 | 14.5 |
| 1939 | 39.4 | 16.4 | 22.9 | 33.4 | 15.1 |

[a]Adjusted demand deposits exclude interbank and U.S. government deposits and cash items in process of collection.

Source: Board of Governors of the Federal Reserve System, *Banking and Monetary Statistics* (Washington, D.C., Board of Governors, 1943), pp. 19, 34–35.

increase in investments went into corporate securities. In short, the credit expansion of the 1920s served to support the large volume of security flotations during the period and the growing speculation in the stock market. It is interesting to note in this connection that demand deposits rose only moderately; the chief increase was in time deposits.[14] There was a growing tendency, encouraged by the banks, to classify relatively idle demand deposits as time deposits, on which a higher interest rate was paid. The increasing volume of such deposits resulted in part from the fact that high security prices encouraged firms to float securities in excess of their immediate needs. Thus, the banks' financing of security operations helped bring these time deposits into existence, made large firms less dependent on the banks for working-capital requirements, and created a reservoir of lendable funds in the hands of nonbank lenders; these funds could find their way into the stock market. To the extent that credit expansion took the form of time

14 See Table 2.4. The narrower version of the money supply ($M_1$), including currency in circulation and adjusted demand deposits, increased at an annual rate of 2.6 percent between 1923 and 1929. The broader version, including time deposits at commercial banks ($M_2$), increased at an annual rate of about 4.1 percent. The rate of increase of both $M_1$ and $M_2$ was considerably faster during 1923–1926 than during 1926–1929.

deposits, which required lower reserves than demand deposits, the lending capacity of the banks was increased.

By earlier standards interest rates were not unduly high during the 1920s. High-grade bond yields and short-term interest rates were relatively stable and showed a moderate tendency to decline between 1923 and 1927. In 1928–1929 all classes of interest rates rose under the stimulus of large-scale speculative demand for credit and the attempts finally made by the Federal Reserve to bring the boom under control.

The Federal Reserve authorities have frequently been criticized for not taking any decisive action to curb the boom until 1928. In 1924 and again in 1927, the Federal Reserve Banks reduced rediscount rates and bought securities in the open market with the twofold objective of alleviating the mild recessions that occurred in those years and creating conditions favorable to the restoration of monetary stability in Europe. (It was only in the early 1920s that the Federal Reserve System developed open-market operations as an important instrument of monetary policy.[15]) The System sold in 1928 somewhat more securities than it had bought in 1927, and the New York Bank's rediscount rate was raised in several steps from 3½ percent in January, 1928 to 5 percent in July. But more than a year went by before the rediscount rate was raised further—to 6 percent in August, 1929. From the middle of 1924 to January, 1928, the rediscount rate did not go above 4 percent.

It is doubtful whether these monetary developments were of primary importance in creating the boom of the 1920s. In the terms used by some business cycle theorists, the "natural rate" of interest was higher than the market rate, and part of the large volume of investment was financed by credit expansion. But the chief reasons for this lay in the nonmonetary sphere—in the developments discussed earlier that made the marginal efficiency of capital high and in the wave of speculative optimism that raised it still higher. In addition, the unwise lending practices of the commercial banks encouraged speculation and unsound promotions, and weakened the banking system's ability to withstand the strains that were to come after 1929. It was the nature rather than the amount of lending that led to later trouble. It is doubtful whether the Federal Reserve System, through any action then within its power, could have prevented the stock market boom and yet permitted a level of investment high enough to maintain business activity close to full-employment levels.

[15]See Anderson, *op. cit.,* pp. 47–54; Friedman and Schwartz, *op. cit.,* chap. 6.

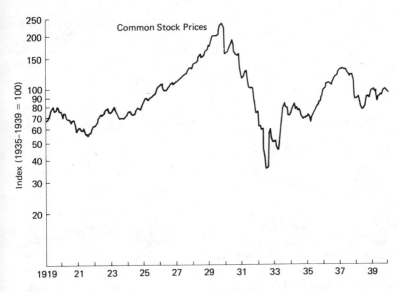

**Figure 2.2**  Common Stock Prices, 1919–1939

(Source: Standard & Poor's Index, as given in Board of Governors of the Federal Reserve System, *Banking and Monetary Statistics.*)

## Speculation and Finance

The most spectacular aspect of the "New Era" was the stock market boom.[16] The extent of the rise in stock prices is indicated in Figure 2.2. Over a billion shares changed hands on the New York Stock Exchange in 1929 and nearly that amount in 1928, compared to an annual average of about 250 million shares during 1922–1924 and even less in the prewar years. With this rise went an enormous expansion in brokers' loans to finance security purchases on margin.

The rise in stock prices, together with the investment opportunities described previously, stimulated the offering of a tremendous volume of new security issues. More than $30 billion worth of new issues were put on the market in the three years 1927–1929 alone. The relative importance of the different types of issuers is suggested by the following figures (in billions of dollars).[17]

[16] For an entertaining account of the stock market boom and collapse, see J. K. Galbraith, *The Great Crash, 1929* (Boston, Houghton Mifflin, 1955).

[17] From Board of Governors of the Federal Reserve System, *Banking and Monetary Statistics*, p. 487.

Issues to raise new capital, 1927–1929

|  |  |  |
|---|---:|---:|
| State and municipal | 4.3 | |
| Federal agencies | 0.2 | |
| Corporate | | |
| Bonds and notes | 7.6 | |
| Stocks | 10.4 | |
| Foreign | 3.3 | |
| | | 25.7 |
| Refunding Issues | | 5.5 |
| Total | | 31.2 |

The magnitude of the amount of new capital raised by corporations, particularly in the form of stocks, is especially noteworthy.[18] The figures also point up the fact that state and local governments were borrowing heavily in this period.

By no means all of the new-capital issues in these years went into capital formation. Indeed, the major part, particularly from 1926 on, seems to have gone into erecting a financial superstructure of holding companies, investment trusts, and other forms of intercorporate security holdings that was to come crashing down in the 1930s. Investment bankers were active in the promotion of companies to hold the securities of other companies, and commercial banks were involved through their own investment banking affiliates and through loans on securities. Large promoters' profits were made, and capital gains from the sale of securities by the former holders inflated consumer demand and spread the speculative fever in widening circles.

Similar speculative developments involving the inflation of capital values occurred in the real-estate field. Houses, apartment houses, office buildings, and hotels were built with almost reckless abandon under the spur of promoters' profits and the ease with which securities could be sold to finance the cost of construction. Banks loaned heavily on bonds and mortgages, without adequate safeguards as to amortization, and later found themselves with "frozen assets" whose values had to be scaled down drastically.

The consequences of these financial developments need no great elaboration. One result was a good deal of real investment that was not justified in terms of long-term profit possibilities. Capital goods were created that were to "hang over the market" and discourage further investment for a decade after 1929. The banking system was seriously weakened. Many weak business ventures were saddled with a load of fixed charges that could eventually lead only to the bank-

[18] Issues of bonds by corporations exceeded their stock issues until 1928.

ruptcy court. Business expectations in many fields became geared to a level of capital values that could not be maintained indefinitely. The rise in security prices created capital gains, particularly in the upper income groups, and thus put an artificial support under the demand for luxury and durable goods that would collapse with the eventual and inevitable break in security prices.

One result of the excesses, as their effects were felt in the financial collapse after 1929, was the banking and securities legislation of the New Deal.

## Agriculture and Raw Materials

It is important to remember that farming constituted a much more important part of the American economy in the 1920s than it did after World War II. Agriculture accounted for nearly 25 percent of total employment in the mid-twenties. By 1970 this figure had fallen below 5 percent.[19] Hence we must pay more attention to agriculture in the interwar period than we are inclined to today.

American agriculture did not share in the boom of the 1920s to the same degree as the rest of the economy. The disruption of European agriculture had led to an unprecedented boom in American farm production, prices, and exports during the war and immediate postwar years, a boom that was bound to end once European agricultural output returned to something like its prewar level. The situation was made worse by the speculative rise in farm land prices and a heavy increase in farm mortgage debt. The increase in debt, which reached a peak in 1921, was a heavy burden after the collapse of farm prices in 1920–1921, and foreclosures of farm property were high throughout the mid-1920s.

Nonetheless, American agriculture cannot be said to have been depressed during the 1920s, though seeds of difficulty lay under the surface that were to ripen all too rapidly once the domestic demand for farm products began to fall after 1929. Between 1921 and 1929 income in agriculture showed a percentage increase not far below that of total national income. But the rise in farm income was largely over by 1925. In short, by 1925 American agriculture had made a substantial recovery from the very low level reached in 1921, but it contributed little to the expansion in total income thereafter. These indications of a stable demand for agricultural products were a result of rising domestic consumption and declining foreign demand. The per-

[19] For the 1920s, see Lebergott, *op. cit.*, p. 512. For the period after World War II, the distribution of employment by industry can be followed in the *Manpower Report of the President*.

centage of total exports made up of agricultural products showed a significant decline over the decade as a whole. Although this result was accentuated by the growth of agricultural protectionism in Europe, it chiefly reflected a tendency associated with the growing industrialization of this country, which had been going on for decades.[20]

Technological developments increased investment and output in agriculture during the 1920s, but the effects were not so marked as elsewhere in the economy. Use of tractors, trucks, and automobiles spread rapidly, and the "all-purpose" tractor tended to encourage the movement toward large-scale farming. The full effect of these and other technological developments, however, was not fully felt until the 1930s. During the 1920s productivity in agriculture increased much less rapidly than in industry, one result being that the ratio of farm to nonfarm prices tended to rise. The combined effect of technological developments and contracting export markets did tend, however, to depress the prices of some important types of farm products, particularly from 1925 on.

The pressure of increasing supplies was even more noticeable in the world markets for a variety of important agricultural products and raw materials. Following the breakdown of a number of international commodity control schemes, particularly from about 1925 on, prices of primary products registered important declines. These falling prices, taken in conjunction with increasing production and, in some cases, rather rapidly accumulating stocks, suggest that a condition of world overproduction in some primary products was developing before the 1929 downturn.

As important as these developments were, they did not bring on or determine the timing of the downturn in 1929. Their cyclical significance lies in the contribution they made to the severity of the Great Depression. This is true also of the international financial and monetary developments in the 1920s, to which we now turn.

## International Developments

The years 1922–1929 were marked by expanding economic activity throughout the world. The relative increase in industrial production outside the United States (but excluding Russia) in these years was, on the average, not greatly different from that in this country. But the rate of expansion was not uniform. Europe was slow to recover after

[20] Cf. H. Barger and H. H. Landsberg, *American Agriculture, 1899–1939* (New York, National Bureau of Economic Research, 1942), p. 293; Margaret S. Gordon, "International Aspects of American Agricultural Policy," *American Economic Review 36* (September, 1946): 598.

the war, whereas countries undergoing rapid industrialization, such as Japan, Russia, and Canada, showed the largest rates of increase.[21]

American loans played a major role in encouraging expansion in other countries. The war had made the United States a great creditor nation, and, as suggested by Table 2.5, it continued to export capital on a large scale through the 1920s. Net payments due to other countries for freight, tourists' expenditures, and other "invisible" items did little more than offset the large sums due the United States on account of interest and dividends (see Table 2.5). There remained the large export surplus from the United States to be paid for, and this was in effect financed by loans.[22]

The nature of international lending during the 1920s did not make for long-run stability. Many of the American loans were unwisely made. American investment bankers, inexperienced in the international field, encouraged foreign firms and governments to borrow more than they could productively use. Germany was the largest borrower during this period, needing capital for internal reconstruction and foreign exchange with which to make reparation payments. The ease with which foreign loans could be secured led to unwise public expenditures, particularly by local German governments; impaired Germany's ability to export by inflating her costs and prices; and temporarily concealed her inability to pay the existing scale of war reparations in the absence of continued borrowing. Similar overborrowing, though on a smaller scale, took place in some of the Latin American countries.[23]

The flow of American capital was sharply reduced after the first part of 1928. The stock market boom and rising interest rates led American investors to keep their capital at home and even induced a movement of foreign funds to the United States. The abrupt decline of capital exports immediately created difficulties in the debtor countries, particularly those that relied on exports of agricultural products and raw materials, whose prices were already falling in world markets. Even in 1928 some of these countries could not export enough to meet the service charges on their external debt, and by 1929 the situation had become acute in a number of countries.

The inherent instability in the international situation was made all the more serious by the increasingly important role being played by

21 Cf. U.S. Department of Commerce, *The United States in the World Economy* (Washington, D.C., GPO, 1943), p. 150; League of Nations, *Industrialization and Foreign Trade* (Geneva, League of Nations, 1945), pp. 134–135; and Lewis, *op. cit.*

22 Direct investment abroad by American corporations did not play the role in the interwar period that it did in the years after World War II.

23 After World War II foreign aid by the federal government took over some of the role played by private foreign loans in the 1920s.

**Table 2.5**  Balance of Payments of the United States, 1920–1937 (In millions of dollars)

| Type of Transaction | 1920 | 1924 | 1928 | 1929 | 1932 | 1937 |
|---|---|---|---|---|---|---|
| A. Current transactions | | | | | | |
| Exports | 8,481 | 4,741 | 5,249 | 5,347 | 1,667 | 3,451 |
| Imports | 5,384 | 3,684 | 4,159 | 4,463 | 1,343 | 3,181 |
| Balance of merchandise trade | +3,097 | +1,057 | +1,090 | +884 | +324 | +270 |
| Net freight payments | +271 | -46 | -88 | -119 | -84 | -130 |
| Net travel expenditures | -123 | -226 | -327 | -344 | -194 | -213 |
| Unilateral transfers | -679 | -364 | -365 | -377 | -238 | -235 |
| Net interest and dividends | +476 | +622 | +805 | +809 | +392 | +282 |
| Other service items | -198 | -56 | -103 | -82 | -31 | +88 |
| Balance of service items | -253 | -70 | -78 | -113 | -155 | -208 |
| Balance of all current transactions | +2,844 | +987 | +1,012 | +771 | +169 | +62 |
| B. Capital movements | | | | | | |
| Net private long-term | -832 | -700 | -847 | -278 | +225 | +521 |
| Net private short-term | —a | +119 | -348 | -4 | -446 | +354 |
| Net government | -175 | +28 | +49 | +38 | +26 | +2 |
| Net capital movements | -1,007 | -553 | -1,146 | -244 | -195 | +877 |
| C. Net gold movements | +68 | -256 | +238 | -143 | -53 | -1,364 |
| D. Unexplained items | -1,905 | -178 | -104 | -384 | +79 | +425 |

aNot available.

Source:  U.S. Bureau of the Census, *Historical Statistics of the United States: Colonial Times to 1957* (Washington, D.C., GPO, 1960), pp. 562, 564. Plus signs represent a demand for dollars; minus signs, a supply of dollars (or demand for foreign currencies).

short-term capital movements. Short-term funds were held in the leading world money markets by European banks and investors, who tended to shift their balances from country to country in response to actual or anticipated changes in money market conditions or exchange rates. (After World War II similar problems developed, particularly after the mid-1950s.) The situation in Great Britain was particularly serious. That country had returned to the gold standard in 1925 at too high a value for the pound (thus making British goods relatively expensive in foreign markets) and then sought to protect a weakened balance-of-payments position by maintaining high interest rates in London. This policy, together with the reestablishment of London as a world financial center after the return of the pound to a gold basis, attracted large amounts of foreign funds to Britain. The sudden exodus of these funds when confidence in the pound was impaired in 1931 was to drive England off the gold standard.

Germany was also a heavy short-term borrower. Here again the flight of short-term capital was to bring a crisis in 1931. France, on the other hand, was an important short-term creditor; the return of capital to France after the official stabilization of the franc at too low a level in 1928 tended to drain gold out of England and other countries.

It is impossible to say what the course of the business cycle would have been in the rest of the world if the American boom had not collapsed in 1929. A downswing of some sort was probably called for by 1929 or 1930 merely as a result of the weak position of many primary world markets, and serious difficulties in the rest of the world would certainly have eventually affected the United States. In retrospect we can see that the turning point in some countries with balance-of-payments difficulties came before that in the United States. But there is no evidence that the weaknesses in the international situation brought the American boom to an end. The immediate causes of the downturn in the United States lay in domestic developments, which we shall look at further in the next section. But international developments did play a crucial role in determining the extent and severity of the depression once the downswing had begun.

## THE TURNING POINTS, 1923–1929

Before examining the critical turning point in 1929, we shall pause briefly to discuss the minor reversals in business activity in 1923–1924 and 1926–1927.[24] These were mild recessions, somewhat similar to those we experienced after World War II. The National Bureau of Economic

24 For a more detailed analysis of these turning points, as well as that in 1929, see the studies by Wilson, Slichter, and Schumpeter listed in footnote 1, p. 17.

Research gives the following dates for the cyclical phases following the low point in 1921:

| | |
|---|---|
| Expansion | July, 1921–May, 1923 |
| Contraction | May, 1923–July, 1924 |
| Expansion | July, 1924–October, 1926 |
| Contraction | October, 1926–November, 1927 |
| Expansion | November, 1927–August, 1929 |

These are the phases of the minor cycles that were superimposed on the major upswing of 1921–1929. The recessions in 1923–1924 and 1926–1927 were quite mild and brief, and were associated, particularly in 1923–1924, with changes in short-term business expectations. The downturn in 1923 stemmed largely from the rapidity of the rise after 1921. With the debacle of 1920–1921 fresh in their minds, businessmen became concerned over the rapid rise in prices in 1922 and the early months of 1923. This concern was reinforced by a slight rise in Federal Reserve discount rates and by warnings in the financial press.[25] Building activity fell off slightly in response to rising costs. Beginning in the late spring of 1923, business firms began to curtail output, and a general decline set in. Thus change in stort-term expectations seems to have been the chief factor bringing on the recession. Minor horizontal maladjustments affecting particular industries contributed to this downward shift in anticipations.

The low point in business was reached in July, 1924. Money conditions were easy, partly in response to open-market purchases and a reduction in rediscount rates by the Federal Reserve System. Inventories had been reduced, and retail sales had fallen relatively little. Building activity increased, and the volume of new security issues was large. A number of foreign developments reacted favorably on business sentiment, and large domestic crops together with poor harvests abroad had a favorable influence on agricultural incomes. Most important of all, underlying investment opportunities remained favorable. Indeed, on the basis of annual data, output and employment in 1924 were not significantly below 1923 levels. Production recovered sharply in the latter part of 1924 and then continued to expand at a more moderate pace in 1925 and 1926.

"The recession which began in the fall of 1926 was so mild that one hesitates to regard it as a recession in general business."[26] The Federal Reserve index of industrial production showed a total decline of only

---

[25] The Federal Reserve Banks also sold securities in the open market during the first half of 1923, but the effect on interest rates was minor.

[26] Slichter, *op. cit.*, p. 11.

about 6 percent. The recession in manufacturing output was entirely in durable goods and occurred chiefly after Ford Motor closed down in the course of changing to a new model. The production of nondurable goods scarcely showed any recession, and neither did department store sales. As indicated in Table 2.1, total GNP (in constant prices) was slightly larger in 1927 than in 1926. Since most of the decline occurred after the Ford shutdown, it is a fair inference that in the absence of this occurrence no noticeable recession would have developed. It is worth pointing out, however, that there were some elements of weakness in the latter part of 1926. Residential construction had shown a a moderate decline from its peak; there had been some reduction in automobile output since the latter part of 1925; wholesale prices had been falling since the middle of 1925, with some resulting decline in farm incomes; and there was a tendency for our foreign trade balance to decline.

The weakness in prices was worldwide and was connected with developments discussed in the preceding section. These deflationary forces were offset for the time being by the easy-money policy of the Federal Reserve authorities in 1927, which induced a temporary outflow of gold and capital from the United States, and by accentuation of the boom in 1928–1929.

By the end of 1927 Ford had announced its new model, and automobile production rose rapidly thereafter. Prices had begun to move upward earlier in the year, and agricultural incomes improved. Construction activity was again expanding, credit was easy, new security issues had continued at a high level, and stock prices had continued their upward course. Business expectations, which had scarcely felt any setback, improved further. Thus began the final spurt before the collapse of 1929.

The expansion in industrial output in 1928–1929 was extremely rapid (see Figure 2.1), the rise in durable-goods production being particularly marked. Gross capital formation expanded sharply between 1928 and 1929. All the increase was in producer durable goods and inventory accumulation; consumption rose at a slower pace.

The sharp upsurge in production was in the face of declining prices from the fall of 1928 on. Nonagricultural prices had been drifting downward slowly since 1925. Nonetheless, profits were high and continued to rise until about the third quarter of 1929. Wage rates rose relatively little, and the relative increase in factory payrolls was not so great as that in factory output. The expansion in business was also in the face of a rise in interest rates after the beginning of 1928, associated with the mounting speculative demand for credit and with attempts of the Federal Reserve System to bring the stock market boom under control.[27] High-grade bond yields rose moderately after the beginning of 1928, following an almost steady, though mild, decline since 1923. New security issues rose to a new high in 1929, and the volume of stock issues—particularly investment trusts and holding companies—was abnormally large.

The stock market crash came in October, but most observers put the turning point in business several months earlier. The National Bureau's date is August, and the peak in the index of industrial production came at about the same time.[28] Some other indicators turned down even earlier. Retail sales, however, did not decline until the last quarter of the year. We may view the period from about March to October as representing the "turning point zone," or critical period, within which the forces making for deflation gradually came into ascendancy.

It is impossible to give a complete and precise statement of the immediate causes of the downturn. Certainly the full explanation of the extent and severity of the Great Depression is not to be found merely in the sequence of events during 1928–1929; we must look at boom of the 1920s as a whole and at the course of developments during 1930–1933.

Nonetheless, it is possible to find in the situation prevailing in 1929 important elements of weakness that were sufficient to create a depression more severe than that of 1924 or 1927. It is clear that the rise in output of durable goods in 1928–1929 was too rapid to be long maintained. Excess capacity was developing in a number of lines, and this meant a decline in demand for capital goods. As a matter of fact new orders for some types of durable goods declined fairly early in 1929. The automobile market was clearly oversold; in addition, the

---

[27] Federal Reserve pressure was exerted in three stages: sale of securities and increase in rediscount rates in the first half of 1928; the famous warning against bank loans for speculative purposes in February, 1929; and increase of the rediscount rate of the New York Reserve Bank to 6 percent in August, 1929. See Friedman and Schwartz, *op. cit.,* pp. 289–291.

[28] The National Bureau's dates for the turning point in several other countries are: France—March, 1930; Great Britain—July, 1929; Germany—April, 1929. In a more comprehensive compilation the Brookings Institution lists the turning point in different countries by quarters as follows: First quarter, 1929—Poland; second quarter—Canada, Argentina; third quarter—United States, Belgium, Italy, Egypt; fourth quarter—Switzerland, Netherlands, Austria, Czechoslovakia, India, British Malaya; first quarter, 1930—United Kingdom, Japan, New Zealand, South Africa; second quarter of 1930 or later—France, Sweden, Ireland, Yugoslavia, Norway, Denmark. See *The Recovery Problem in the United States* (Washington, D.C., Brookings, 1936), chart following p. 28.

industry's capacity exceeded even the peak production of 1929. The tire industry had been overbuilt, and tire production had fallen sharply in the latter part of 1928. The textile industries had been suffering from overcapacity for some time. Residential construction had been declining sharply since the beginning of 1928, and an overbuilt situation obviously existed in that area. Some of these developments may be described as a result of the belated and rough working of the acceleration principle, although it should be emphasized that we can trace no simple correlation between the short-term changes in the rate of increase in output and the demand for capital goods.

The tendency for buyers' markets to develop in 1929 probably weakened business expectations, and some concern was created by fears arising out of the final excesses of the stock market boom. Accumulating surpluses in agricultural products and raw materials also created a vulnerable situation; this, however, was not fully revealed until after the stock market crash. There was increasing pressure on the balance of payments of various foreign countries as the stock market boom and high interest rates in the United States stopped the outward flow of capital, but the fundamental weaknesses in the international economic situation were not to be fully revealed until the depression had gathered momentum in 1930–1931.

Except in a few sectors, the decline in activity was not severe until after the stock market collapse, which undoubtedly led to a sharp downward revision in expectations and had a considerable effect on the demand for luxury and durable goods. As would be expected, the decline, once it began, was particularly severe in the durable-goods industries.

Although we cannot complete our explanation of the causes of the Great Depression until we look at developments during the 1930s, we can dispose of a number of possible hypotheses as to the major cause of the downturn in 1929. It was clearly not due to an encroachment of costs on profits. Raw-material prices showed some tendency to sag, and wages rose relatively little, despite the relatively low level of unemployment during 1923–1929. (The Phillips curve that prevailed in the 1920s clearly was significantly to the left—that is, less inflationary than that which characterized the American economy after World War II.[29]) While finished-goods prices were also declining as supply pressed on demand, profits were high and rising through the third quarter of the year.

29 The Phillips curve shows the relation between unemployment and the rate of change in wages or prices. Thus the lower the level of unemployment, the higher the rate of increase in wages and prices, other things being given.

Nor can the downturn be explained by monetary developments. The rise in interest rates was not great enough to discourage business borrowing; the Federal Reserve authorities were careful not to restrict credit for legitimate business purposes. We have already seen that business was becoming increasingly independent of the banks, and commercial loans did not begin to decline until after the stock market crash.[30] The tightness of credit affected speculation, but this is another matter. It is also clear that a shortage of capital (savings) was not responsible. Had there been such a shortage, prices and wages should have risen markedly as the capital- and consumer-goods industries bid against each other for labor and materials. Clearly, also, there was no bumping against a ceiling, as is called for in Hicks' version of a multiplier-accelerator theory.[31] Nor did the capital markets show any inability to absorb new security issues until after the break in stock prices. True, there was a moderate rise in bond yields, but this was scarcely enough to discourage much new investment.[32] Indeed, new security issues were in surprisingly large volume even in 1930; the decline in that year was in stock issues, as more new capital was being raised by bonds than in 1929.

We shall return to the problem of causes in the next chapter. Whatever the reasons for the immediate downturn, business activity began to decline in about August, 1929, and in October the bottom dropped out of the stock market. Thus began what we now call the Great Depression. The title is well deserved.

[30] Cf. Nancy Dorfman, "The Role of Money in the Investment Boom of the Twenties and the 1929 Turning Point," *Journal of Finance 23* (September, 1968): 683–684.

[31] John R. Hicks, *A Contribution to the Theory of the Trade Cycle* (Oxford, Clarendon Press, 1950).

[32] It may have had some effect on construction, but here overbuilding was clearly more important than high interest rates.

# 3

# The Great Depression

The downswing that began in 1929 developed into the worst depression in modern history. It spread throughout the world, feeding on the weaknesses in the international situation described in Chapter 2. Although it was worldwide, the depression was more severe and developed more rapidly in the United States than in most other industrial countries. To make matters worse, recovery in the United States after 1933 was slow and painful, and was still far from complete when war broke out again in Europe in 1939. In 1932–1933 virtually 25 percent of the American labor force was unemployed (a figure that today seems inconceivable); the unemployment rate was still as high as 17 percent in 1939.

The loss in potential output during the 1930s is suggested by these unemployment figures and be can further traced in Figure 2.1 (page 18). A rough calculation suggests that the cumulative loss of potential output during the years 1930–1939 was on the order of $490 billion in 1958 prices ($715 billion in 1972 prices), or about twice the annual potential output the economy was capable of producing (at 4 percent unemployment) at the end of the decade. These bare figures, however, are an inadequate measure of the human suffering, economic and social disorganization, and political tensions (domestic and international) that were spawned by the Great Depression.[1]

## ECONOMIC COLLAPSE, 1929–1933

### Extent and Severity of the Decline

Some measure of the magnitude of the contraction after 1929 is provided by the figures in Table 3.1. The GNP in real terms fell by about 30 percent—45 percent when expressed in current prices. Industrial

[1] There is a large literature on the social and economic consequences of the Depression and on the recovery and reform efforts of the New Deal. One of the best, with a detailed bibliography, is Dixon Wecter, *The Age of the Great Depression, 1929–1941* (New York, Macmillan, 1948). Two more recent and journalistic accounts, with some additional bibliography, are Caroline Bird, *The Invisible Scar* (New York, McKay, 1966) and Milton Meltzer, *Brother, Can You Spare a Dime? The Great Depression, 1929–1933* (New York, Knopf, 1969).

**Table 3.1** Measures of the Severity of the Great Depression and of the Extent of Recovery by 1937

|  | 1929 High | 1932–1933 Low | 1937 High |
|---|---|---|---|
| *Annual data* |  |  |  |
| Billions of 1958 dollars |  |  |  |
| GNP | 203.6 | 141.5 | 203.2 |
| Gross private domestic investment | 40.4 | 4.7 | 29.9 |
| Consumer expenditures | 139.6 | 112.8 | 143.1 |
| In current prices, billions of dollars |  |  |  |
| GNP | 103.1 | 55.6 | 90.4 |
| Gross private domestic investment | 16.2 | 1.0 | 11.8 |
| Disposable income | 83.3 | 45.5 | 71.2 |
| Consumer expenditures | 77.2 | 45.5 | 71.2 |
| Total new construction | 10.8 | 2.9 | 7.0 |
| Outside demand deposits | 18.3 | 11.3 | 19.3 |
| Loans, all commercial banks | 36.0 | 14.9[a] | 17.4 |
| Deposits of suspended commercial banks | 0.23 | 3.60 | 0.02 |
| Unemployment rate (percent) | 3.2 | 24.9 | 14.3 |
| *Monthly data* |  |  |  |
| Industrial production (1957–1959 = 100) | 40.1 | 18.7 | 42.3 |
| Durable manufactures | 41.1 | 9.5 | 39.3 |
| Nondurable manufactures | 39.1 | 26.1 | 47.2 |
| Wholesale commodity prices (1926 = 100) |  |  |  |
| All commodities | 98.0 | 59.8 | 88.0 |
| Farm products | 107.6 | 40.9 | 94.1 |
| Stock prices (1935–1939 = 100) | 238 | 36 | 137 |

[a]Figure for June 30, 1935, when low for this series was reached.

Source: Data are from official sources, chiefly Department of Commerce, Bureau of Labor Statistics, and Board of Governors of the Federal Reserve System. Stock prices are the Standard & Poor's index.

production was reduced by more than one-half. Private investment collapsed completely; gross private domestic investment in constant prices fell by nearly 90 percent, to a level much below that needed merely for replacement. The fall in prices was catastrophic both because of the magnitude of the overall decline and because of the distortions created in the price structure. Farm prices declined to less than 40 percent of their 1929 peak, while industrial prices fell much less. In this country the decline in prices and capital values was so great and extensive as eventually to threaten the collapse of our entire banking system and to jeopardize the solvency of many of our financial institutions. Internationally the Depression completely destroyed the monetary stability painfully built up in the 1920s, demoralized trading and financial relations between countries, and generally created a condition of international economic paralysis.

The international scale of the depression is suggested by the figures in Table 3.2.[2] On this side of the Atlantic, Canada was hit nearly as hard as the United States but then had a more rapid recovery. In Europe, the worst sufferer was Germany; the severity of the Depression in that country, which was still saddled with war debts and had never fully recovered from World War I and the peace settlement, had much to do with Hitler's rise to power. Declines in industrial production and national income of one-quarter to one-third were common among the industrial nations listed.

Table 3.2 also suggests that recovery after 1932–1933 was slower in the United States than in most other countries. In 1937 industrial production was significantly above the 1929 level in a number of countries; it had barely regained that level in the United States. The recovery in national income (not adjusted for price changes) was less than in industrial or total output because prices in 1937 were still lower than they were in 1929. One country that did worse than the United States during the recovery was France, the leading member of a group of "gold bloc" countries that stubbornly kept their currencies pegged to gold at preexisting parities after the rest had devalued their currencies.

The National Bureau of Economic Research places the lower turning point in March, 1933. Thus the downswing continued for 43 months, longer than any other business contraction but one since the Civil War. (The downswing following the crisis of 1873 lasted 65 months.) But if we take into account the extent of the decline, the amount of distress caused, the international ramifications, and the slowness of recovery after 1933, we need have little hesitation in rating the Depression of the 1930s the most severe in our history.[3] It was truly the Great Depression.

2 The underlying data from which the percentage changes in Table 3.2 were calculated are from early United Nations publications; some, including the American figures, have since been revised.

3 This is clearly the case for the period since the Civil War, before which our records are too incomplete for meaningful comparison. Cf. A. R. Eckler, "A Measure of the Severity of Depressions, 1873–1932," *Review of Economic Statistics 15* (May, 1933): 75–81, and J. B. Hubbard, "Business Declines and Recoveries," in the same journal, *18* (February, 1936): 16–23.

**Table 3.2** Extent of the Decline and Recovery in National Income and Industrial Production, Selected Countries, 1929–1937

| | Percentage Change | | | |
|---|---|---|---|---|
| | 1929–1930 Peak to 1932–1933 Trough[a] | | 1929–1930 Peak to 1937 | |
| Country | National Income[b] | Industrial Production | National Income[b] | Industrial Production |
| United States | −54.7 | −47.4 | −15.7 | +3.1 |
| Canada | −49.1 | −33.7 | −14.3 | +16.3 |
| Germany | −40.5 | −41.9 | −2.8 | +16.3 |
| Hungary | −33.0 | −18.2 | −13.3 | +29.9 |
| Poland | — | −37.0 | — | +8.7 |
| Italy | — | −33.0 | — | 0 |
| Belgium | — | −31.1 | — | −2.9 |
| Netherlands | −30.4 | −15.7 | −21.4 | +12.4 |
| France | — | −26.2 | — | −18.0 |
| Austria | −27.6 | −38.3 | −5.5 | +6.4 |
| Australia | −25.8 | — | +14.6 | — |
| Czechoslovakia | −23.0 | −39.4 | −12.4 | −3.9 |
| Switzerland | −21.5 | — | −13.8 | — |
| Chile | — | −23.4 | — | +29.9 |
| Norway | — | −22.8 | — | +26.6 |
| Mexico | −19.7 | — | +73.0 | — |
| Sweden | −16.8 | −13.2 | +25.0 | +47.1 |
| South Africa | −15.6 | — | +45.9 | — |
| New Zealand | — | −18.4 | — | +31.6 |
| United Kingdom | −14.6 | −16.5[c] | +10.5 | +23.6[c] |
| Japan | — | −8.4[c] | — | +70.8[c] |

[a]In some cases a year before 1929 may have been the peak, but the data used were available only beginning in 1929 in the case of national income and 1928 in the case of industrial production. In some cases these percentages are based on a trough that occurred later than 1933.

[b]National income figures are in current prices.

[c]Source: League of Nations, *Monthly Bulletin of Statistics 20* (January, 1939): 12.

Source: United Nations, *Statistical Yearbook,* 1948, 1951.

## The Course of the Downswing

That a depression of unusual severity was developing did not become clearly apparent until the second half of 1930. After the collapse of the stock market and the sharp decline in business activity in the last quarter of 1929, there was a slight, abortive recovery in the early months of 1930, associated particularly with a partial recovery in automobile production and some improvement in nonresidential construction.[4] Wage rates were well maintained throughout 1930, and there were public statements against the desirability of wage cuts. But the decline in prices and production and the collapse in the speculative boom that had already taken place had led by mid-1930 to a marked downward revision in both short- and long-term expectations. The decline began to uncover the serious weaknesses in the domestic financial situation, in the position of some of the basic agricultural and raw-material markets, and in the international balance-of-payments position of various countries—particularly those exporting primary commodities and those that had borrowed heavily during the 1920s.

Prices continued to decline through 1930. The rise in automobile production proved short-lived, drought conditions added to the effect of collapsing agricultural prices in reducing farm incomes, nonresidential construction fell off sharply after the middle of 1930, and other private investment also declined markedly. Inventories decreased sharply after the third quarter, and the decline in equipment expenditures accelerated in the second half of the year. The freezing of bank loans associated with the fall in agricultural, real-estate, and security prices began to sap the public's confidence in the banking system; bank failures increased, particularly toward the end of the year. (It should be remembered that there was no deposit insurance in those days to maintain the public's confidence in the solvency of the banks.) Business continued to contract despite a decline in interest rates and a general and substantial easing of credit conditions.

Contracting world trade uncovered oversupply positions in various agricultural and raw-material staples. As a result, prices of these commodities dropped sharply, in turn reducing the demand by agricultural and raw-material-producing countries for the products of industrial nations. By the middle of 1930 the depression was worldwide. In the face of sharply falling prices, the position of debtor countries began to be intolerable, and the situation was made worse by the cessation of international lending. A few countries had been forced to depreciate their currencies as early as December, 1929, and others followed in 1930, although the acute financial crisis did not come until 1931.[5]

---

[4] Apparently a considerable amount of investment planned in 1929 was carried over into 1930. The railroad and electric-power industries spent more for plant and equipment in 1930 than in 1929.

[5] For a picture of the steady abandonment of the gold standard in the 1930s, see the useful summary table in Margaret S. Gordon, *Barriers to World Trade* (New York, Macmillan, 1941), pp. 40–41. This entire book provides an excellent survey of the breakdown of the world trading system in the thirties. For an excel-

Passage of the American Smoot-Hawley Tariff in 1930 induced a wave of retaliation against American trade and set in motion an epidemic of restrictive trade measures by various countries that tended further to strangle world trade. These measures became more severe and discriminatory as the depression developed.

In the early months of 1931, the American economy again seemed to be attempting to stage a recovery. Production in a number of lines expanded, the decline in retail trade leveled off, and there was some minor temporary improvement in private investment. It seemed as if the extreme liquidation of the preceding months might have been sufficient to induce some recovery. At this point, in the late spring of 1931, the international financial structure collapsed completely, and a financial crisis starting in Europe began a new wave of liquidation through the world and deepened the depression in the United States.

The crisis began in May with the failure of the Credit Anstalt, the largest bank in Austria, spread to Germany and the rest of central Europe, and then precipitated a run on the pound sterling that led to the suspension of the gold standard by England and the other countries of the "sterling area" in September. This in turn started a run on the dollar. Gold left this country in large volume in the wake of a flight of short-term capital; interest rates generally increased, and rediscounts with the Reserve Banks rose sharply as the crisis led to renewed currency hoarding and to additional pressure on a banking system already weakened by the impairment of its earning assets. The number of bank failures increased sharply, and business confidence deteriorated still further.[6]

The European financial crisis of 1931 was the direct result of the weak foundations on which the world's financial structure had been built in the 1920s. The recovery of central Europe in the 1920s, as well as Germany's ability to pay reparations, rested on foreign loans, which declined rapidly after 1928. Also, as we saw at an earlier point, short-term capital movements played a much more important role in the 1920s than they did before World War I. Short-term capital could quickly move out of a country and, in so doing, put violent pressure on its balance of payments. The spread of the crisis in the

---

lent study of international monetary relations during the entire interwar period, see League of Nations, *International Currency Experience* (Geneva, League of Nations, 1944).

[6] We shall discuss this episode further in the section on government policy. In the face of massive unemployment and continued worsening in business conditions, the Federal Reserve authorities sought to protect the dollar and stop the gold outflow by a restrictive credit policy.

summer of 1931 was marked by this sort of panicky flight of capital as confidence in currency stability was impaired in one country after another. It was the flight of short-term capital from England that drove that country off the gold standard in 1931, though the steady decline in world prices and in its exports might well have forced it to take this step eventually.

The United States withstood the assult on her monetary standard, but the slight recovery in the first part of 1931 was wiped out. All components of aggregate demand again began a steady decline that continued until the summer of 1932. It was not until this phase of the Depression that wage cuts became substantial. But the reductions were made piecemeal, and each cut merely led to expectations of further reductions in wages and prices.

This phase of the contraction was marked by extreme monetary and financial liquidation—frequent bank failures, currency hoarding, a sharp upsurge of business bankruptcies, severe inventory liquidation, another run on the dollar in the spring of 1932, sharply falling stock prices, and other signs of the almost complete destruction of business confidence. The wave of liquidation subsided in the summer of 1932. Beginning in the third quarter, noticeable improvement began to be evident in the United States and other countries. The increase in production was particularly pronounced in textiles and was undoubtedly due in part to the need to replace depleted inventories after a prolonged period in which production had fallen much more than retail sales. Commodity prices began to show resistance to further declines, and even construction activity began to show signs of improvement.

In the United States this recovery was struck a severe blow at the beginning of 1933 by an outbreak of bank closings beginning in the Middle West and spreading rapidly through the rest of the country. A final wave of hysteria undermined completely the foundation of confidence on which modern banking rests, and by the end of the first week of March all banks in the United States were closed. For many statistical series, this month marks the low point of the Depression. For many others, the summer of 1932 was the low point. Most other countries date their recovery from 1932 rather than 1933. The behavior of the American economy in early 1933 is associated particularly with the final liquidation of the weak spots in our banking system—and perhaps to a minor degree with uncertainty arising out of the imminent change of administration in Washington.

On March 4, 1933, with all banks in the United States closed, Franklin Roosevelt was inaugurated President, and the frantic first "hundred days" of the New Deal began. "The only thing we have to fear is fear itself," declared the new President in his inaugural address. Prompt and energetic action led to rapid reopening of solvent banks, and confidence in the banking system returned immediately. With this hurdle cleared and evidence of a vigorous new leadership in the White House, business and public expectations improved dramatically, and economic recovery in the United States unmistakably began. So did the New Deal measures of recovery and reform that were permanently and radically to change the role of the federal government in the American economy.

Let us now turn back and examine the relevant policies of the government during 1929–1933.

## ECONOMIC POLICY IN DEFAULT

### Federal Reserve Policy

The massive business decline between 1929 and 1933 was accompanied by financial liquidation on an unprecedented scale. The money supply (adjusted demand deposits plus currency in circulation) fell by nearly 30 percent between August, 1929 and March, 1933. Beginning in the fall of 1930 there was a run on the banks of mounting intensity, and between October, 1930 and March, 1933 the amount of currency in circulation increased by over 50 percent despite the decline in production and trade. One wave of bank failures succeeded another; during the years 1930–1933 more than 9,000 banks, with deposits totaling nearly $7 billion, closed their doors. During these traumatic years, when vigorous countercyclical monetary policy was so urgently needed, the Federal Reserve System followed a "passive, defensive, hesitant policy" that in effect permitted the liquidation to run its course.[7] "In retrospect the Federal Reserve's monetary policy, or lack of policy, was a disaster."[8]

Immediately following the stock market crash, the Federal Reserve Bank of New York did take action to provide adequate liquidity for the New York banks, both through a liberal policy of discounting and through open-market purchases (which were made without prior ap-

[7] The quoted phrase is from Milton Friedman and Anna J. Schwartz, *A Monetary History of the United States, 1867–1960* (Princeton, N. J., Princeton University Press, 1963), p. 411. Our discussion of monetary policy in the thirties leans heavily on the analysis of these authors. Their chapter on the 1929–1933 period has been reprinted in paperback as *The Great Contraction, 1929–1933* (Princeton, N. J., Princeton University Press, 1965).

[8] G. L. Bach, *Making Monetary and Fiscal Policy* (Washington, D.C., Brookings, 1971), p. 71.

proval by the Federal Reserve Board). Thereafter the New York Bank favored reducing discount rates and further open-market purchases, but it met with little sympathy from the Federal Reserve Board or from a number of other Reserve Banks.[9]

Federal Reserve action from the end of 1929 to mid-1931 to cope with the Depression was minimal. Discount rates were reduced, but open-market purchases were of modest amount and reluctantly made. The system's holdings of bills and securities were actually reduced somewhat in the early months of 1931. Then came the international financial crisis in September, 1931; gold flowed out of the country, and the Federal Reserve System sharply increased discount rates. Protection of the gold standard was the dominant objective of monetary policy, regardless of what was happening to the domestic economy.

About a billion dollars of government securities were bought between February and August, 1932, in good part because of prodding from Congress. This was the end of any significant expansionary action by the Federal Reserve. The monetary authorities stood by, apparently without any positive policy, in the final wave of liquidation that led to the closing of all banks in March, 1933.

Thus did the Federal Reserve System default on its responsibilities during the worst depression in American history. Monetary policy during these years was truly "a disaster."

### Fiscal Policy in Reverse

If monetary policy during 1929–1933 can be called a disaster, little better can be said for fiscal policy. With respect to the latter, there are some extenuating circumstances: the underdeveloped state of macroeconomic analysis, the almost universal emphasis on the need for "sound" government finance, the small size of the federal budget relative to national income (so that large increases in expenditures were administratively difficult), and the fear, particularly in 1931 at the time of the international financial crisis, that continued large federal deficits and the accompanying increase in the public debt would

---

[9] At issue here was not merely a conflict as to appropriate policy but a jurisdictional dispute as to the authority of the New York Bank vis-à-vis the Board. Until Benjamin Strong died in 1928, his leadership had given the New York Bank the dominant role in the formulation of Federal Reserve policy, but his successor was not able to maintain this dominance. The Board gradually began to exercise its authority, although not without a struggle. The issue of centralizing authority for policy in the hands of the Federal Reserve Board was finally settled by Congress in the Banking Acts of 1933 and 1935.

tighten credit, impair business confidence, and cause an international loss of confidence.[10]

With a continuing budgetary surplus in prospect for fiscal 1930, President Hoover proposed a small and temporary reduction in income taxes at the end of 1929. This was the last stimulative action from the side of taxes during the contraction. Indeed, the tax cut was restored a year later. Pressure was put on state and local governments and on business firms to increase their capital expenditures, and the federal government began to make modest increases in its own expenditures on public works. But President Hoover firmly rejected the proposals that came to him from individual congressmen and various sectors of the public for a much-enlarged program of public works. One such proposal, also rejected, come from a committee that the President himself had set up.

The one really important act of fiscal stimulation by the federal government occurred in 1931. Congress passed a billion-dollar veterans' bonus—over the veto of the President. This, combined with the automatic declines in tax revenues as the Depression deepened, meant that between 1929 and 1931 the federal budget took a substantial swing from surplus to deficit.

The story of federal fiscal policy during the contraction ends with the *deflationary* action of a large tax increase in 1932. This action was initiated by President Hoover at the end of 1931, against the background of the same international financial crisis that precipitated restrictive action by the Federal Reserve System. The increase proposed was a heavy one, in both excise and income taxes, estimated to yield increased revenues equal to about one-third of existing tax receipts. Congressional opposition was largely confined to the nature of the tax increase; the desirability of such a large increase with millions unemployed was not an issue. The increase went into effect in June, 1932, close to the bottom of the Depression.[11]

The rationale behind this action, beyond Hoover's belief in the virtues of a balanced budget, lay in the domestic monetary conditions created by the international financial crisis, which, as we have seen, were exacerbated by restrictive Federal Reserve action. The administra-

[10] This and the ensuing discussion leans heavily on Herbert Stein, *The Fiscal Revolution in America* (Chicago, University of Chicago Press, 1969), chap. 2.

[11] Cf. Stein, *op. cit.*, pp. 31 ff. The Revenue Act of 1932 virtually doubled full-employment tax yields and seriously impeded recovery in the remainder of the decade. See E. Cary Brown, "Fiscal Policy in the 'Thirties: A Reappraisal," *American Economic Review 46* (December, 1956): 868–869.

tion, and many outside the government, feared that continued substantial sales of government securities to finance a large deficit—in the face of tight credit conditions, the weakened banking structure, and an outflow of gold—would further depress security prices, make it difficult for business to borrow, impair public confidence, and thus impede recovery. The administration was not alone in these views.

One moral of this story is the importance of coordinating monetary and fiscal policy. Another is that preoccupation with maintaining balance-of-payments equilibrium at a fixed gold parity can jeopardize efforts to stimulate the domestic economy. An expansionary monetary policy in 1931 and less official concern about the outflow of gold would have made the tax increase seem less necessary to the administration in 1931–1932.

## THE RECOVERY BEGINS

By the fall of 1932 a number of factors were beginning to make for recovery: depleted inventories, the need for some replacement of equipment, the elimination of weak firms and finally a sharp decline in the number of bankruptcies, the tendency of many prices to become stabilized, indications of improvement in some foreign countries and in some primary world markets, and so on. In addition, government measures like the creation of the Reconstruction Finance Corporation in 1932 alleviated some financial distress, and sizable government deficits in 1931 and 1932, even if unwillingly incurred, provided a mild stimulus. Wage rates had declined significantly in 1931–1932, but it is difficult to say whether the stimulating effect of the cost reductions thus achieved offset the depressing effect of business expectations that wages might go still lower.

In any event the banking crisis overwhelmed the tendencies making for recovery at the end of 1932. A new, and this time sustained, recovery began in March, 1933 with the successful efforts of the Roosevelt administration to reopen the banks. Business sentiment immediately improved and then became actively optimistic in response to the further measures of the government to raise prices and incomes during the hectic "hundred days."[12]

The upswing that followed was completely unlike any in our history, and its course aroused more controversy than that of any earlier

[12] See Wecter, *op. cit.*; Basil Rauch, *The History of the New Deal* (New York, Creative Age Press, 1944); and Arthur M. Schlesinger, Jr., *The Age of Roosevelt: The Coming of the New Deal* (Boston, Houghton Mifflin, 1958).

business cycle.[13] The expansion was the longest on record up to that time—50 months between March, 1933 and the National Bureau's date of May, 1937 for the peak. Yet the recovery was weak and irregular, and at the peak in 1937 total output had barely recovered to the 1929 level. Output per capita was less than in 1929. Even during the boom of 1936–1937, there were seven to eight million unemployed. The expansion took place in a setting of far more government intervention in economic affairs than this country had ever before experienced; it was accompanied by unprecedented peacetime government deficits and by a storm of controversy over far-reaching measures of social reform; and it occurred in a world setting of restrictive trade barriers and mounting political tension that eventually ignited the flames of World War II.

## Characteristics of the Upswing

Some of the main features of the cycle of 1933–1938 are summarized in Figure 2.1 (page 18), and additional information is supplied by Tables 3.1 and 3.3. We shall first look at the general characteristics of the expansion and then go on to consider the boom in 1936–1937 and the apparent causes of the downturn that followed.

Employment and output rose sharply in the second quarter of 1933 under the spur of renewed business confidence and anticipations of rising prices resulting from various government measures.[14] A speculative boom ensued that collapsed in the latter part of the year. Business activity recovered further in the first half of 1934, suffered some setback in the second half, and then began a fairly steady advance that accelerated into a moderate boom in 1936 and the early months of 1937. Even at the peak, however, there was widespread unemployment; the national unemployment rate in 1937 was about 14 percent. Wholesale prices rose sharply in 1933 and more moderately in 1934 and then remained relatively stable until a final spurt in the latter part

[13] For more extended discussion of this cycle, see League of Nations, *World Economic Survey* (annual); Thomas Wilson, *Fluctuations in Income and Employment*, 3rd ed. (New York, Pitman, 1948), chap. 18; S. H. Slichter, "The Downturn of 1937," *Review of Economic Statistics 20* (August, 1938): 97–110; J. A. Schumpeter, *Business Cycles* (New York, McGraw-Hill, 1939), vol. 2, pp. 1011 ff.; A. H. Hansen, *Full Recovery or Stagnation?* (New York, Norton, 1938), chaps. 16–17; and K. D. Roose, *The Economics of Recession and Revival* (New Haven, Conn., Yale University Press, 1954).

[14] Including emergency banking legislation and suspension of the gold standard, the Agricultural Adjustment and National Industrial Recovery Acts, measures aimed at providing financial relief to various types of debtors, etc.

**Table 3.3** Gross National Product and Components, 1929 and 1933–1939 (in billions of dollars)

| | 1929 | 1933 | 1934 | 1935 | 1936 | 1937 | 1938 | 1939 |
|---|---|---|---|---|---|---|---|---|
| Total GNP | 103.1 | 55.6 | 65.1 | 72.2 | 82.5 | 90.4 | 84.7 | 90.5 |
| Consumption expenditures | 77.2 | 45.8 | 51.3 | 55.7 | 61.9 | 66.5 | 63.9 | 66.8 |
| Durable goods | 9.2 | 3.5 | 4.2 | 5.1 | 6.3 | 6.9 | 5.7 | 6.7 |
| Nondurable goods | 37.7 | 22.3 | 26.7 | 29.3 | 32.9 | 35.2 | 34.0 | 35.1 |
| Services | 30.3 | 20.1 | 20.4 | 21.3 | 22.8 | 24.4 | 24.3 | 25.0 |
| Private domestic investment | 16.2 | 1.4 | 3.3 | 6.4 | 8.5 | 11.8 | 6.5 | 9.3 |
| Residential construction | 4.0 | 0.6 | 0.9 | 1.2 | 1.6 | 1.9 | 2.0 | 2.9 |
| Nonresidential construction | 5.0 | 0.9 | 1.1 | 1.2 | 1.6 | 2.4 | 1.9 | 2.0 |
| Producer durables | 5.6 | 1.5 | 2.2 | 2.9 | 4.0 | 4.9 | 3.5 | 4.0 |
| Inventory change | 1.7 | -1.6 | -0.7 | 1.1 | 1.3 | 2.5 | -0.9 | 0.4 |
| Net foreign investment | 1.1 | 0.4 | 0.6 | 0.1 | 0.1 | 0.3 | 1.3 | 1.1 |
| Government expenditures | 8.5 | 8.0 | 9.8 | 10.0 | 12.0 | 11.9 | 13.0 | 13.3 |
| Federal | 1.3 | 2.0 | 3.0 | 2.9 | 4.9 | 4.7 | 5.4 | 5.1 |
| State and local | 7.2 | 6.0 | 6.8 | 7.1 | 7.0 | 7.2 | 7.6 | 8.2 |

Source: U.S. Department of Commerce, *The National Income and Product Accounts of the United States, 1929–1965*, p. 2.

of 1936 and the first part of 1937. Even in 1937 prices were considerably below the levels of the late 1920s.

The failure of private long-term investment to achieve anything approaching a full-employment level is the outstanding characteristic of the 1933–1937 upswing in the United States. The deficiency was particularly great in construction expenditures (see Table 3.3). The recovery in producer durable goods was more satisfactory, though here again the 1929 level was not regained. Exports also lagged, and net foreign investment created little in the way of employment opportunities between 1933 and 1937.

It is clear that the marginal efficiency of capital was relatively low in the 1930s. As a result recovery tended to lag, and large government deficits failed to prime the pump. The chief gains between 1933 and 1937 were in consumption rather than investment, and compared to 1929 the output of consumer and nondurable goods made a better recovery than did the production of durable and capital goods.

New private construction in 1937 was about $4 billion less than in 1929 and about $5 billion less than in 1926. Construction was particularly laggard in the residential, public-utility, and commercial fields. Although factory building was also at a low level, the deficiency here was not so great, either absolutely or relatively, as in the other areas mentioned.

Business displayed a notable unwillingness to undertake long-term investment projects, either in new directions or in the lines that had attracted most investment funds in the 1920s. The fact that equipment expenditures made a better showing than business construction suggests that firms were willing to make capital expenditures only as necessary to replace and modernize equipment and to meet relatively minor changes in demand. In manufacturing, sufficient plant capacity had apparently been built during the 1920s to satisfy the demand for products from existing industries, and the demand for capital from new or young industries was not very great. The chief difficulties, however, seem to have been in fields other than manufacturing. Residential construction had obviously been overdone in the 1920s; the normal corrective forces, retarded by a decline in the rate of population growth, had not yet generated the upper levels of a new building cycle. Similar factors were at work to hold down the amount of commercial building (stores, hotels, etc.). Declining rates of growth, calling into play the long-run working of the acceleration principle, restricted investment in some of the industries that had expanded rapidly during the 1920s—the public utilities, for example, and those that depended on the production and use of automobiles.

In addition to these underlying influences, the business fears and antagonism created by various government measures undoubtedly tended to retard investment in some directions, and its has been frequently argued that the New Deal's regulation of the capital markets and tax legislation interfered with the flow of savings, particularly into the more risky types of long-term investment. We can safely dismiss the argument that New Deal policies were the *sole* factor retarding investment, but it is highly probable that they did play some, and perhaps an important, restrictive role. The most serious effect may have been on public-utility investment.

The "deflationary gap" left by private investment was partly filled by government deficits. The effect of the federal budget on the economy is suggested by the figures in Table 3.4. The federal deficit, in response to increased expenditures on relief, public works, agricultural benefits, and so on, rose from $1.4 billion in 1933 to $3.9 billion in 1936. The deficit in 1936 was swollen by the large soldiers' bonus paid in that year. In addition to the ordinary budget, we must consider the effect of the government's social security transactions, which were relatively unimportant until 1937, when the full effect of the large tax payments required by the Social Security Act of 1935 began to be felt. The excess of these receipts over benefit payments was a major offset to the ordinary deficits incurred by the government from 1937 on. We shall return to the subject of the New Deal's fiscal policies in the next section.

**Table 3.4**  Excess of Federal Government Expenditures over Receipts, Including and Excluding Social Security Accounts, 1933–1939 (In millions of dollars)

| Year | (1)<br>Federal Deficit,<br>Excluding Social<br>Security Accounts | (2)<br>Surplus on<br>Social Security<br>Accounts | (3)<br>Net<br>Deficit |
|------|------|------|------|
| 1933 | 1,373 | 58 | 1,315 |
| 1934 | 2,902 | 49 | 2,853 |
| 1935 | 2,633 | 62 | 2,571 |
| 1936 | 3,910 | 281 | 3,629 |
| 1937 | 1,810 | 1,452 | 358 |
| 1938 | 3,213 | 1,084 | 2,129 |
| 1939 | 3,354 | 1,145 | 2,209 |

Source: U.S. Department of Commerce, *The National Income and Product Accounts of the United States, 1929–1965,* Tables 3.1 and 3.7. Column (1) is computed by adding columns (2) and (3).

On the monetary side the 1933–1937 upswing was characterized by exceptionally easy credit conditions, and yet both commercial loans by the banks and the volume of new security issues remained abnormally low. Heavy gold imports added to the excess reserves of member banks, which reached a peak of about $3 billion at the end of 1935. Commercial loans failed to show any increase until 1936 and then remained far below the level of the 1920s. Bank deposits rose, partly as a result of gold imports but chiefly through purchases of government bonds by the commercial banks. Bonds rather than business loans became the chief earning assets of the banks.

The lack of private demand for credit and the extreme liquidity of the banking system led to a marked decline in all types of interest rates in the face of expanding business activity. While firms took advantage of the low interest rates to refund outstanding security issues bearing higher-interest coupons, the volume of corporate issues to raise new capital was extremely low. Stock issues were particularly restricted during the 1930s.

Profits were relatively low throughout the upswing of the 1930s and were lower in 1936–1937 than in 1928–1929. On the other hand, under the stimulus of favorable legislation and the spread of collective bargaining, wage rates rose (despite the high level of unemployment) until in 1937 average hourly earnings of industrial workers were higher than in 1929. The relative rise in money wage rates between 1933 and 1937 was greater than that in either the cost of living or the wholesale prices of finished products. (Real wages in the mid-thirties were significantly higher than in 1929.) The rise in wage rates was only partly offset by increases in labor productivity. Unit labor costs in manufacturing rose rather sharply between 1933 and 1934, and again between 1936 and 1937. As a result of these tendencies operating to increase wages, to some extent at the expense of profits,[15] wage and salary income rose as fast as GNP and somewhat faster than total income payments or disposable income. Despite this indication of a shift toward lower incomes with a higher propensity to consume, personal savings in 1936 and 1937 were about as large a percentage of disposable income as in 1929. Corporate saving, however, was far smaller.

---

[15] According to Spurgeon Bell's data, the ratio of unit labor costs in manufacturing to prices of finished manufactured goods was higher in 1937 than in 1929, though this was not true in 1936. See his *Productivity, Wages, and National Income* (Washington, D.C., Brookings, 1940), p. 270. However, more recent data suggest that, if anything, unit labor costs in 1937 were slightly lower relative to manufactured-good prices than in 1929. See Bureau of Labor Statistics, *Handbook of Labor Statistics*, 1947 ed. (Washington, D.C., GPO).

The factors thus far discussed that impeded recovery in the United States were apparently absent in most other countries. Nearly everywhere the expansion following 1932 was more vigorous than in this country, though the advance was far from uniform. The main exceptions were the countries, of which France was the most important, that maintained a deflationary policy after 1932 in an attempt to remain on the gold standard at pre-Depression parities. By 1937 the world index of manufacturing production (excluding Russia) was above the 1929 level. This was true of the index of capital goods as well as that of consumer goods.

The substantial advance in production and national income in the rest of the world occurred despite the continuance of international trade restrictions on a far greater scale than in the 1920s. Currency management and restrictions on imports permitted various countries to adopt measures to stimulate domestic expansion, and the process was aided (to different degrees in different countries) by public-works programs, rearmament, and continued industrialization.

## Recovery Policy Under the New Deal

Prompt action by the new administration in March, 1933 led to the reopening of solvent banks and restoration of the public's confidence in the banking system. At the same time, the gold standard was suspended and gold exports temporarily embargoed. With the banking crisis over and the balance-of-payments constraint removed, the New Deal could concentrate its efforts on domestic recovery and reform.

Franklin Roosevelt assumed the presidency in 1933 firmly believing in the virtues of a balanced budget, and one of his early acts was to ask for authorization to reduce *regular* government expenditures.[16] At the same time he was committed to a program of larger government expenditures on an emergency basis to cope with the suffering created by mass unemployment and the decline in farm incomes. His method of reconciling these conflicting objectives in his first proposal for a large-scale spending program in 1933 was to request an increase in taxes to finance the interest and amortization payments on the increase in the federal debt that would result. Neither then nor for several years afterward did the notion of the multiplier effects of increased government spending play any role in the New Deal's

16 The discussion of New Deal fiscal policy in this section leans heavily on Stein, *op cit.*, chaps. 3–7. For a retrospective review and defense of New Deal policy by the leading American Keynesian of the time, see Alvin H. Hansen, "Was Fiscal Policy in the Thirties a Failure?" *Review of Economics and Statistics* 45 (August, 1963): 320–323.

fiscal strategy. The aim was relief of distress and placing the unemployed directly in jobs. Thus the intials PWA, WPA, CCC, and others quickly became part of the nation's vocabulary.[17]

In the beginning government spending did not rank high on the New Deal's list of recovery measures. On the monetary side emphasis was placed on banking reform, monetary expansion, and raising the price of gold. Beyond this and increased federal spending for relief and public works, the stress was on the need to "restore purchasing power" through raising wages and prices. This was to be done through the National Recovery Administration (NRA) and the Agricultural Adjustment Administration (AAA), both struck down as unconstitutional by the Supreme Court in 1935–1936. Roosevelt's ambivalent attitude regarding government spending is further reflected in his veto of the veterans' bonus bill in 1935, which Congress overrode in 1936.

Whatever the President's lingering commitment to the notion of "sound" government finance, New Deal efforts to relieve distress both in the city and on the farm, to provide jobs, and to bring about measures of structural reform led to growing government expenditures and a large and rising deficit through 1936.[18]

By early 1937, with revenues increasing as business improved and with the bonus out of the way, the administration thought it might be possible to balance the budget in fiscal 1938. The pressure to do so was increased by monetary developments similar to those in 1931—a restrictive monetary policy, rising interest rates, and a weakening market for government bonds. But efforts to balance the budget ended with the recession of 1937–1938, which was soon followed by the defense program and then our entry into World War II.

We have already noted (Table 3.4) the sharp decline that occurred in the federal cash deficit in 1937 when we include the new

---

[17] The initials cited refer to the Public Works Administration, the Works Progress Administration, and the Civilian Conservation Corps (a resource conservation program for unemployed youth). Another emergency program in the winter of 1933–1934 was the Civil Works Administration (CWA).

[18] See Table 3.4. Neither expenditures nor the deficit rose uninterruptedly. Outlays in fiscal 1935, for example, were slightly less than in fiscal 1934. They then rose sharply with the payment of the veterans' bonus in 1936. The deficit also reached a peak in fiscal 1936. Because of rising incomes (as well as some tax increases), federal revenues rose each year after fiscal 1933. In this connection it might be mentioned that taxes were increased in 1935 and in 1936. The tax increases, reflecting New Deal philosophy, were aimed at the wealthy and at corporate business. For a quantitative evaluation of fiscal policy in the 1930s, see Brown, *op. cit.*

social security taxes.[19] As we shall see in the next section, this was an important contributing factor in the sharp business contraction of 1937–1938.

This recession played an important role in the development of modern fiscal policy in the United States. In April, 1938, after business activity had been falling for nearly a year, the government inaugurated a large-scale spending program. The aim was not merely relief but to stimulate the economy, taking into account multiplier effects. This was the New Deal's first deliberate use of expansionary fiscal policy on modern Keynesian grounds. Even so, it was only a limited version of the New Economics of the Kennedy Administration a quarter-century later. In the 1960s, expansionary fiscal policy was to be used until full employment was reached. In 1938, increased public spending was viewed as a countercyclical device to stop an economic decline and to stimulate recovery but not necessarily to be continued after substantial improvement had been achieved.[20]

Indeed, at no point in the 1930s was New Deal fiscal (or monetary) policy guided by the goal of full employment in its modern sense. It was desirable to balance the budget even if unemployment remained far above its level in 1929, so long as economic activity had been restored to levels equal to or above those of the late 1920s. If surplus labor still existed at this level of total output, it would have to be dealt with in other ways, including (at least in part) reducing the labor supply through, for example, longer schooling, shorter hours, earlier retirement, and so on. At least this seemed to be the dominant view within the administration.[21]

One final aspect of New Deal fiscal policy may be mentioned. Fiscal stimulus was conceived entirely in terms of increases in government spending; there was no use of tax reductions. Indeed, taxes were actually increased on several occasions. The emphasis on expenditures as the fiscal tool to use was fairly common among economists through the 1930s. The shift to preferring changes in tax rates came gradually after World War II.

---

[19] The Social Security Act was passed in 1935.

[20] Alvin Hansen, the leading American disciple of Keynes in the late thirties, believed that incentives to private investment were more or less permanently impaired (see p. 73) and that therefore a higher level of government spending would have to be continued indefinitely. For a retrospective review of the influence of Keynes and his American disciples on New Deal policy, see Alan Sweezy, "The Keynesians and Government Policy, 1933–1939," *American Economic Review 62 (Papers and Proceedings,* May, 1972): 116–124.

[21] See Stein, *op. cit.,* pp. 91–92, 116–117.

Let us turn now to monetary policy.[22] The essential basis for recovery in 1933 was restoration of confidence in the banking system. As we have seen, this was promptly achieved. A crucial step in this connection, and the most important single contribution by the government to the avoidance of future financial crises, was the establishment of federal deposit insurance.

As we have already noted, another of the New Deal's first actions was to suspend convertibility of the dollar into gold, which was followed by Treasury purchases of gold in order to depress the gold value of the dollar. When restricted convertibility was reestablished in January, 1934 at $35 an ounce (a rate that was to endure until August, 1971), the resulting undervaluation of the dollar led to a massive inflow of gold. This in turn created a large increase in the reserves of commercial banks. By the end of 1935 excess reserves of member banks amounted to more than half of the banks' total reserves. Thus an ample basis existed for credit expansion, provided business had the incentive to borrow.[23]

The Banking Acts of 1933 and 1935 ended uncertainty regarding the locus of power within the Federal Reserve System. Authority was firmly placed in the hands of the Board of Governors, the Federal Open Market Committee was established in its present form, to direct open-market operations, and the Board was given various other powers.

With the large inflow of gold rapidly increasing member-bank reserves, additional Federal Reserve action of an expansionary nature did not seem necessary. Thus open-market operations played no significant role in the recovery after 1933. The one important act of discretionary monetary policy, in 1936–1937, was to *tighten* credit as the recovery picked up speed and the rise in prices accelerated. Federal Reserve action in this case took the form of a sharp increase in member-bank reserve requirements. We shall describe this incident in more detail in the next section.

An important development in the thirties was the shift by economists and policy makers away from monetary and toward fiscal policy. This attitude had begun to develop even before the publication of Keynes' *General Theory*, which accelerated the shift in emphasis. This was to

22 Monetary policy in this period is described in Bach, *op. cit.*, pp. 72–78, and Friedman and Schwartz, *op. cit.*, chaps. 8–9.

23 To some extent, however, as Friedman and Schwartz point out, these larger excess reserves—as well as the extent to which the commercial banks shifted their portfolios toward security investments rather than loans—reflected the banks' increased desire for liquidity and not merely the restricted business demand for bank credit.

be the situation for roughly the next 20 years. Renewed interest in the use of monetary policy began to appear in the 1950s and became much stronger in the late 1960s.

## The Boom and Turning Point

Beginning in the spring of 1936, hesitant recovery gave way to rapid expansion. Industrial production increased by nearly 30 percent between March, 1936 and March, 1937, and then moved virtually horizontally through August. Prices rose sharply in the latter part of 1936 and the first few months of 1937. The increase was particularly marked in farm and raw-material prices. At the same time commercial loans began to expand rapidly, there was a general and pronounced rise in inventories, and other characteristics of a speculative boom began to be evident. Wage rates rose sharply in late 1936 and early 1937; other costs increased too; and some bottlenecks began to appear, though total unemployment remained substantial. In the middle of 1936 payment of the veterans' bonus increased incomes and added to the upward movement.

The peak was reached about May, 1937, but a sharp decline did not begin until autumn. The rise in raw-material, farm, and stock prices came to an end in March, and industrial production ceased to advance after that month—though no significant decline occurred until September. A number of other series also show an approximate plateau for a good part of the second and third quarters. Business expectations remained generally favorable, but falling prises, large inventories, and other elements of uncertainty led businessmen to exercise caution by curtailing orders for new goods. Beginning about September, production and employment began to fall as old orders were filled and new ones failed to appear, and an extremely sharp downswing began that lasted until about June, 1938 (compare Figure 2.1, page 18). This recession was primarily an American phenomenon. Production in some foreign countries fell moderately, but in others expansion continued with little or no interruption.

The question is immediately raised: Why was the recovery cut short when business activity was still considerably below the full-employment level? Before attempting to answer this question, it is necessary to review several policy developments that occurred during 1936–1937.

The Federal Reserve authorities had for some months been uneasy about the inflationary possibilities inherent in the large excess reserves of member banks, and these fears were accentuated by the beginnings of the speculative boom. Hence in August, 1936, reserve requirements were increased by 50 percent; they were raised a further 33⅓ percent in two steps between March and May, 1937. The total effect was to double reserve requirements (the maximum increase permitted by law) and to reduce excess reserves from about $3 billion to less than $1 billion. In December, 1936, the Treasury reinforced this action by announcing a program to "sterilize" gold imports—that is, to prevent them from adding to bank reserves. These restrictive measures led to large-scale selling of bonds by the banks, particularly in the first half of 1937. As a consequence there was some increase in bond yields, which may have had an unfavorable effect on the long-term capital market. Commercial loans and short-term interest rates (except on government securities) were not appreciably affected. The issue is still open, but the consensus among authorities has been that monetary policy was not a major cause of the downswing, though it probably had some effect, especially through psychological channels.[24]

The reduction in the federal deficit in 1937, to which we have already referred, was more clearly deflationary. As noted in Table 3.4 (page 60), the ordinary deficit was reduced from $3.9 billion in 1936 to $1.8 billion in 1937, and this lower deficit was nearly offset by the influx of social security taxes. As a result the federal government reduced its net contribution to aggregate demand, including social security funds, from $3.6 billion in 1936, when the deficit was swollen by the bonus payment, to nearly zero in 1937. This deflationary force was particularly operative from about March on; that is, it occurred in the critical period when business was already hesitating for other reasons. Consequently the decline in the deficit was not offset by an increase in private investment. Indeed, by tending to depress incomes and consumption it probably tended to reduce private investment also, since, as we saw earlier, the latter was closely geared to short-term expectations.

In an important sense federal fiscal policy was exceptionally inept in 1936–1937. The large bonus payment added to the boom in 1936, and the sudden reduction in the deficit in 1937 helped tip the balance at a time when business was hesitating.

It is probable that wage and labor developments also played a role of some importance in 1936–1937. The organizing drives of the CIO and union pressure in general led to a sharp increase in wage rates

[24] Kenneth Roose concluded that "Federal Reserve policy cannot be cleared of important responsibility in the recession" because it made more difficult the flotation of any except the highest-grade securities and unfavorably affected business expectations (*op. cit.*, p. 117). As might be expected, given the well-known monetary views of the senior author, Friedman and Schwartz attach considerable importance to monetary restriction in 1936–1937 (*op. cit.*, pp. 520–534, 543–545).

from the end of 1936 to the middle of 1937, and the number of strikes increased rapidly in the first few months of 1937. Higher wages led to anticipations of higher prices, which at first tended to expand advance ordering by business. During the critical period from March on, however, the continuance of wage increases and the rise in some important material costs tended to cut into profits and reduce profit expectations, at least in some lines. At the same time increased building costs had an unfavorable effect on the volume of construction. Under more favorable conditions the increase in costs could have been absorbed by an expanding demand fed by a rising volume of private investment, but in 1937 the depressing effect of the rise in costs was not offset by continued expansion of demand.

## Downswing and Recovery

After September an extremely sharp decline in business activity took place. Industrial production declined by 30 percent in the eight months between September, 1937 and May, 1938. Prices, particularly of farm products, fell rapidly, and so did stock prices (compare Figures 2.1 and 2.2 on pages 18 and 34). Unemployment rose sharply, averaging about 19 percent in 1938. The decline in output considerably exceeded the reduction in retail sales and consumption expenditures, with the result that inventories were reduced rapidly.

Production of nondurable goods ceased to decline after the end of 1937, and expectations in these lines gradually improved. Output of durable goods continued to fall until June, 1938, but at a decreasing rate after the beginning of the year. Nonresidential construction held up relatively well, and residential building, which had shown a significant decline during the latter part of 1937, rose rapidly after January, 1938. In April, as we have seen, the federal government announced a new "spend-lend" program, which undoubtedly improved business expectations even before incomes were enlarged by increased government spending from June on. Exports held up, and a decline in imports increased the export balance. Credit conditions eased rapidly. Reserve requirements were reduced in April, the Treasury stopped sterilizing gold imports and began to spend the proceeds of the gold previously sterilized, and total and excess bank reserves rose throughout 1938.

The low point in business was reached by about June. The turning point may be ascribed to the normal corrective forces operating in a minor depression, particularly liquidation of inventories, plus the stimulating effect of renewed large government deficits. These factors caused short-term expectations to improve. No serious maladjustments or financial weaknesses developed to delay recovery, and there was no fundamental change in long-term expectations. The latter were relatively poor in 1937 (which is why the economy was so vulnerable then) and not much better in 1938—except that the passage of time steadily accumulated more replacement needs and gradually reduced the excess capacity inherited from the 1920s.

We may now turn back and try to summarize the causes of the downswing of 1937–1938. The setting was that of a minor cycle against the background of a deficiency of long-term investment. Short-term expectations were inflated by the speculative boom in 1936, and the increase in inventories and the absence of long-term investment incentives made business highly vulnerable to unfavorable developments that might affect short-period expectations. The fall in commodity and stock prices in the spring of 1937 had just this effect, and so, to some extent, did the action of the monetary authorities. Labor difficulties and the increase in costs also tended to depress profit expectations. A leveling off in retail sales made the economy all the more vulnerable in view of the previous accumulation of inventories. In these circumstances, given the general unsatisfactory level of profits in many lines and the unwillingness or inability of business to invest in long-term projects on any considerable scale, the sharp decline in the government deficit probably provided the factor that tipped the balance. The extent to which private investment was geared to short-term expectations largely explains the sharpness of the decline.

## The Situation in 1939

Business recovered rapidly in the second half of 1938. Minor hesitation in the first half of 1939 was followed by a new upsurge after the outbreak of the war in Europe. By the end of 1939 business in the United States had reached or exceeded the peak attained in 1937. For the year as a whole, the GNP and its various components were approximately the same as in 1937[25] (see Table 3.3). Internationally, the business scene in 1938–1939 was dominated by preparation for and the final outbreak of war, and these developments are reflected in the high level of exports from the United States and in the tremendous influx of gold and short-term capital into this country.

---

[25] The chief differences were the absence of marked inventory accumulation, larger government expenditures, and an increase in foreign investment.

## A LOOK BACK

We are now ready to try to summarize the causes of the Great Depression. Three questions need to be answered. First, what were the factors immediately responsible for the downturn in 1929? Second, how do we account for the length and severity of the downswing that followed? And third, what caused the recovery in the United States after 1933 to be so weak and halting, and to stop so far short of full employment?[26]

The immediate causes of the 1929 turning point have already been suggested and may be summarized as follows:

1. There was a weakening of short-term expectations associated with (a) the development of buyers' markets in particular lines and (b) concern over the stock market boom. Oversupply in the automobile industry was particularly important in this connection.
2. Deflationary pressure accumulated as a result of the decline in residential building that had been going on since early 1928. This was offset only so long as other forms of investment were increasing.
3. Most important, the abnormally high level of investment in 1928–1929—on top of the substantial investment in the several preceding years—was beginning to create conditions of overcapacity in particular industries. This was one of the causes of the weakening of short-term expectations previously mentioned, but, more important, it led to a change in long-term expectations.
4. The developments mentioned were sufficient to begin the downswing. Then in October the stock market crash provided the *coup de grâce*—depressing expectations, removing a cheap source of long-term capital, and reducing consumer demand for luxuries and durable goods.[27]

The international factors—the cessation of international lending and the pressure of supply on the prices of important primary products—were in a sense an independent set of causes operating chiefly on other countries, at least as far as the immediate causes of the downturn are concerned. They were not important in bringing the boom in the United States to an end.

The situation in 1929 was quite different from that in existence at the time of the earlier downturns in the 1920s. Whereas in 1921, 1924,

26 Erik Lundberg seeks to answer essentially the same questions in *Instability and Economic Growth* (New Haven, Conn., Yale University Press, 1968), pp. 74–84.

27 These factors have been stressed by J. K. Galbraith in *The Great Crash, 1929* (Boston, Houghton Mifflin, 1955), pp. 191–193.

and 1927 the maladjustments could be corrected by a brief curtailment of output and liquidation of inventories, in 1929 businessmen began to doubt the profitability of continuing to invest in new plant and equipment at the rate prevailing in 1928 and the first half of 1929. Speculative optimism and technology had inspired in the middle and late 1920s a rate of investment in particular lines that could not be indefinitely maintained, and the acceleration of investment expenditures in 1928–1929 aggravated this tendency. Unlike the earlier downturns in the 1920s, a downward shift in short-term expectations in 1929 involved also a fundamental change in long-term expectations.

It is more accurate to say that the downturn in 1929 was due primarily to "overinvestment" than to ascribe the difficulty to "underconsumption." True, overinvestment was in relation to the demand for final products. But it is difficult to conceive of any increase in *total* consumption that would have maintained investment in a number of areas at the rate that had been reached before the turning point. It is true that wages did not rise as rapidly as productivity and that the propensity to consume apparently fell somewhat in 1929, but it can scarcely be argued that a moderately higher level of consumption could have prevented for very long, if at all, a decline in investment in residential and commercial building, in the automobile and related industries, and in other areas that had been expanding most rapidly. There was overinvestment in the late 1920s in the sense that capacity in numerous lines had been expanding at a rate that could not be maintained indefinitely.

All this, however, does not explain the length or severity of the Depression or its international ramifications. What we have said in earlier sections suggests that the following factors were chiefly responsible for the magnitude of the catastrophe that occurred.

1. The exhaustion of investment opportunities resulting from (a) the working of the acceleration principle in industries approaching maturity and (b) the creation of considerable excess capacity, particularly in residential and commercial building.
2. The financial excesses of the 1920s, which at the same time led to too rapid a rate of real investment in some industries and created a superstructure of inflated capital values whose collapse weakened the banking system and caused both borrowers and lenders to take a pessimistic view of the feasibility of further investment.
3. The unwise lending policies of the commercial banks, which created "frozen assets" on such a scale as to undermine the public's confidence in the entire banking system.

4. Inept and blundering monetary and fiscal policies during 1929–1933, which undoubtedly accentuated the severity of the Depression. Collapse of the banking system could have been avoided by vigorous action. By today's standards the passiveness of the Federal Reserve System between the end of 1929 and mid-1931 and again in early 1933, and its restrictive policy following England's suspension of the gold standard seem inexcusable.[28] Nor did the lack of an expansionary fiscal policy during 1929–1932 help matters. The decline in aggregate demand would have been slowed, and halted sooner, by larger government spending and by tax reductions instead of tax increases, particularly if accompanied by an expansive monetary policy and more vigorous aid to distressed banks.

5. International balance-of-payments difficulties arising out of (a) the decline in American foreign lending, (b) the erratic movement of short-term capital, and (c) the serious oversupply situation in world primary markets, including some of the principal products of American agriculture.

It was these weaknesses, particularly the last four, that continued and deepened the downswing from 1931 on. The combination of these factors made the Depression more severe than the other "major depressions" we have had since the Civil War.

There remains the question: Why was the recovery of the 1930s so slow and halting in the United States, and why did it stop so far short of full employment? We have seen that the trouble lay primarily in the lack of inducement to invest. Even with abnormally low interest rates, the economy was unable to generate a volume of investment high enough, given the propensity to consume, to raise aggregate demand to the full-employment level. What made the general propensity to invest so low is a question that is still being debated.

One answer points to the reform measures of the Roosevelt administration. We have already expressed our own view that New Deal policies cannot be held completely responsible, though they undoubtedly had a restrictive effect on long-term business expectations. There is no reason to believe that different government measures would have restored residential or commercial construction to the inflated levels of the 1920s, and the federal government can scarcely be blamed for the flattening out of growth curves in particular industries or for the "once-

28 One does not need to be a "monetarist" to agree with Friedman and Schwartz (*op. cit.*) that vigorous action by the Fed could have substantially reduced the severity of the depression.

burned-twice-shy" attitude developed by many investors after the financial collapse beginning in 1929.[29] But we may grant, without further analysis, that willingness to invest in long-term projects was impaired to some unknown extent by the way business reacted to the activities of the federal government during those years. Needless to say, this conclusion carries no implications regarding the social desirability, from one or another point of view, of the measures that were taken.

Although much work remains to be done on the interwar period, the author is inclined to believe that government policies were not the most important factor holding back investment in the 1930s. There seems to have been a lack of underlying investment opportunities, apart from the depressing effects of government actions and attitudes. To this should perhaps be added a greater aversion to risk on the part of both institutional and individual investors as a result of the excesses of the twenties and the financial liquidation that followed.

One group of writers holds that a fundamental change in the character of the American economy had occurred by the 1930s, with the result that the level of investment could be expected to be normally deficient in the future, given the existing propensity to consume. In the opinion of Alvin Hansen, the leading proponent of this view, rapid population growth and the opening up of new territory in various parts of the world were responsible for perhaps half of the total net investment in the nineteenth century. Technology was responsible for the remainder. In the 1930s, according to this view, we began to see the effect of the decline in population growth and territorial expansion. Technology alone could not be expected to generate as high a rate of investment as all three stimuli working together, and in the 1930s even technology did not provide as strong a stimulus as it had in earlier decades, when the railroad or the automobile and electric power were expanding most rapidly.[30] Thus in the 1930s the American economy

[29] Schumpeter offers a persuasive argument that New Deal policies helped crystallize a "climate of opinion" unfavorable to business and that this largely explains the disappointing nature of the recovery in the 1930s. In addition, he says, the economy was still riding the downswing of a long wave, but this should not have made the situation any worse than major upswings superimposed on declining phases of earlier long waves. Cf. *op. cit.*, vol. 2, pp. 1038–1050.

[30] Cf. A. H. Hansen, *Fiscal Policy and Business Cycles* (New York, Norton, 1941), chap. 17; also his *Full Recovery or Stagnation? op. cit.*, chaps. 16–18. Later, in *Business Cycles and National Income* (New York, Norton, 1964), Hansen did not deal with secular stagnation as a separate problem but merged it into his discussion of cycles, long waves, and the conditions necessary for steady growth. The resemblances between the 1930s and the 1870s and 1890s were emphasized more, the big difference being the decline in the rate of population

was suffering from "secular stagnation" or "economic maturity"—a drying up of private investment opportunities. If the argument is granted, the solution is obvious. If aggregate demand is equal to the sum of $C + I + G$, and if $I$ remains too low for full employment, the answer lies in increased government spending or measures to raise the propensity to consume, or both.

This is not the place to attempt a critical evaluation of the secular-stagnation thesis, which has attracted much less attention in the inflationary years following World War II than it did in the 1930s.[31] There is unquestionably an important element of truth in the argument—particularly the part that stresses the effect of a declining rate of population growth on opportunities for investment—in residential building, for example, and in the further expansion of old industries. Even if technology prevents a secular decline in the level of investment, "under-employment equilibrium" may still be a danger. For as technology raises potential output, it is not sufficient that the level of investment remain constant. The volume of investment must rise to absorb an increased flow of saving. If this does not occur, the propensity to consume must increase, or government spending must absorb the increased savings not absorbed by an expansion in private investment.

A plausible view is that stagnation existed in the 1930s but did not necessarily have secular significance. Investment opportunities were restricted then because they had been so thoroughly exploited in the 1920s and because the severity of the financial liquidation after 1929 led businessmen and investors to view with a jaundiced eye the opportunities that were available. We would add that, given such a situation, the relative inflexibility of some prices (for example, building costs) prevented investment from being as high as it might otherwise have been. And, as noted before, the reaction of business to New Deal policies made the situation still worse.

By the end of the 1930s, a good deal of excess capacity had been

---

growth in the 1930s. But he no longer assumed that this decline in population growth would automatically continue. He still believed that "there is the danger that we may not achieve, on a sustained basis, our growth potential." *Ibid.*, p. 488.

31 The most vigorous attack on the secular-stagnation thesis has been made by George Terborgh in *The Bogey of Economic Maturity* (Chicago, Machinery and Allied Products Institute, 1945). For a range of views on this subject, see the Twentieth Century Fund symposium, *Financing American Prosperity* (New York, Twentieth Century Fund, 1945), *passim.* For further discussion and bibliography, see Benjamin Higgins, "Concepts and Criteria of Secular Stagnation," in *Income, Employment, and Public Policy: Essays in Honor of Alvin H. Hansen* (New York, Norton, 1948).

liquidated, residential construction was showing encouraging signs of revival, and technology was creating new investment opportunities. Had the war not intervened, private investment might or might not have increased to the point where full employment would have been possible without major government intervention. We shall never know, of course. In the years since World War II, the combination of private investment, a high level of government expenditures, and acceptance of the need to maintain a high level of employment has been sufficient to give us sustained prosperity interrupted by only relatively mild recessions—although the rate of growth through most of the 1950s was disappointing and the level of unemployment remained above 5 percent from 1958 through 1964 and again from mid-1970 through 1972.

# 4

# From World War II to Korea

Hitler's march into Poland touched off the second world war in a generation—and initiated a new set of economic forces that were to dominate the course of economic activity in the United States and most other countries in the decades that followed. In this chapter we shall deal with the period from the outbreak of the war in 1939 to the beginning of the Korean conflict in 1950. The two following chapters will carry the story up to the efforts of the Nixon administration to curb inflation in 1971–1973.[1]

## AFTER 1939: A BRIEF PREVIEW

The general course of economic activity in the war and postwar years can be followed in the charts in this and the next two chapters. There we can trace the wartime boom of output and the initial upsurge in prices brought on by the war, the pronounced inflation in the immediate postwar period, the irregular growth in output in subsequent years, the failure of the economy to achieve its potential in most years after 1948 (except when stimulated by military spending during the Korean and Vietnam wars), and the accelerating inflation after 1965. One trend that is not portrayed in these charts is the deterioration in the balance-of-payments position of the United States from the late 1950s on, a deterioration that finally reached crisis proportions in 1971 and resulted in devaluation of the dollar.

[1] For the postwar period up to 1958, a good general source is Bert G. Hickman, *Growth and Stability of the Postwar Economy* (Washington, D.C., Brookings, 1960). An excellent comparative study, covering the experience of a number of other countries as well, is Erik Lundberg, *Instability and Economic Growth* (New Haven, Conn., Yale University Press, 1968).

**Figure 4.1** Selected Indicators of Economic Activity, 1939–1950

(Source: For actual and potential GNP, U.S. Department of Commerce, *Long Term Economic Growth, 1860–1965,* and *Economic Report of the President,* January, 1972. Other series are from U.S. Department of Labor, Bureau of Labor Statistics, and Board of Governors of the Federal Reserve System.)

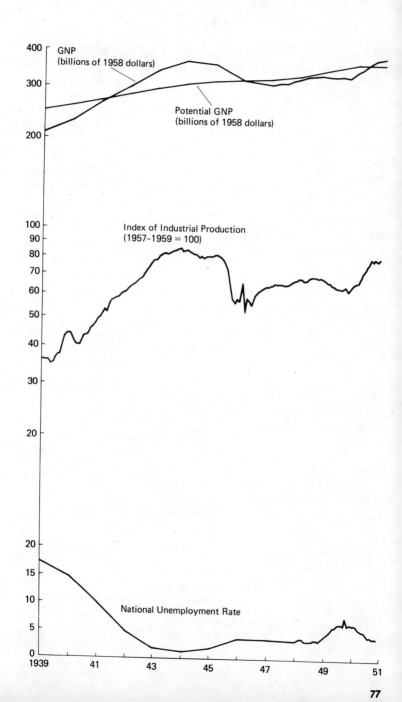

400 ┤ GNP
      (billions of 1958 dollars)

300

200 ┤ Potential GNP
      (billions of 1958 dollars)

100
90
80
70
60
50

40

30

20 ┤ Index of Industrial Production
      (1957–1959 = 100)

20
15
10 ┤ National Unemployment Rate
5
0

1939    41    43    45    47    49    51

From our point of view the most important contrasts between the interwar and postwar periods are (1) the greater stability of the economy after the war (in terms of output and employment), (2) the new commitment by government to maintain high levels of employment, and (3) the development of new inflationary pressures that kept prices rising, with few interruptions, throughout the postwar years. Obviously these changes are all interrelated. All of these contrasts hold not only for the United States but also, and even more strongly, for other advanced economies. In Western Europe and Japan another marked contrast is the much faster rate of growth after the war than in the prewar period, even if the decade of the thirties is excluded from the comparison.[2] One result of the greater stability and, in the case of Western Europe, the faster rate of growth was that the employment record on both sides of the Atlantic was much better than it had been before World War II. However, from the mid-fifties on the American economy performed less well in this respect than Japan or the countries of Western Europe. One price that had to be paid by all countries for high employment and rapid growth was an uncomfortable rate of inflation.

Between October, 1945 (the trough of the mild recession at the end of World War II) and the end of 1970, the United States experienced five complete business cycles, with the cyclical troughs coming in 1949, 1954, 1958, 1961, and 1970. On the average, expansions were longer and recessions briefer and milder than in the prewar period. Since the war we have escaped completely not only the catastrophe of another Great Depression but also such sharp declines as those of 1907–1908, 1920–1921, and 1937–1938. Clearly the economy has been more stable than before the war, and this change has been even more pronounced in other advanced economies.

A number of structural changes account for this greater stability. We shall confine ourselves to the United States, but similar developments have occurred in other countries also. Probably the most important are the following ones.[3]

2 See Table 1.1, p. 2. An excellent study of the causes of rapid growth after World War II is Angus Maddison, *Economic Growth in the West* (New York, Twentieth Century, 1964).

3 For a useful discussion of these changes, see A. F. Burns, "Progress Towards Economic Stability," *American Economic Review 50* (March, 1960): 1–19; Hickman, *op. cit.;* and Lundberg, *op. cit.,* especially chap. 2. For a review of European developments, see Angus Maddison, "The Postwar Business Cycle in Western Europe and the Role of Government Policy," *Banca Nazionale del Lavoro Quarterly Review* (June, 1960): 99–148.

1. *Banking and financial reforms,* which have greatly strengthened the banking system, reduced the extent of financial speculation, and otherwise improved financial practices. These reforms include deposit insurance, regulation of security issues and security trading, the development of amortized mortages (and of guaranteed and insured mortgages), and so on. We should also include here improvement in the conduct of monetary policy.

2. *The greatly increased importance of the "automatic stabilizers,"* which help hold up disposable income and consumer expenditures when GNP declines. These "stabilizers" include social security payments (particularly unemployment compensation), other transfer payments to individuals by the government, corporation and personal income taxes, and undistributed corporate profits. Thus if the GNP begins to decline, undistributed profits and income taxes will fall more than proportionately, and unemployment compensation and other transfer payments will rise. Consequently the decline in disposable income and consumption is much less than it otherwise would be, resulting in milder business recessions than would occur in the absence of these stabilizers.

3. *Government spending is a much larger fraction of GNP than before World War II,* and private investment (when measured in constant prices) is a somewhat smaller fraction of GNP than it was before the 1930s. Thus as long as government spending is maintained, a given percentage change in private investment represents a smaller fraction of GNP than was once the case, and the destabilizing influence of changes in investment is further weakened by the effect of the automatic stabilizers.

4. *The structure of employment has been changing in a stabilizing direction.* Government, the service trades, and white-collar jobs generally are not subject to the wide cyclical swings in employment characteristic of manufacturing, mining, construction, and freight transportation, and it is these relatively stable kinds of employment that have shown the most rapid increases in recent decades.

5. *The government's commitment to maintaining a high level of employment,* which was given concrete expression in the Employment Act of 1946, has undoubtedly influenced business and consumer expectations in a way that is favorable to stability. In particular, business firms and consumers are not so likely to rush to contract their expenditures if they are confident that government intervention will stop a recession before it has gone very far. And contracyclical action by government is much more likely to occur than before.

6. *Business has begun to manage its investment planning and its inventories more wisely*—through, for example, long-term capital budgeting and economizing in the use of inventories. Plant and equipment expenditures can still be cut back in recessions, and inventory investment is still highly volatile, but better business planning has probably made some contribution to greater stability.

7. *For a variety of reasons prices and costs seem to be less variable over the cycle than was once the case, and increasingly businessmen and consumers have come to plan their expenditures on the assumption that prices will continue to rise.* Businessmen do not defer expenditures in recessions or try to liquidate inventories simply because they expect prices to fall rapidly. At the same time the steady upward pressure on wages may help support workers' incomes during business contractions, although the evidence on this point is by no means clear.

8. Finally, *certain secular forces* have operated in the postwar period to create strong booms and mild depressions. These include the rapid rate of population growth (until very recently) and the acceleration of technological change, to which should probably be added the steady rise in prices. It is probable also that, with the greater emphasis on systematic laboratory research, technological change has been proceeding more smoothly and steadily than in the past.

These changes (and others not mentioned) have undoubtedly made the American economy more stable than it was before World War II, although some degree of short-run economic instability remains. At least this is true as far as the behavior of output and employment is concerned. But on the side of prices, as we shall see in this and the following chapters, new inflationary pressures were unleashed after the war that had not yet been brought under control when our story ends.

Let us now examine the decade of the 1940s in some detail. This is the decade of World War II and its aftermath.

## THE DEFENSE PERIOD, 1940–1941

World War II did not begin to have its full effect on the American economy until after the German invasion of Western Europe in the spring of 1940. The situation changed radically after Hitler's triumphant

**Figure 4.2**  Gross National Product and Major Components, 1939–1951 (billions of 1958 dollars)

(Source: U.S. Department of Commerce, *The National Income and Product Accounts of the United States, 1929–1965.*)

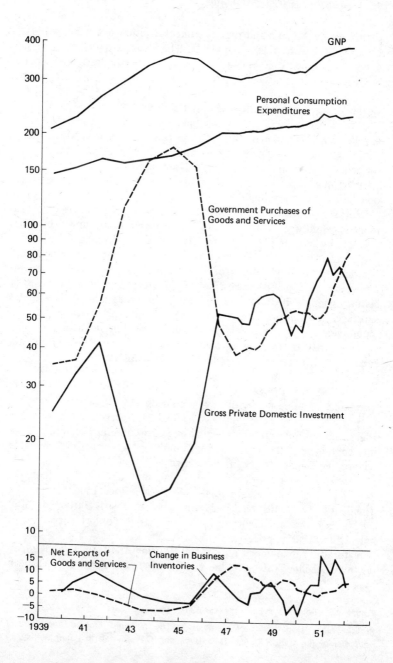

400

GNP

300

Personal Consumption
Expenditures

200

150

Government Purchases of
Goods and Services

100
90
80
70
60
50

40

30

Gross Private Domestic Investment

20

10

Net Exports of          Change in Business
Goods and Services      Inventories

15
10
5
0
−5
−10

1939    41        43        45        47        49        51

81

march to the Atlantic and the consequent decision of the United States to arm itself as rapidly as possible. The American defense program dates from June, 1940. From this point on, the rapid acceleration of military spending injected a powerful new stimulus into the economy.

## Behavior of Government and Private Spending

The factors operating to expand business activity during 1940–1941 can be traced through the data on the components of GNP in Figure 4.2. While defense appropriations increased rapidly after May, 1940, the expansion of military orders did not result in a marked increase of government spending until the fourth quarter of the year. From then on, the rise in government outlays was very rapid.

Working through the familiar multiplier effect, the increased government expenditures led to a rise in incomes and in consumer spending. Private investment expanded rapidly also. The demand for military goods called for new specialized facilities, particularly machinery and equipment. The rapid influx of workers into the war production centers created a demand for new housing. Increased incomes and sales of civilian goods called for new productive facilities, and fears of later shortages led business firms to accelerate their plans for expansion, modernization, and replacement. At the same time, with prices rising and the threat of shortages growing, business firms ordered ahead and accumulated inventories as rapidly as they could.

## Production and Prices

The effect of these powerful new stimuli on industrial production can be seen in Figure 4.1, page 77. The Federal Reserve index of industrial production began a spectacular rise that continued almost without interruption until the end of 1943. Commodity prices began to increase toward the end of 1940, and the rise was quite sharp during 1941 (Figure 4.3). Farm prices in particular shot up rapidly. Much the largest part of the increase in the Wholesale Price Index during the decade of the 1940s occurred either before Pearl Harbor or after the end of the war. During 1942–1945 price control succeeded in holding the rise in prices fairly well in check.

Naturally employment rose rapidly during 1940–1941, and unemployment declined. Even at the end of 1941, however, the American

**Figure 4.3**  Selected Price Indexes, 1937–1954

(Source: U.S. Department of Commerce, *The National Income and Product Accounts of the United States, 1929–1965*, and U.S. Bureau of Labor Statistics.)

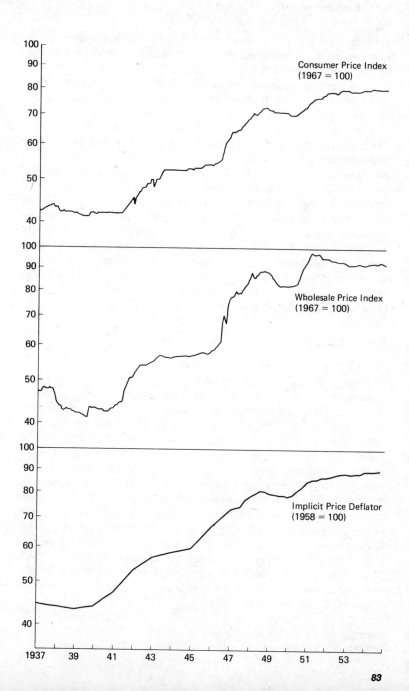

Consumer Price Index
(1967 = 100)

Wholesale Price Index
(1967 = 100)

Implicit Price Deflator
(1958 = 100)

economy had not yet achieved a position of full employment. Total unemployment in December, 1941 was estimated to be about 7 percent of the total civilian labor force.[4] Even so, labor shortages in some occupations and industries and in some sections of the country began to be felt even in 1941. Wage rates began to rise and continued to increase rapidly until they were finally stabilized in 1943.

When aggregate demand increases as rapidly as it did in 1940–1941, prices and wages are likely to rise considerably even before labor and other resources are fully employed. Short-period supply curves may be quite inelastic, particularly when sellers anticipate that demand, costs, and prices will continue to rise, and the supply of agricultural products is relatively fixed in the short run. The rapid accumulation of inventories in 1941 had the effect of both increasing demand and reducing supply for various types of goods. Wage increases began to accelerate well before full employment was reached. This was particularly true where the increase in demand was concentrated in certain areas or industries. Local labor shortages led to localized wage increases to attract labor from other industries or sections of the country, and these wage increases spread rapidly.

## FROM PEARL HARBOR TO RECONVERSION

### The Expansion in Spending and Output

The main outlines of the tremendous expansion in the American economy during the years 1942–1945 are summarized in figures 4.1 and 4.2. Total GNP in current prices jumped from $125 billion in 1941 to $212 billion in 1945, when it was more than twice the figure for 1940. Total government expenditures on goods and services rose to $96.5 billion in 1944,[5] which was more than the entire gross national product during any year of the 1930s. In terms of constant (1958) prices, the GNP increased from $209 billion in 1939 to a peak of $361 million in 1944. In the same constant prices, purchases of goods and services by the federal government were $12.5 billion in 1939, $36 billion in 1941, and $165 billion in 1944. Despite this increase in the share of total output taken by government, private consumption was able to expand moderately (in constant prices) between 1941 and 1945. While gross private domestic and foreign investment declined sharply, the total of private consumption and investment during the war years never fell below the level of 1939.

4 *Survey of Current Business* (January, 1943): 5.
5 This includes state and local expenditures, which declined during the war.

These figures suggest the great elasticity of the American productive system at the time of Pearl Harbor. The increase in war production was secured primarily by expanding total output and, to a minor extent, by reducing private investment. Total consumption did not decline at all. However, neither did it rise as rapidly as disposable income. And of course some types of consumer goods suffered a reduction in supply or were not available at all. Thus, despite the maintenance of consumption, a backlog of pent-up demand accumulated throughout the war. This was to have an important effect on the course of developments after the war was over.

Toward the middle of 1942 the United States reached a position of full employment for the first time since 1929. Even before, labor shortages were becoming acute in some areas and occupations. From 1942 on, the expansion of the armed forces was greater than the increase in the total labor supply, with the result that the *civilian* labor force declined. Unemployment averaged about 1.7 percent during 1943–1945, which was much less than the normal frictional amount.

## Financing Government Expenditures

The federal deficit mounted rapidly as tax receipts lagged the rise in expenditures. The government financed less than half its total expenditures by taxation during the war years. For the entire period from mid-1939 to June, 1946, 45 percent of total expenditures was met by taxes. About 35 percent was borrowed from nonbank investors and did not directly add to the money supply; about 20 percent came from the banking system and gave rise to a corresponding increase in the supply of money in the hands of the public.[6]

The gross public debt rose from about $50 billion at the end of 1940 to more than $275 billion at the end of 1945. Something more than $20 billion of this increase represented merely the building up of Treasury deposits, which were used after the war to cancel a corresponding part of the outstanding debt. If we adjust for this item, we get the results shown in Table 4.1. Between June, 1939 and June, 1946, the federal government borrowed a total of $215 billion, of which 38 percent was provided by the banking system and the remainder by nonbank investors.

By the standards both of past wars and of the experience of other countries in World War II, this was a relatively good performance, although both Canada and the United Kingdom met a larger percentage

[6] H. C. Murphy, *The National Debt in War and Transition* (New York, McGraw-Hill, 1950), p. 258.

**Table 4.1**  Net Amounts Borrowed by the Federal Government from Each Principal Investor Class, June 30, 1939–June 30, 1946

| Investor Class | Billions of Dollars | Percentage of Total |
|---|---|---|
| Commercial banks | 60.2 | 28 |
| Federal Reserve Banks | 21.2 | 10 |
| Total banking system | 81.4 | 38 |
| Individuals | 53.9 | 25 |
| Insurance companies | 19.1 | 9 |
| Mutual savings banks | 8.5 | 4 |
| Other corps. and assocs. | 22.8 | 10 |
| State and local governments | 6.1 | 3 |
| U.S. govt. agencies and trust funds | 23.2 | 11 |
| Total nonbank investors | 133.6 | 62 |
| Net amount borrowed | 215.0 | 100 |

Source:  Reproduced by permission from p. 259 of *The National Debt in War and Transition,* by H. C. Murphy. Copyright, 1950, by McGraw-Hill Book Company, Inc.

of their expenditures by taxation than did the United States. Nonetheless, the (roughly) $200 billion of deficit financing created a huge inflationary potential that could not be held in check once the war was over.

The magnitude of this inflationary potential can be shown in various ways. Total adjusted deposits and currency in circulation more than doubled between 1939 and 1945.[7] The expansion in the money supply was much greater than the increase in private spending, with the result that the income velocity of money (adjusted to exclude both government spending and the government's deposits) fell sharply. The public found its supply of cash rising rapidly relative to its spending. "Excess" cash was accumulating, which firms and households would try to spend once direct controls were terminated and goods were again freely available.

In addition to the increase in the money supply, two other monetary effects, both inflationary, resulted from the government's deficit-

[7] Adjusted deposits are total demand and time deposits minus checks in process of collection and minus U.S. government and interbank deposits.

financing program. First, the public's total supply of liquid assets increased far beyond the expansion in the money supply. As is shown in Table 4.1, nonbank investors absorbed more than $100 billion in government bonds between 1939 and 1946. These bonds were readily convertible into cash, either by direct redemption (as in the case of savings bonds) or by sale in the market. Once the war was over, this greatly increased supply of "near-monies" made the public much more willing and able to spend than would otherwise have been the case. As we shall see later, consumption did rise much faster than disposable income after the war, largely owing to the large accumulation of liquid assets in the hands of the public.[8]

## Monetary Policy and Debt Management
The other inflationary result arose out of the obligation the Federal Reserve authorities assumed, and carried over into the postwar period, to support the government bond market. This meant that the Federal Reserve Banks could not engage freely in open-market operations to limit the supply of bank reserves and thus the volume of bank lending. This was not a major issue during the war. The Federal Reserve Banks had to make available to the banking system the reserves required to meet the great expansion of currency in circulation and the rise in deposits that resulted from government bond sales to the banks. The trouble came after the war. Since the Federal Reserve had to maintain government bond prices, it could not sell government securities freely in order to reduce bank reserves or even to offset the effect of the large gold imports after the war. And it also had to support the bond market while insurance companies and other business firms liquidated part of their bondholdings in order to use the funds in ways that increased the volume of private spending. One result was that the commercial banks were able to expand their loans rapidly after the war, secure in the knowledge that their large holdings of government securities were a highly liquid secondary reserve that could be turned into cash reserves as needed.

By agreement with the Treasury the monetary authorities maintained a fixed pattern of interest rates on the various maturities of government securities by intervening in the market to the extent necessary. The Federal Reserve authorities then proceeded to supply the banking system with the additional funds needed to meet the large flow of currency into circulation and to provide the additional reserves required

[8] For an analysis of monetary developments during the war, see Milton Friedman and Anna J. Schwartz, *A Monetary History of the United States, 1867–1960* (Princeton, N. J., Princeton University Press, 1963), chap. 10.

by the steady expansion in bank deposits. Between Pearl Harbor and the end of 1945, the Federal Reserve Banks increased their holdings of government securities from about $2 billion to approximately $24 billion, thus permitting total reserves to rise by no more than the amount required to back the expansion in deposits. *Excess* reserves declined steadily through 1943 and remained approximately constant thereafter.

## Control of Consumption and Investment

Both consumer expenditures and private investment were far lower during the war than they would have been in the absence of government controls. Gross private domestic investment declined by almost 70 percent between 1941 and 1943. Private capital expenditures were not large enough to take care of current wear and tear and obsolescence, although this deficiency was offset to some extent by new government-financed facilities that are not included in the figures for private investment. Private capital expenditures were held to a low level by a battery of direct controls. Under a system of priorities and allocations, scarce materials were not available for uses other than those considered essential to the war effort; nonessential building was prohibited; and the production of some types of goods was limited by direct order or forbidden outright.

On the basis of the prewar relationship of consumption to disposable income, all types of consumer expenditures were abnormally low during the years 1942–1945. A number of factors contributed to holding down consumption. The mere fact that some goods were unavailable or of inferior quality caused many consumers to save a larger part of their income. Price control also tended to hold down consumption and to increase personal savings. In the absence of price ceilings, the excess of demand over supply would have led to much higher prices, and consumer expenditures would have risen correspondingly without any increase in the actual quantities of goods available. Thus the combination of scarcities and price control tended to hold down consumer spending and to increase saving, although some income did spill over into black markets.

Price control needed the support of a rationing program, and a variety of consumer goods, chiefly foods, were rationed. This again held down consumption and increased the proportion of consumer incomes that was saved.

The government also acted to stimulate saving directly through a vigorous campaign to sell bonds to nonbank investors. An integral part of this campaign was the savings bond designed for the small investor and the program for systematic purchase of these securities through payroll deductions.

So far we have mentioned the main ways in which the propensity to consume disposable income was reduced during the war. In addition, of course, the government attempted to slow down the rise in disposable incomes by increasing taxes. Personal tax payments to the federal government rose from $2 billion in 1941 to about $20 billion in 1945. In 1943 the federal income tax was put on a pay-as-you-go basis, a major reform that was carried over into the postwar period.

## Wage and Price Controls

We have noted the sharp rise in wholesale prices in 1940–1941 and the continued rise of retail prices through 1942. Wages rose steadily during 1941–1942 and were not effectively stabilized until 1943. With the inflationary gap creating a large excess of demand over supply in the private sector and wages and prices pursuing each other upward in an inflationary spiral, all-embracing wage and price controls became necessary.

Price ceilings were imposed on a number of scarce commodities during 1941, but general price control was not instituted until the spring of 1942. Most farm prices were not brought under effective control until 1943.

Price control could not hope to be effective without the stabilization of wages. Wage rates were finally brought under control by application of the "Little Steel formula," which limited the rise in wage rates to 15 percent above the level of January, 1941, with adjustments permitted to remove inequities and to meet special needs. Despite the stabilization of *wage rates,* average hourly earnings continued to rise as the result of the upgrading of workers to higher-paid jobs and an increasing amount of overtime. With longer hours, weekly earnings rose faster than hourly earnings. Despite higher taxes, the take-home pay of the average American factory worker rose significantly more during 1941–1945 than did the cost of living. Part of this gain was due to the increase in the length of the workweek. When the workweek was again reduced after the war, labor sought to offset the consequent reduction in take-home pay through higher wage rates.

## Summing Up

Price and wage control in World War II was surprisingly successful. There were many inequities; some black markets flourished; and perhaps some goods would have been in larger supply or of better quality in the absence of price control. On net balance, however, price and wage controls clearly aided the war effort. As long as it was politically impossible to meet the full cost of the war by taxes, price and wage controls prevented a sharp inflationary spiral that would have created grave political and social tensions, and would have distributed the burden of the war effort in a highly inequitable manner. But this success was only temporary. The end of price control in 1946 let loose the inflationary pressures that had been bottled up, with the effect on prices shown in Figure 4.3.

On net balance, then, this country managed the economic side of the war quite well. It was able to put forth a prodigous productive effort, which resulted in a tremendous flow of armaments of all types. It was able to do this while putting 12 million men and women into the armed services and at the same time maintaining the living standards of the civilian population. Resources were diverted promptly to war uses through a system of direct allocation controls. While deficit financing created a large inflationary potential, prices were held in check, and the real burden of the war was distributed reasonably equitably through direct controls involving rationing and price and wage controls as well as through heavy, progressive taxation. As one economist has put it, this country did a good job of managing a "disequilibrium system" during the war.[9] An "equilibrium system" would have entailed a much heavier burden of taxation to cut down consumer demand or a much higher level of prices to equate the inadequate supply of civilian goods to the inflated level of demand.

## THE PROCESS OF RECONVERSION

Government expenditures reached their peak in the first quarter of 1945. Government war orders declined rapidly after V-E Day and precipitously after the Japanese surrender. Total government purchases of goods and services fell from an annual rate of nearly $100 billion in the first three months of 1945 to about $35 billion in the first quarter of 1946 (see Table 4.2). Thus in the short period of a year the government reduced its contribution to aggregate demand by an amount equal to almost 30 percent of the total GNP at the beginning of the period.

It is not surprising that many observers doubted the ability of the economy to adjust itself to a deflationary force of such magnitude without a serious recession. In the summer of 1945 the belief was fairly

9 J. K. Galbraith, "The Disequilibrium System," *American Economic Review 37* (June, 1947): 287–302.

**Table 4.2** Components of Gross National Product for Selected Calendar Quarters, 1945–1946 (Seasonally adjusted annual rates; in billions of dollars)

|  | First Quarter, 1945 | First Quarter, 1946 | Fourth Quarter, 1946 |
|---|---|---|---|
| Consumption expenditures | 119.0 | 137.2 | 156.1 |
| Gross private domestic investment | 7.7 | 24.5 | 30.3 |
| Net foreign investment | −2.7 | 2.6 | 4.8 |
| Government expenditures | 98.6 | 35.4 | 29.2 |
| Gross national product | 222.6 | 199.7 | 220.4 |
| National income | 191.8 | 169.7 | 190.3 |
| Less: Corporate profits | 23.5 | 14.7 | 21.5 |
| Other deductions[a] | 5.8 | 6.9 | 5.8 |
| Plus: Govt. transfer payments | 3.5 | 12.0 | 9.7 |
| Other additions[b] | 8.5 | 10.2 | 10.4 |
| Personal income | 174.4 | 170.3 | 184.2 |
| Less: Personal taxes | 21.3 | 17.8 | 19.6 |
| Disposable income | 153.1 | 152.5 | 164.6 |
| Consumption expenditures | 119.0 | 137.6 | 156.1 |
| Personal saving | 34.1 | 15.3 | 8.5 |

[a]Chiefly social security contributions.

[b]Includes government interest payments, corporation dividends, and business transfer payments.

Source: *Survey of Current Business* (July, 1950): 30–33. These figures have since been slightly revised, but the changes are not important and in no way alter the interpretation offered in the text.

widely held that unemployment would be a serious problem during the winter of 1945–1946, and a strong deflationary tendency was predicted.

## The Mildness of the Recession

These forecasts, of course, were completely wrong. Total GNP declined by considerably less than half the drop in government spending and had about regained its wartime peak by the end of 1946 (see Table 4.2). Unemployment did not rise as high as 4 percent. Consumer expenditures did not decline at all and, indeed, rose with startling rapidity after V-J Day. Beginning early in 1946, as controls were relaxed, prices began to rise rapidly. In 1946 as during the war, the problem was one of insufficient supplies of goods and excessive demand. Even with the decline in government spending, aggregate demand was sufficient to maintain full employment. By the middle of 1946 a vigorous inflationary boom was in full swing.

Why was the "reconversion recession" so brief and mild—in the face of such a tremendous decline in government spending and a decline of 35 percent in industrial production between February, 1945 and February, 1946? One way of answering this question is to examine in detail the behavior of the components of GNP during this period. Table 4.2 provides a basis for doing this.

## The Behavior of Private Investment

Despite the tremendous decline in government spending, both consumption and private investment rose rapidly. Between the first quarter of 1945 and the first quarter of 1946, private spending increased by about $40 billion. As can be seen in Table 4.2, consumption, domestic investment, and foreign investment all contributed to this expansion. Let us look first at private investment.

The outstanding influence here was the existence of tremendous pent-up demand. Expenditures had to be made as quickly as possible to convert facilities to civilian production and to build up inventories at all stages of production and distribution. Deferred replacement and modernization had to be undertaken. There was a desperate shortage of housing and also other types of buildings. In addition, capacity had to be expanded in many lines to meet the high level of demand that existed or was anticipated.

Businessmen were encouraged to go ahead by the quick lifting of wartime controls and an efficient machinery for handling war contract cancellations. As a result industry was free to absorb labor and materials almost as quickly as they were released by the decline in government orders. Firms reconverting from war to civilian production retained most of their employees to aid in the reconversion process. In addition, workers laid off in some plants were quickly hired by other manufacturers and by the trade and service industries, which had been starved for manpower during the war, or else they were absorbed in the burgeoning construction industry. Another factor moderating the decline in employment was the shortening of the workweek.

In addition to the expansion of domestic investment, Table 4.2 indicates that there was a large increase in net foreign investment as privately financed exports spurted to meet the insistent demand of foreign countries for American goods. The rise in privately financed shipments partially offset the decline in Lend-Lease exports, which had been included in government expenditures in the GNP accounts.

## The Spurt in Consumer Expenditures

The increase in private investment was only a modest offset to the much larger decline in government expenditures on goods and services. In view of this fact the behavior of consumption in this period is quite remakable. There was no multiplier effect leading to a decline in consumer expenditures. On the contrary, consumption increased rapidly in the face of a decline in the GNP. Here lies the major part of the answer to the mildness of the reconversion recession.

There were two main reasons for this. First, disposable incomes of individuals remained virtually constant during the year despite the decline in total GNP. Second, there were powerful forces operating to increase the ratio of consumption to disposable income and to reduce the volume of personal savings.

The stability of disposable income in the face of a decline in GNP is explained primarily by three facts, all of which are brought out in Table 4.2. First, there was a sharp rise in government transfer payments, which increased disposable income without affecting GNP. This chiefly represented benefits paid to veterans as they were rapidly released from the armed services. Second and less important, a decline in personal taxes helped support disposable income. The third factor had to do with the behavior of profits. Corporate profits fell by $9 billion between the first quarters of 1945 and 1946, but dividend payments did not decline. To this extent the decrease in GNP had no effect on disposable income. We shall encounter the same stabilizing behavior of profits and dividends in the later postwar recessions.

Now we come to the rapid rise in the ratio of consumption to disposable incomes in 1945–1946. Here we get into the most important set of influences holding up demand during the reconversion period—and perhaps the most important cause of the inflated level of demand during the postwar boom that followed.

As we have already seen, consumer expenditures were abnormally low during the war years; the propensity to consume was held down by shortages, rationing, price control, and the wartime saving campaign. The deficiency in consumption was most striking in the case of durable goods. By the end of the war there had accumulated a tremendous pent-up consumer demand and also un unprecedented amount of liquid assets to make this demand effective.

Once the war was over and rationing ended, consumers went on a buying spree. What surprised economists was the extent to which this pent-up demand made itself felt in the field of nondurable goods—with the result that expenditures on such goods rose rapidly to a level well above the prewar relationship to disposable income. Expenditures on durables increased rapidly also, but continued shortages limited the amount that could be spent. Returning veterans, supplied with accumulated savings and demobilization benefits, added to the swelling demand for consumer goods. The continued buoyancy in the demand for nondurables and steadily rising expenditures on durable goods made consumer demand an active inflationary force during the postwar boom.

## THE POSTWAR BOOM

The low point of the mild reconversion recession came in the last quarter of 1945. There followed a vigorous inflationary boom that carried the money value of the GNP well above the wartime peak. This boom was characterized by rapidly rising prices and wages, an unprecedented volume of private investment of all types, an unparalleled volume of exports, and a seemingly insatiable demand for consumer goods. Signs of tapering off appeared in 1948, to be followed by a brief and mild recession that reached its low point in the second half of 1949. A vigorous recovery got under way in the first six months of 1950. At this point the outbreak of hostilities in Korea unleashed a new set of inflationary forces.[10]

### Comparison with the Boom After World War I

The period 1946–1949 has certain resemblances to the postwar boom of 1919–1920 and some even more striking differences. The mild recession in 1945 was matched by the mild reconversion dip of 1918–1919. In both cases a sharp inflationary boom ensued that had its basic causes in a great pent-up demand by consumers and businessmen, a swollen foreign demand for American goods, a greatly increased money supply and stock of liquid assets in the hands of the public, and an elastic credit supply that expanded rapidly as business firms sought to enlarge their inventories, plant, and equipment. But here the resemblance largely ends. The boom after World War I was heavily speculative and closely geared to short-term expectations, and the backlog of pent-up demand and the accumulation of liquid assets were nowhere as great as after World War II. In addition, the expansion of 1919–1920 was subject to three deflationary shocks that were largely absent in the later period. Government spending continued at the wartime level well into 1919 and then was sharply curtailed. (In 1945–1946 this deflationary force was out of the way before the boom

---

10 For a detailed analysis of this first complete postwar cycle, see C. A. Blyth, *American Business Cycles, 1945–50* (New York, Praeger, 1969), which also contains references to earlier studies.

began.) Moreover, the monetary authorities deliberately and substantially tightened credit in 1920, whereas monetary ease was the rule throughout the period 1946–1950. And finally, foreign demand weakened significantly in 1920, whereas after World War II the Marshall Plan and other forms of American aid helped maintain exports for a much longer period.

As a result the 1919–1920 boom was quickly over, and because of its short-term, speculative character it was followed by the quite severe depression of 1921. The outstanding characteristic of this episode was the extreme decline in prices that occurred. Nothing like this happened after 1945. Though the boom was highly inflationary and prices rose substantially, there was little speculative accumulation of inventories. While bank credit expanded, business firms remained in a healthy and relatively liquid position. The pent-up demand for consumer goods, the great demand for plant and equipment for replacement, modernization, and expansion, and the acute housing shortage, all backed by the great increase in the money supply and in the public's stock of liquid assets, created a set of expansionary forces that were largely independent of changes in short-term business expectations and other minor deflationary shocks. Essentially, this is why the underlying boom persisted so long and why the minor deflationary forces operating in 1948–1949 led to only a mild and brief dip in business activity.

### General Features of the Boom

Perhaps the outstanding feature of the postwar boom was the rise in prices (see Figure 4.3). Both wages and prices bean to rise rapidly early in 1946, and the upward course of prices was accelerated after the abandonment of price controls in the second half of that year. Protected by steadily expanding aggregate demand and spurred by the sharp increase in the cost of living, organized labor successfully negotiated a series of wage increases that were quickly passed on in higher prices. Food prices, however, rose faster than industrial prices.

Because of the much higher price level, the money value of the GNP quickly surpassed its wartime peak, but the physical volume of production remained below the highest levels reached during the war. This is to be explained in large part by the return to a shorter workweek and by the fact that labor productivity in many peacetime lines was lower than in the highly mechanized war industries. The economy operated at or above the full-employment level; unemployment averaged about 3.9 percent during 1946–1948.

The rise in aggregate demand during the postwar years reflected the behavior of private spending, both consumption and private investment. Although government expenditures on goods and services remained much higher than before the war, they averaged about the same fraction of total GNP as in 1939. On a cash basis the federal budget showed a substantial surplus during the period of most rapid expansion in private spending. There was also a significant decline in the size of the public debt between the end of 1945 and the end of 1948. However, bank loans expanded rapidly. As a result, despite the decline in the commercial banks' holdings of government securities, the money supply in the hands of the public showed a net increase during 1946–1947.

## Behavior of Consumption

Consumer expenditures increased faster during 1946–1947 than could be explained by the rise in income, and an increase in the propensity to consume was an independent influence inflating the level of aggregate demand. The final tapering off in the expansion of consumer demand in 1948 was an important factor in the mild business recession that occurred in 1949.[11]

As we should expect, there was a heavy pent-up demand for consumer durable goods, particularly automobiles, which had not been available during the war. Sales of consumer durables rose as rapidly as expanding production permitted, but it was not until 1948 that consumer expenditures on durables approximated the prewar relationship to disposable income. Even then the backlog of deferred demand for some goods, particularly automobiles, had not been fully satisfied.

Consumer demand for durables (as well as for housing and nondurables) was supported by the large accumulation of liquid assets carried over from the war. Individuals also borrowed heavily, and the volume of installment credit outstanding increased rapidly between the end of World War II and the outbreak of the Korean crisis. Even so, the ratio of such credit to personal income was not as high as during 1939–1941, though much higher than in 1929.

The rapid rise in expenditures on durable goods was not surprising. What was surprising was the level of demand for nondurables. We have already commented on the spurt in this type of expenditures in 1946, when retail sales of nondurables rose to a level considerably above the prewar relationship to disposable income and continued at an abnormally high level during the several years following.

We cannot explore in detail all the possible reasons for this behavior of nondurable-goods consumption. The large volume of ac-

---

[11] On the behavior of consumption, see Blyth, *op. cit.,* chaps. 2–4.

cumulated liquid assets probably played a role of some importance. The distribution of income had changed in favor of low-income groups, and this tended to raise the overall propensity to consume. For a variety of reasons the consumption of food per capita was higher in the postwar period than before the war, and the public did not readily reduce its consumption as prices rose. The percentage of disposable income spent on food was significantly higher during 1946–1947 than before the war.[12] Other factors also undoubtedly played a role in expanding consumption: the desire to spend freely after three years of shortages and rationing, the needs of veterans as they were re-absorbed into civilian life, and in general a free-spending psychology induced by high and rising incomes, full employment, and anticipation of still higher prices. The expansion in consumer expenditures began to level off in 1948, and the volume of personal savings began to rise after the middle of 1947, suggesting that some of the forces operating to create an abnormal level of demand were perhaps beginning to lose their strength. We shall look further at the behavior of consumption and saving in the next section.[13]

### Private Investment in the Postwar Period

Perhaps at no time in our history were the forces tending to expand private investment as strong as they were after World War II (see Figure 4.4). As a result gross private domestic investment rose sharply between 1945 and 1946, from about $10 billion to $30 billion, and then continued to expand further to a temporary peak in 1948. Even if we allow for the higher level of prices after World War II, private investment during 1946–1948 was considerably larger than in 1929.

American business emerged from World War II with a heavy pent-up demand for plant and equipment of all types. There had been little expansion or modernization of capacity during the 1930s, and stringent controls prevented much private investment during the war years. Against this background business faced a demand for goods after the war that was much greater than anything that had been experienced before. Thus there were two driving reasons to invest in new plant and equipment: to satisfy the accumulated needs for replacement and modernization and to expand capacity to meet the new high level of demand.

[12] For an analysis for food consumption and expenditures in the immediate postwar period, see *Survey of Current Business* (January, 1948): 12–16.

[13] See also Irwin Friend, "Personal Saving in the Postwar Period," *Survey of Current Business* (September, 1949).

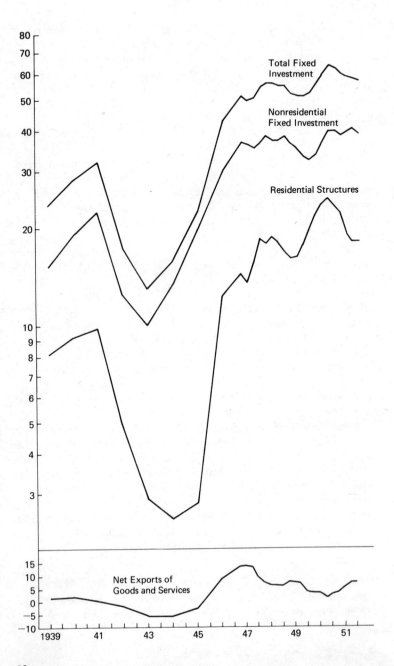

As a result expenditures on nonfarm plant and equipment in each of the years 1947–1950 were more than double the level of 1929 and 1941, the two previous peak years. (Of course allowance must be made for the higher level of prices after World War II.) The rise in plant and equipment expenditures was particularly marked in manufacturing and in electric power and gas.

By 1949 some evidence was beginning to accumulate that the most urgent part of the pent-up demand for plant and equipment had been met, although a substantial backlog of demand for replacement and modernization still existed. In some industries—for example, electric power—the need for further expansion of capacity remained urgent. It seems likely that if the Korean crisis had not occurred business expenditures on plant and equipment would have remained at a high level for several more years but with some tendency to recede gradually from the peak rate reached in 1948.[14]

The high level of residential building was another important factor in the postwar investment boom. An acute housing shortage existed at the end of the war, and residential construction mounted rapidly despite the rise in building costs. During 1948–1949 the volume of residential building exceeded even the peak rate reached in the building boom of the 1920s.

In addition to the shortage inherited from the war, a number of other factors operated to raise the demand for housing: a continued high marriage rate, the high level of incomes, the large volume of liquid assets, and the liberal terms under which mortgage credit could be secured. Here was a strong and largely autonomous stimulus to investment that provided powerful support to the postwar level of business activity and was largely immune to minor deflationary shocks.

During 1946–1948, builders concentrated on higher-priced single-family dwellings. By 1948, supply was beginning to catch up with demand for this type of housing, and tightening credit conditions began to restrict the supply of mortgage credit; a short decline in building activity resulted. This was enough to bring about some reductions in building costs and to stimulate builders to enter the lower-

[14] The forces operating on business investment during these years are surveyed in Blyth, *op. cit.*, especially chaps. 2–4.

**Figure 4.4** Components of Gross Capital Formation, 1939–1951 (billions of 1958 dollars)

(Source: U.S. Department of Commerce, *The National Income and Product Accounts of the United States, 1929–1965.*)

priced field. In addition, federal legislation made the financing of multifamily rental projects easier. As a result residential construction began to rise very rapidly early in 1949, and the expansion continued into 1950 at an accelerated rate. This behavior of residential building is one of the main reasons for the mildness of the 1949 recession.

The accumulation of business inventories also helped support the postwar investment boom, particularly in 1946. In 1947 and again in 1949, however, the tendency toward inventory accumulation was reversed. In 1947 other factors offset the decline in inventory investment, so there was no general recession in business activity. In 1949, however, the decline in inventory investment was larger. This was not offset by expansion in other types of investment, and a mild recession resulted.

Although there was a substantial net accumulation of inventories between V-J Day and the Korean crisis, nearly all of this was required to fill the pipelines between producer and consumer. Despite the rise in prices there was little speculative accumulation of inventories, and businessmen generally followed a conservative inventory policy.

The foreign demand for American goods also played a role of considerable importance in supporting the level of aggregate demand. Both total exports and our export surplus rose rapidly to a peak in 1947. While both declined thereafter, the volume of exports remained abnormally large.

By 1947 foreign countries had virtually exhausted their free reserves of gold and dollars, which they had been using to pay for needed imports from the United States. This situation and continued recovery abroad, which lessened the need for American goods, were responsible for the decline in exports after 1947. A worldwide dollar shortage continued after 1947, and despite American assistance Great Britain and many other foreign countries were forced to devalue their currencies in 1949. The marked rise in American imports in 1950 made a substantial contribution toward relieving the dollar shortage in the rest of the world.

The $5 billion decline in the net export surplus from 1947 to 1948 undoubtedly contributed to the mild recession of 1948–1949, but it was only one of the contributing factors and not the most important. (Figure 4.4 shows that the peak in the export surplus was reached in the third quarter of 1947, a year or more before the business downturn began.) The course of business activity was largely dominated by domestic influences. But the decline in foreign demand did serve to moderate somewhat the inflationary pressures operating on the American economy in 1947–1948, and this in itself contributed to the business downswing that began in the closing months of 1948.

## THE 1949 RECESSION

The rapid rise in prices came to a halt in 1948; farm prices reached a peak early in the year, and the general wholesale index reached its pre-Korean maximum in August (see Figure 4.3). In the latter part of the year, a general business recession set in that was not reversed until the second half of 1949. The recession was mild and brief. Industrial production fell by only about 10 percent, GNP declined by only about 3 percent, and consumer expenditures hardly declined at all. Unemployment increased but remained below 7 percent except for one month during a strike in the steel industry. The contraction lasted 11 months, from November, 1948 to October, 1949. By June, 1950, even before the invasion of South Korea, virtually all the ground lost in 1949 had been regained.[15]

### Causes of the Downswing

The causes of the 1949 decline can be summarized fairly briefly. Three sets of influences were operating in 1948 to bring the steady rise in aggregate demand and in the price level to at least a temporary halt.

1. Increasing supplies of goods, both in the United States and abroad, exerted downward pressure on prices and led eventually to a reaction to the rapid rise in prices that had been in progress. The reaction was sharpest where the rise in prices had been most rapid —that is, in the case of farm prices.
2. The abnormal expansion in consumer demand began to level off, and personal saving began to rise. There were a number of reasons for this. The backlog of demand for most durable goods (except automobiles) had been or was close to being satisfied. In addition, the inflationary stimulus arising from the swollen supply of liquid assets was beginning to lose some of its force. The rise in prices had reduced the real value of the public's stock of liquid assets, and there had also been a movement of these assets away from those who wanted to buy goods to those in the higher income groups who

---

[15] For a useful summary of the developments leading up to the 1948 downturn and an appraisal of the factors responsible for the recession, see Hickman, *op. cit.*, chap. 4, and Blyth, *op. cit.* Other recent references can be found in the latter source.

were willing to hold them. At the same time the steady rise in consumer debt eventually began to act as a check on the continued expansion in consumer spending. Also, as consumers satisfied their most urgent needs there was increasing resistance to high prices.[16]

3. Finally, private investment stopped expanding at its former rate and showed a tendency to decline. Residential building fell off in the final quarter of 1948 for reasons that we have already examined, and industry was beginning to satisfy its most urgent demands for new plant and equipment.[17] New firms had been an important source of demand for plant, equipment, and inventories during 1946–1947, but in 1948 the number of new businesses declined significantly.[18] There was also a sharp decline in our export surplus between 1947 and 1948.

These deflationary forces all came from the private sector of the economy. Paradoxically, the federal budget had been a deflationary force in 1946–1947, when the inflationary boom was at its height, and turned expansionary during 1948, shortly before the downturn in business. Congress reduced tax rates in the spring of 1948, and during the same year adoption of the Marshall Plan and a stepped-up defense program led to increased government expenditures. The excess of receipts over expenditures by the federal government declined from an annual rate of about $15 billion in the fourth quarter of 1947 to $3 billion in the final quarter of 1948.[19]

What happened in 1949 is a good example of how certain influences tend to generate minor business recessions. The decline in prices, the leveling off in consumer demand, and the return to a buyers' market in many lines led to a change in *short-term* expectations, which was reflected in a rapid decline in inventory investment. But underlying long-term investment opportunities remained favorable and, in the important field of residential construction, took a marked turn for the better as credit conditions eased. Also, government spending remained at a high level. Thus, despite the decline in inventory investment, the maintenance of government spending and private long-term investment served to prevent incomes and consumer demand from

16 Cf. D. Hamberg, "The Recession of 1948–49 in the United States," *Economic Journal 62* (March, 1952): 1–14; also Hickman, *op. cit.,* chap. 4.

17 The role of plant and equipment expenditures in the 1949 recession has been carefully examined by Blyth, *op. cit.,* esp. pp. 118–124 and *passim.*

18 See *Survey of Current Business* (February, 1949): 2.

19 U.S. Department of Commerce, *The National Income and Product Accounts of the United States, 1929–1965,* p. 52.

falling very far. Consumer expenditures actually rose slightly in the face of a small decline in disposable income.

## The Mildness of the Recession

The nature of these influences can be readily seen in Table 4.3. Here are presented the main components of the GNP for the fourth quarters of 1948 and 1949, which marked the beginning and end of the decline, respectively, and for the last quarter before the Korean crisis.

The upper half of the table indicates clearly why this is called an inventory recession. The decline in inventory investment ($9.6 billion) was slightly greater than that in total GNP. Consumer expenditures rose during 1949,[20] while there was a small drop in private long-term investment (i.e., investment other than in inventories). A moderate decline in expenditures on nonresidential construction and equipment was partially offset by a rise in residential construction in the second half of the year.

The lower part of the table helps explain why consumption was so well maintained. Although GNP fell by about $9 billion, disposable income declined by only about $6 billion. Three "automatic stabilizers" account for the failure of disposable income to fall any further. First, corporations maintained dividends despite a decline in profits. Second, an increase in unemployment and the need to support farm prices led to a rise in government transfer payments. And third, personal taxes were lower. Thus disposable income declined by much less than GNP. Consumption, however, did not fall at all. Instead, consumers reduced their savings and slightly increased their rate of spending.

With consumption so well maintained, manufacturers and retailers were able quickly to liquidate excess stocks of goods. By the beginning of 1950 they were finding it necessary to replace depleted inventories. Industry began to expand its orders even before the end of 1949, and a widespread and vigorous recovery occurred after the turn of the year. The extent of the recovery up to the time of the Korean crisis is indicated by the last column in Table 4.3, as well as by Figure 4.1, page 77. An outstanding feature of the upswing was the almost spectacular increase in residential building—a rise that was already under way in the first half of 1949, before the low point in general business activity was reached. The recovery was also supported by larger plant and equipment expenditures. However, the most important single factor in the expansion of private investment in the first half of 1950 was the cessation of inventory liquidation.

[20] Expenditures on nondurables declined by about $3 billion, but this was more than offset by an increase in spending on durable goods and on services.

**Table 4.3** Components of Gross National Product for Selected Calendar Quarters, 1948–1950 (Seasonally adjusted annual rates; in billions of dollars)

|  | Fourth Quarter, 1948 | Fourth Quarter, 1949 | Second Quarter, 1950 |
|---|---|---|---|
| Consumption expenditures | 176.6 | 178.8 | 185.8 |
| Durables | 23.1 | 26.3 | 27.9 |
| Nondurables | 96.9 | 94.0 | 96.2 |
| Services | 56.5 | 58.5 | 61.7 |
| Gross private domestic investment | 46.3 | 33.8 | 50.8 |
| New construction | 23.2 | 23.3 | 28.1 |
| Producer durables | 18.8 | 15.7 | 17.9 |
| Change in inventories | 4.3 | −5.3 | 4.8 |
| Net exports | 5.5 | 3.8 | 2.6 |
| Government expenditures[a] | 35.6 | 38.6 | 36.2 |
| Gross national product | 263.9 | 255.0 | 275.4 |
| National income | 229.8 | 214.0 | 232.7 |
| Less: Corporate profits | 34.4 | 28.4 | 35.5 |
| Other deductions[b] | 5.4 | 5.7 | 6.7 |
| Plus: Government transfer payments | 10.1 | 12.3 | 14.1 |
| Other additions[c] | 14.3 | 15.0 | 16.3 |
| Personal income | 214.5 | 207.1 | 220.9 |
| Less: Personal taxes | 20.3 | 18.2 | 19.4 |
| Disposable income | 194.2 | 187.9 | 201.5 |
| Personal saving[d] | 15.4 | 9.3 | 12.9 |

[a]On goods and services. Excludes transfer payments.

[b]Chiefly social security contributions.

[c]Includes government interest payments, corporation dividends, and business transfer payments.

[d]Personal saving in the national income accounts is less than the difference between disposable income and consumption expenditures. The discrepancy is accounted for by consumer interest and personal transfer payments to foreigners.

Source: U.S. Department of Commerce, *The National Income and Product Accounts of the United States, 1929–1965.*

## Summary and Evaluation

The downswing in 1949 was what we have called a minor recession, reflected primarily in a sharp change in inventory investment. Long-term investment opportunities remained favorable throughout the downswing; hence there was only a modest decline in long-term investment. Since government spending was also maintained, incomes could not fall very far. There was no serious impairment of business expectations, both because long-term investment opportunities remained favorable and because businessmen did not believe that a catastrophic decline in prices was "in the cards." A number of factors were responsible for this latter belief: the government's support program for farm prices, the easy credit situation and favorable financial position of business generally, and the feeling that high wages and other elements in the cost structure would keep prices high. The moderate price decline that did occur probably contributed to the removal of some maladjustments in particular markets and thus helped bring on recovery.

Though the change in expectations was of the short-term variety, there was the beginning of a change in the underlying situation in 1948. In particular, the most urgent pent-up demands by consumers and business were beginning to be satisfied. Apparently this required at the time no more than a tapering off in the previous rapid rate of advance. Underlying investment opportunities in particular were still sufficiently widespread and profitable to call for a continued high level of investment. This was most strikingly the case in the field of housing, but it seemed also to be true for business plant and equipment.

Wages continued to rise during 1949, and although consumer prices fell the decline was very modest. As we shall see in the next two chapters, the wage-price structure became increasingly invulnerable to downward pressure in the mild recessions of the postwar period. Another troublesome feature of the 1949 recession was the slowness with which excess unemployment was eliminated once recovery began. By the middle of 1950 both industrial production and GNP in constant prices were above their 1948 peaks, yet the unemployment rate was still as high as 5 percent. The economy had not achieved a position of full employment at the time the Korean War broke out in June, 1950. Although 1948 output levels had been exceeded, the substantial increase in the labor force since 1948 had not yet been fully absorbed.[21]

## GOVERNMENT POLICY, 1946–1949

To what extent did government policy affect the course of economic activity during the boom of 1946–1948 and the recession that followed? Like other major countries the United States emerged from World War II with the resolve that a Great Depression must not occur again and that a major goal of public policy should be the maintenance of a

[21] The slowness of the decline of unemployment after the recession of 1969–1970 was even more pronounced.

high level of employment. One result was the Employment Act of 1946.

Passage of the Employment Act, however, did not mean that the federal government immediately proceeded, deliberately and continuously, to use the monetary and fiscal instruments at its disposal to maintain employment and control inflation. Differences of opinion about precise goals as well as methods of achieving them persisted both inside and outside of government. Numerous other objectives, in addition to the standard macroeconomic goals, strongly influenced fiscal policy—rapid conversion to a peacetime economy, the needs of returning veterans, foreign aid, coping with the farm problem, defense needs, and so on. And on the monetary side Federal Reserve policy was largely subordinated to the debt-management needs of the Treasury.

The federal budget shifted from a huge deficit in 1945 to a moderate surplus in 1946 and a considerably larger surplus in 1947. Government expenditures were determined by considerations entirely apart from stabilization policy and, beginning in the second half of 1947, began to increase again after the massive cutback immediately after the war, despite the inflationary pressures from the private sector of the economy.

The single most important act of discretionary fiscal policy during 1946–1949 was a large tax reduction imposed by Congress in 1948 over President Truman's veto. In retrospect Congress appears to have been prescient, since the recession began within about six months, but there is serious doubt that the proponents of the tax reduction either foresaw the downturn or weighed carefully the effects of the fiscal stimulus if a decline occurred. As for President Truman, he was still recommending a tax increase for more than six months after the recession began.[22]

No discretionary fiscal action was taken during 1949 specifically to deal with the recession. The automatic stabilizers led to a decline in tax revenues while government expenditures (including transfer payments) remained roughly constant, with the result that a moderate deficit emerged for the year beginning in the second quarter of 1949. This covered the second half of the downswing and the early months of the ensuing recovery. In brief, federal fiscal policy was essentially passive during the recession, but by then it was generally accepted

---

[22] Federal fiscal policy during these years is reviewed in Herbert Stein, *The Fiscal Revolution in America* (Chicago, University of Chicago Press, 1969), chap. 9, and Wilfred Lewis, Jr., *Federal Fiscal Policy in the Postwar Recessions* (Washington, D.C., Brookings, 1962), chap. 4. See also Blyth, *op. cit.*, chap. 5, which also deals with monetary policy during the boom and the recession.

that no attempt should be made to balance the budget during a period of rising unemployment.

Monetary policy during the early postwar years was seriously restricted by the obligation imposed on the Federal Reserve System to maintain very low interest rates and thus place a floor under government bond prices. As a result the Fed could not engage in open-market sales of government securities to reduce member-bank reserves as a way of combating inflationary pressures during 1946–1948. Restrictive Federal Reserve action was limited in good part to increasing member-bank reserve requirements in three steps in 1948, but it then had to buy the securities that the commercial banks sold in order to meet the higher reserve requirements. Interest rates remained very low, although the Fed did succeed, against opposition from the Treasury, in bringing about some increase in rates on short-term government securities. Consumer credit controls were also used in 1946–1947 and then again in 1948, with some restraining effect on consumer expenditures for durables.[23] It is fair to say, however, that the Federal Reserve did little to restrain the boom and that restrictive monetary action had little to do with bringing on the downturn.[24]

In the first half of 1949, with the recession well under way, Federal Reserve policy was actually deflationary as it engaged in open-market *sales* to prevent what it considered an undesirably rapid rise in the price of government securities. But beginning in the spring of 1949, it did take a series of expansionary actions—easing credit controls, relaxing stock margin requirements (which had been increased during the boom), reducing reserve requirements in a series of steps, and, in June, ceasing its open-market sales and permitting bond prices to rise. These measures may well have contributed to speeding recovery, which began in the final months of 1949.[25] The Federal Reserve System was not able fully to reestablish its right to an independent monetary policy, free of the obligation to maintain the prices of government securities, until the famous Treasury–Federal Reserve "Accord" of 1951. But that is a subject for the next chapter.

[23] Wartime controls over consumer credit were terminated by Congress in November, 1947 but were temporarily reinstated in August, 1948.

[24] Cf. Friedman and Schwartz, *op. cit.,* pp. 574–585. On the struggle between the Treasury and the Federal Reserve, see also Stein, *op. cit.,* pp. 244 ff.

[25] Federal Reserve policy in 1949 is briefly described in Friedman and Schwartz, *op. cit.,* pp. 606–607.

# 5

# The Decade of the Fifties

By June, 1950 the American economy had almost fully recovered from the mild recession of 1949. Industrial production had already exceeded its 1948 peak, substantial inroads were being made into the unemployment remaining from the recession, and prices were again rising moderately in the fashion typical of cyclical expansions. Then came the invasion of South Korea; the United States found itself again in a "shooting war" and a new set of inflationary pressures was released.

In this chapter we shall look at the American record from the outbreak of the Korean war to the inauguration of President Kennedy in January, 1961. Our ending date is significant in two respects. A business recession reached its low point in February, 1961. And more important, the 1960s inaugurated a new period of vigorous government intervention to restore and maintain full employment.

The period 1950–1961 spans three complete business cycles. The expansion phase of the first—from October, 1949 to July, 1953—was heavily influenced by the Korean war. The ensuing recession in 1953–1954 was again mild, and this was followed by a vigorous capital-goods boom that was the outstanding feature of the long cyclical expansion ending in July, 1957. Again the economy escaped with a mild and brief recession. But the next upswing, from April, 1958 to May, 1960, was a brief and weak one, with the unemployment rate remaining stubbornly above 5 percent. Indeed, the annual average unemployment rate remained above 5 percent from 1958 through 1964, a period of no less than seven years, leading to a national debate regarding the possible growing importance of "structural" unemployment. This debate was to be renewed in somewhat different form at the beginning of the 1970s.

Growth in output during the 1950s was slower than in the preceding or following decades (see Table 1.2, page 12). This was particularly true between the cyclical peak years of 1953 and 1960, a reflection of the much higher unemployment rate in the latter year (5.5 percent) than in the former (2.9 percent). There is also some evidence that the rate of growth of potential output temporarily declined during this period.

Price inflation continued to plague the United States—and, indeed, most of the rest of the world—through the larger part of the decade. The Korean war touched off a new but brief wave of sharply rising prices in 1950–1951. Then came a lull that lasted through 1955, after which prices began to rise again, fairly rapidly in 1956–1957 and more slowly thereafter, with no offsetting decline during the 1958 or 1960 recession. Concern about "creeping" inflation was being widely expressed as the decade ended.

In the closing years of the decade, the combination of uncomfortably high unemployment and a continuing although modest rate of inflation generated a vigorous debate as to how the American economy could best reconcile the seemingly conflicting goals of full employment and rapid growth on the one hand and price stability on the other.[1] This issue was being debated even more urgently a decade later as the economy moved into the 1970s.

## THE KOREAN PERIOD

The Communist invasion of South Korea immediately unleashed a wave of anticipatory buying by both consumers and businessmen; as a result prices rose rapidly during the remainder of 1950 and into the early months of 1951.[2] Although the federal government immediately moved to increase military expenditures as rapidly as possible, this was a process that took time. Consequently, the inflationary pressures during the second half of 1950 and the early months of 1951 came chiefly from the private sector, supplemented by the initial placement of orders for armaments that led private manufacturers to increase their orders for parts and materials, and to step up their hiring of workers. But the big rise in actual government spending came in 1951.

Anticipating price increases and future shortages, consumers sharply increased their purchases in the third quarter of 1950. Indeed, the

[1] See the numerous volumes of hearings and staff reports published by the Joint Economic Committee under the general title *Study of Employment, Growth, and Price Levels* (86th Congress, 1st and 2nd Sessions, 1959–1960).

[2] For a more detailed analysis of developments during the Korean war, see Bert G. Hickman, *Growth and Stability of the Postwar Economy* (Washington, D.C., Brookings, 1960), chap. 5, and the *Economic Report of the President* for the appropriate years.

increase in retail sales was so large that for the time being business was frustrated in its attempts to build up inventories. In the fourth quarter retail sales fell off, and a huge increase in inventory investment occurred. In the meantime business was expanding its capital budgets to provide for larger expenditures on plant and equipment.

The federal government moved promptly and vigorously to control these inflationary pressures. Personal and corporate income taxes were substantially increased in September, an excess profits tax was enacted, controls were reimposed on installment credit, and new restrictions on mortgage credit were put into effect to curb the housing boom. Since tax revenues increased immediately as a result of both the rise in incomes and the higher tax rates, while government expenditures rose much more slowly, a large budgetary surplus accumulated in the second half of the year and particularly in the first quarter of 1951.[3]

These measures were not enough to bring the rise in prices to a prompt halt, nor were they able to prevent a new wave of anticipatory buying and inventory accumulation that broke out after the Chinese communists entered the war in November.

This second buying wave subsided by the end of the first quarter of 1951. Early in the year general price and wage controls were reimposed on the economy. From the end of the first quarter of 1951 until the fall of 1952, the economy was surprisingly stable (see Figure 5.1). Wholesale prices declined gradually through the rest of 1951 and all of 1952. The Consumer Price Index did not fall, but its rise after early 1951 was very moderate (see Figure 6.2, page 144). The rise in consumer expenditures became more gradual. Inventory accumulation fell off sharply after the second quarter of 1951,[4] and noninventory investment began to move more or less horizontally, with the result that gross private domestic investment declined through the second half of 1951 and the first half of 1952.

It was during this period, after the end of 1950, that the big rise in military expenditures occurred and a substantial budgetary surplus was converted into a sizable deficit. Federal expenditures on new goods and services more than doubled, to an annual rate of $46.7 billion, between the fourth quarters of 1950 and 1951. (They continued to

---

[3] On the financing of the Korean war, see A. E. Holmans, *United States Fiscal Policy, 1945–1959* (London, Oxford University Press, 1961), chaps. 8–9.

[4] The decline in inventory investment was concentrated in wholesale and retail trade, and in manufacturing industries producing consumer goods. The defense buildup required rapid accumulation of inventories of military goods and materials throughout the year.

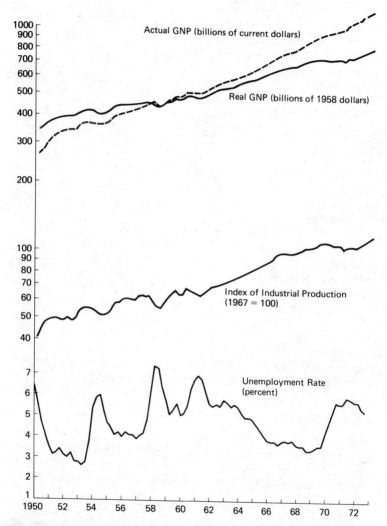

**Figure 5.1** Gross National Product, Industrial Production, and Unemployment, 1950–1972

(Source: *Business Conditions Digest,* June, 1972; January, 1973; and *Industrial Production,* 1971 Edition.)

rise, though more slowly, to a peak of $57.8 billion in the second quarter of 1953.)[5]

Undoubtedly government controls had something to do with the stability of the economy following the early months of 1951. Price controls removed some fears regarding runaway inflation and thus reduced speculative buying, wage controls helped reduce inflationary pressures emanating from tight labor markets and strong trade unions, and the battery of credit and allocation controls worked to hold back consumer and business spending.

While all of this is true, the chief reason for the economy's stability during 1951–1952 probably lay in another direction. Consumers and businessmen had stocked up so well in the two big buying waves in the fall and winter of 1950–1951 that some recession in private buying was virtually inevitable.[6] Even with the diversion of resources to military production, capacity to produce civilian goods proved ample, and businessmen found that their inventories were larger than their sales required.[7]

Thus, to use Hickman's phrase, we had a "divided economy" during 1951–1952. Government expeditures and the production of military goods rose rapidly, but consumer expenditures remained relatively stable and production of many types of consumer goods actually declined. While consumer restraint and inventory disinvestment were largely responsible for these developments, government controls played an important contributing role. Higher tax rates restrained the rise in disposable incomes, selective credit and allocation controls helped curb nonessential private investment, and wage and price controls not only had some direct influence but also helped create consumer and business expectations that were favorable to economic stability.

## THE 1953 DOWNTURN

With government spending continuing to rise, business activity expanded further during the first nine months of 1952, although a steel strike caused some interruption during the summer. In general the lull in consumer spending and in the behavior of prices continued until

[5] U.S. Department of Commerce, *The National Income and Product Accounts of the United States, 1929–1965*, p. 3.

[6] As John P. Lewis has put it, referring to the relative price stability after early 1951, "we could not have gotten the sobriety of the lull without the excesses that immediately preceded it." "The Lull That Came to Stay," *Journal of Political Economy* 63 (February, 1955): 7.

[7] Cf. Hickman, *op. cit.*, chap. 5. See also the article by Lewis cited in the preceding footnote.

about September. At that point there was a spurt in private spending by both consumers and business; output and employment increased sharply in the closing months of 1952 and then began to level off in the spring of 1953. This was the last phase of the expansion that finally reached its peak in July, 1953. By then unemployment had fallen to 2.5 percent after averaging about 3 percent in 1952.

## Causes of the Downturn

Following the steel strike in July, 1952, private demand expanded rapidly, especially for durable goods. Inventories had to be replenished after the steel strike. Government controls had been relaxed as the rise in military expenditures began to level off, capacity continued to increase, and a larger supply of scarce materials could be released for civilian use. Also, after a year-and-a-half of fairly restrained buying, consumers stepped up their purchases, particularly of durable goods.

As a result consumer expenditures increased sharply in the fourth quarter of 1952, and business investment also rose. Rapidly expanding production and payrolls increased disposable income, but consumer spending increased faster still. At the same time other elements of aggregate demand continued to rise—for example, residential building, military expenditures, and the spending of state and local governments.

Retail sales leveled off rapidly in the first half of 1953. *Total* consumer expenditures continued to rise about in line with the rise in disposable income, but most of the increase went into services rather than durable or nondurable goods. Services, unlike tangible commodities, do not require a pipeline of inventories in the hands of retailers, wholesalers, and manufacturers.

Given the flattening out in retail sales, the level of output achieved by the early months of 1953 could not be maintained. The rapid rise in production, especially of durable goods, in late 1952 and early 1953 was geared to (1) the current increase in consumer demand, (2) expectations of further expansion of demand in 1953, (3) the need to replenish inventories depleted by the steel strike, and (4) the need not merely to replenish inventories but to increase them in line with the actual and anticipated increase in sales. The flattening out in sales caused a similar movement in output, and this more or less horizontal movement meant that the current level of production could no longer be maintained. Part of current output was going into inventories, and inventories were already adequate if not excessive.

Another factor was emerging that called for a decline in inventory investment. This was the tapering off of the military program. Defense expenditures reached a peak in the second quarter of 1953, but by then the government had already begun to reduce its new orders to manufacturers.

Thus the foundation was laid for an inventory recession. In addition to the forces at work to reduce inventory investment, two other sets of factors played some part in the downturn. One was monetary tightness; the other was the substantial decline in federal government expenditures that began in the third quarter of 1953.

In Chapter 4 we commented on the easy-money policy the Federal Reserve authorities had pursued during the war and immediate postwar years. This period came to an end with the famous agreement, or Accord, between the Federal Reserve and the Treasury in March, 1951. Under this agreement the Federal Reserve authorities again acquired the ability to pursue a restrictive credit policy if they thought such a policy desirable, even though the result might be a rise in interest rates and a consequent decline in the prices of government bonds. Actually interest rates had been rising gradually since the end of the 1949 recession. This rise accelerated toward the end of 1952 and became quite sharp in the spring of 1953 as the Fed proceeded to exercise its restored independence. The Federal Reserve did not supply reserves to the banking system as fast as the demand for bank credit was expanding; as a result member banks were forced to rediscount from the Reserve Banks, sell some of their holdings of government securities, and restrain the expansion in loans. Credit continued to tighten until June, 1953. In general the rise in interest rates during this period was not extreme, and even at their peak short-term interest rates and long-term bond yields were both much below the levels reached after 1955.

Concerned about the degree of credit tightness that was developing and the effect it was having on anticipations, the Federal Reserve authorities executed a quick reversal, and credit conditions eased rapidly from June on. This unusually early reversal of monetary policy probably contributed to the mildness of the recession that followed.[8]

It is doubtful if these monetary developments played more than a minor role in the downturn.[9] First of all, money market conditions

[8] For a review of monetary developments during the 1950s, see Milton Friedman and Anna J. Schwartz, *A Monetary History of the United States, 1867–1960* (Princeton, N.J., Princeton University Press, 1963), chap. 11, and G. L. Bach, *Making Monetary and Fiscal Policy* (Washington, D.C., Brookings, 1971), pp. 80–85 and chap. 5.

[9] This is also Hickman's view (*op. cit.*, chap. 6). Even Friedman and Schwartz, with their emphasis on the role of money, are cautious about ascribing a major role to monetary influences in the 1953 downturn (*op. cit.*, p. 599).

began to ease a month or more before the downturn. Even though falling bond prices in the spring led to postponement of some security issues, there is little evidence that tight money had much effect on actual capital expenditures. Nor can we attribute the eventual decline in inventories to high interest rates. As we have already seen, the behavior of sales required a decline in inventory accumulation, regardless of the level of interest rates.

More important than temporary monetary stringency was the cutback in military procurement. Defense expenditures started to decline in the third quarter of 1953, but the flow of new defense orders began to diminish before the business peak in July. Once the downturn began, declining government expenditures acted as a deflationary force for a year or more.

## The 1953–1954 Recession

The contraction lasted 13 months, until August, 1954. Industrial production fell about 10 percent, GNP declined only about 2 percent, and the unemployment rate rose from 2.5 to about 6 percent. Prices moved more or less horizontally, and wages continued to rise, though more slowly than in earlier postwar years. It is significant to note that from 1953–1954 through the next two decades prices became increasingly resistant to downward pressure during business recessions.

Examination of Table 5.1 quickly reveals that the downswing can be explained in terms of declines in just two components of aggregate demand: inventory investment and federal government expenditures. These two together declined by a total of $16 billion between the second quarters of 1953 and 1954. This was considerably more than the decline in total GNP.

Clearly this is another inventory recession—a recession that might have been so mild as hardly to be noticeable had it not been for the decline in federal military expenditures. Noninventory investment did not fall at all, a small decrease in expenditures on producer durables being offset by an increase in construction (both residential and nonresidential); there was a large increase in state and local expenditures, and—despite the decline in GNP and rise in unemployment—consumer expenditures actually increased.

Why did consumer expenditures rise, and why was long-term investment so stable? To answer the first question we need to look at the lower part of Table 5.1. First of all, the automatic stabilizers were powerfully at work. Corporate profits declined by more than $5 billion, but dividends hardly declined at all. This alone offset about

**Table 5.1** Components of Gross National Product for Selected Calendar Quarters, 1950–1954 (Seasonally adjusted annual rates; in billions of dollars)

|  | Second Quarter, 1950 | Second Quarter, 1953 | Second Quarter, 1954 |
|---|---|---|---|
| Consumption expenditures | 185.8 | 230.1 | 234.6 |
| Durables | 27.9 | 33.5 | 32.5 |
| Nondurables | 96.2 | 117.2 | 117.4 |
| Services | 61.7 | 79.5 | 84.6 |
| Gross private domestic investment | 50.8 | 55.4 | 49.7 |
| Nonresidential construction | 8.8 | 12.6 | 13.0 |
| Producer durables | 17.9 | 21.3 | 20.4 |
| Residential construction | 19.3 | 18.3 | 18.9 |
| Change in inventories | 4.8 | 3.2 | −2.7 |
| Net exports | 2.6 | 0.1 | 1.7 |
| Government expenditures[a] | 36.2 | 81.9 | 74.3 |
| Federal | 17.1 | 57.8 | 47.4 |
| State and local | 19.2 | 24.1 | 27.0 |
| Gross national product | 275.4 | 367.5 | 360.4 |
| National income | 232.7 | 307.9 | 299.5 |
| Less: Corporate profits | 35.5 | 41.9 | 36.6 |
| Other deductions[b] | 6.7 | 8.9 | 9.7 |
| Plus: Government transfer payments | 14.1 | 12.5 | 14.8 |
| Other additions[c] | 16.3 | 19.4 | 19.3 |
| Personal income | 220.9 | 289.1 | 287.2 |
| Less: Personal taxes | 19.4 | 35.7 | 32.5 |
| Disposable income | 201.5 | 253.4 | 254.7 |
| Personal saving[d] | 12.9 | 19.0 | 15.7 |

[a]On goods and services. Excludes transfer payments.

[b]Chiefly social security contributions.

[c]Includes government interest payments, corporation dividends, and business transfer payments.

[d]Personal saving in the national income accounts is less than the difference between disposable income and consumption expenditures. The discrepancy is accounted for by consumer interest and personal transfer payments to foreigners.

Source: U.S. Department of Commerce, *The National Income and Product Accounts of the United States, 1929–1965.*

two-thirds of the decline in GNP. In addition, transfer payments increased by over $2 billion.

On top of this, personal taxes declined by $3 billion. For the most part, however, this did not represent an automatic stabilizer at work. A tax cut had for some time been scheduled to go into effect in January, 1954, and after the Korean truce the administration decided not to seek to defer the reduction that had been scheduled. The total tax saving was about $3 billion.[10] Here we have an example of *discretionary* fiscal policy that turned out, largely by chance (as in 1948), to have just the right timing.

The net result of all these influences was that disposable income rose slightly in the face of a decline in GNP. In addition, consumers increased their spending more than the increase in disposable income. Thus there was no multiplier effect at all from the decrease in defense spending and inventory investment. Indeed, not only was there no decline in disposable income but there was also a modest upward shift in the short-run consumption function. This was only one of a number of occasions in the postwar years when consumer spending proved to be an autonomous factor in the movement of aggregate demand.

Despite the stabilizers and the favorable behavior of consumer expenditures, the 1954 recession would have been much more severe than it was had it not been for the behavior of long-term investment. The decline in business expenditures for producer durables was very mild, and new construction actually increased. Clearly autonomous forces were at work to maintain a high level of long-term investment. Hence the needed adjustment in inventories was quickly effected, and the economy was able without difficulty to absorb the decline in government expenditures. Of the autonomous forces operating to sustain and expand long-term investment, the following in particular should be noted.

1. Residential building continued to support aggregate demand. The underlying demand for new housing remained strong throughout the 1950s. Equally important, the short-run behavior of residential building tended to have a stabilizing effect in postwar recessions, falling little after business turned down and then beginning to expand again before the general business revival set in.[11] Two sets of reasons account for this stabilizing behavior. First, the federal government

---

[10] Offset to a minor extent by an increase in social security taxes. On this see *Economic Report of the President,* January, 1955, p. 19.

[11] The recession of 1960–1961 was an exception (see p. 131).

acted in 1954, as it did in the other postwar recessions, to stimulate residential building, particularly by liberalizing the terms on which mortgage credit could be secured. Second and more important, the operation of the postwar money and capital markets had the effect of causing residential building to behave almost as if it were an automatic stabilizer. When interest rates rose and credit became tight during a cyclical boom, lenders diverted more of their funds from residential mortgages, particularly guaranteed and insured mortgages with relatively fixed interest rates, to other types of securities. When credit became easy in a recession and yields on nonmortgage securities fell, life insurance companies and other lenders sought to invest in residential mortgages. This happened on a large scale in 1954, with the result that mortgage lending and residential building began to expand rapidly from about the beginning of 1954. New-housing starts rose about 40 percent between December, 1953 and December, 1954.[12]

2. There was a strong and rising demand for commercial buildings of all types, and in the 1950s the United States had its first commercial building boom since the 1920s.

3. Plant and equipment expenditures declined only moderately. Investment opportunities were still large in a variety of industries under the spur of rapid technological change and continued growth of population and income. Although this type of investment did not rise until after the general upturn in business, it did not fall very far in 1954, and it provided a powerful stimulus to expansion during 1955–1957.

4. Capital expenditures of state and local governments continued to rise steadily during the 1953–1954 recession, as they have every year since World War II. The decline in interest rates and the better market for state and local bonds made it easier to meet some of the seemingly insatiable demands for schools, roads and streets, and other essential public improvements.

---

12 See Leo Grebler, *Housing Issues in Economic Stabilization Policy*, National Bureau of Economic Research Occasional Paper 72 (1960), esp. chap. 2. Residential building tended to follow this partly countercyclical behavior in subsequent recessions also, although the precise nature of the mechanism at work changed somewhat. Today a very important factor is the movement of funds into savings and loan associations and mutual savings banks when market interest rates are low (as in recessions) and a reverse flow away from these mortgage lenders when market yields rise. This latter reverse flow has come to be called "disintermediation."

## THE CYCLE OF 1954–1958

Rapid recovery got under way in the latter part of 1954, sparked particularly by the new boom in residential building and the steady expansion in consumer expenditures. Inventory disinvestment ceased after the third quarter, the decline in federal government expenditures tapered off after the second quarter, and easy credit conditions stimulated building activity and installment buying. An important stimulus from the fourth quarter on was the public's enthusiastic acceptance of the 1955 automobile models. Plant and equipment expenditures lagged at the upturn, but once recovery began business firms rapidly revised their investment plans upward.[13]

### The Durable-Goods Boom, 1955–1957

Expansion was extremely rapid during 1955. Industrial production then flattened out but remained at a high level during 1956 and most of 1957 (see Figure 5.1). A number of features make this cyclical expansion of particular interest.

1. It was the first postwar boom not to be dominated either by pent-up demands inherited from a war or by actual war.
2. The boom was particularly concentrated in the durable-goods industries. This was associated with a very rapid rise in plant and equipment expenditures, a boom in residential and commercial construction, and the rush to buy automobiles in 1955.
3. The economy teetered on the brink of contraction for an unusually long period, from early in 1956 until the peak was finally reached in July, 1957.
4. The period of price stability that had begun in 1951 finally ended. Both consumer and wholesale prices rose rapidly during 1956 and 1957, and they even continued to increase moderately during the 1957–1958 recession (see Figure 6.2, page 144).
5. The investment boom led to a rapid increase in capacity, but surprisingly, the improvement in labor productivity was unusually small in 1956 and 1957. At the same time wages rose rapidly, with a consequent increase in unit labor costs not completely offset by rising prices. As a result there was some deterioration in profit margins in the later stages of the boom.
6. Despite the vigor of the expansion, unemployment did not fall below 4 percent, and the growth in total output during 1956–1957

[13] This discussion of the 1954–1958 cycle owes a good deal to the excellent analysis in Hickman, *op. cit.*, esp. chap. 7. See also the *Economic Report of the President* for these years.

was not very large. At the same time 1955–1957 are the only years between 1929 and the early 1970s when unemployment was close to 4 percent without the stimulus of either pent-up demands inherited from the war (1946–1948) or increased military spending (World War II, Korea, and Vietnam).

7. The monetary authorities found themselves in a particularly unhappy situation. The rapid rise in prices and the vigorous investment boom induced them to follow a restrictive monetary policy, while the slow growth in output after 1955 and the existence of pockets of unemployment led many observers to advocate a policy of monetary ease.

Let us now look at the boom in greater detail.

Expansion in 1955 was rapid and extended to virtually all private sectors of the economy. The lead had already been taken in 1954 by a sharp rise in residential building. This was followed in late 1954 and early 1955 by a big spurt in expenditures on consumer durables, particularly automobiles, and by a large increase in inventory investment. Beginning in the first quarter of 1955, plant and equipment expenditures also began to rise rapidly.

The boom flattened out in the closing months of 1955 (see Table 5.2 and Figure 5.1). The peak in consumer expenditures on durables was reached as early as the third quarter of 1955. Residential building also began to decline at that point, particularly because of tight credit conditions. What kept the boom going during 1956 and into 1957 was the continued rise in plant and equipment expenditures by business, the steady upward trend in state and local government expenditures, and the increase in consumer expenditures on nondurables and services. Federal government expenditures were stable through 1955 and the early months of 1956, rose moderately during the rest of the year, and increased significantly further in the first quarter of 1957 to a level that was maintained during the remainder of the year. Net exports provided an additional stimulus.

The result of these various forces can be traced in the index of industrial production (see Figure 5.1). The index rose rapidly to an initial peak in December, 1955 and then moved more or less horizontally. There was a further slight increase at the end of 1956, but at no time during 1956–1957 did the index rise more than 2.5 percent above its level in December, 1955.[14]

---

[14] These figures refer to the Federal Reserve index, including utilities. Cf. *Federal Reserve Bulletin* (December, 1959): 1474.

**Table 5.2** Components of Gross National Product for Selected Calendar Quarters, 1954–1958 (Seasonally adjusted annual rates; in billions of dollars)

| | Second Quarter, 1954 | Fourth Quarter, 1955 | Third Quarter, 1957 | First Quarter, 1958 |
|---|---|---|---|---|
| Consumption expenditures | 234.6 | 260.4 | 283.8 | 284.5 |
| Durables | 32.5 | 40.1 | 40.6 | 37.9 |
| Nondurables | 117.4 | 126.1 | 137.7 | 137.8 |
| Services | 84.6 | 94.2 | 105.6 | 108.9 |
| Gross private domestic investment | 49.7 | 71.3 | 70.4 | 57.3 |
| Nonresidential construction | 13.0 | 15.2 | 18.1 | 17.3 |
| Producer durables | 20.4 | 26.5 | 29.1 | 25.7 |
| Residential construction | 18.9 | 22.5 | 20.0 | 19.7 |
| Change in inventories | −2.7 | 7.1 | 3.2 | −5.4 |
| Net exports | 1.7 | 1.6 | 5.5 | 2.6 |
| Government expenditures[a] | 74.3 | 75.5 | 86.6 | 90.2 |
| Federal | 47.4 | 44.7 | 49.7 | 51.3 |
| State and local | 27.0 | 30.8 | 36.9 | 38.9 |
| Gross national product | 360.4 | 408.8 | 446.3 | 434.7 |
| National income | 299.5 | 340.9 | 369.5 | 357.9 |
| Less: Corporate profits | 36.6 | 48.1 | 45.9 | 36.4 |
| Other deductions[b] | 9.7 | 11.5 | 14.7 | 15.2 |
| Plus: Govt. transfer payments | 14.8 | 16.2 | 20.0 | 22.7 |
| Other additions[c] | 19.3 | 22.6 | 25.7 | 25.3 |
| Personal income | 287.2 | 320.3 | 354.7 | 354.2 |
| Less: Personal taxes | 32.5 | 37.1 | 43.0 | 42.0 |
| Disposable income | 254.7 | 283.2 | 311.6 | 312.2 |
| Personal saving[d] | 15.7 | 17.3 | 21.5 | 21.2 |

[a]On goods and services. Excludes transfer payments.

[b]Chiefly social security contributions.

[c]Includes government interest payments, corporation dividends, and business transfer payments.

[d]Personal saving in the national income accounts is less than the difference between disposable income and consumption expenditures. The discrepancy is accounted for by consumer interest and personal transfer payments to foreigners.

Source: U.S. Department of Commerce, *The National Income and Product Accounts of the United States, 1929–1965.*

By the beginning of 1956 the economy was operating close to full capacity, and bottlenecks were appearing in various durable-goods industries, where there was clearest evidence that demand was threatening to outstrip supply. But on the whole the more or less horizontal movement of total output in 1956 and the first half of 1957 was due more to the failure of aggregate demand to continue to expand sufficiently than to an overall insufficiency of supply. Capacity expanded rapidly in 1956–1957, and so did the labor force. A slackening in demand was felt particularly in the automobile industry, housebuilding, and related lines.[15]

Deflated for price changes, consumer expenditures for items other than services flattened out markedly in 1956, and the portion of income saved began to rise. One result was that inventory investment declined all through 1956 and into the first quarter of 1957.

All this suggests that a minor recession might well have begun sometime in 1956. What saved the situation was the continued expansion in business fixed investment, a rapid increase in exports, and a rise in federal government expenditures after the middle of 1956. The continued expansion in private long-term investment in the face of a marked retardation in demand requires some explanation.

Long-term investment continued to rise for two reasons. First, much investment was autonomous and only loosely related to short-run changes in demand. This was particularly true of commercial and some other types of construction. It was probably also true of a good deal of investment inspired by technological change and the rise in labor costs. Second, substantial lags were involved in many types of investment. Expenditures made in the late 1956 and early 1957 represented commitments that had been incurred some time earlier. Decisions made in the second half of 1956 to curtail investment would be reflected in an actual decline in expenditures only some months later.[16]

Just about the time the boom began to flatten out, from the beginning of 1956 on, prices began to rise rapidly. The decline in farm prices ended. Industrial prices rose, particularly in the durable-good's industries.[17] At the consumer level, price increases in 1956–1957 were

[15] For additional evidence on the failure of aggregate demand to rise as rapidly as capacity in 1956–1957, see Joint Economic Committee, *Staff Report on Employment, Growth, and Price Levels* (86th Congress, 1st Session, 1959), pp. 74 ff.

[16] Thus capital appropriations in manufacturing reached a peak in the first half of 1956, although actual investment expenditures for the same companies continued to rise until the third quarter of 1957. Cf. *The Conference Board Business Record*, March, 1958.

[17] Cf. Joint Economic Committee, *op. cit.*, pp. 123–125. See also Hickman, *op. cit.*, chap. 14 for a discussion of price movements during this and the preceding

particularly marked in food and services. Wages rose rapidly, as indeed they had throughout the postwar period (except for brief pauses during recession periods).

The boom was also marked by a considerable degree of monetary tightness. Short-term interest rates reached a low in the middle of 1954 and then began a rise that continued for three years. Long-term bond yields rose sharply beginning early in 1956. The capital-goods boom, continued government borrowing, and the rising need for working capital put heavy demands on the money and capital markets. The Federal Reserve authorities followed a restrictive credit policy, keeping pressure on member-bank reserves. As a result commercial banks were forced to sell government securities and to rediscount at the Federal Reserve Banks. The money supply rose much less rapidly than the money value of GNP, with a consequent reduction in the liquidity of the economy. By the peak of 1957 interest rates were higher than they had been in more than 20 years. Far higher rates were to obtain in the second half of the 1960s, however.

## The Downturn in 1957

The expansion showed signs of new life in the latter part of 1956, helped by the recovery from a steel strike, a rise in federal government expenditures, a boom in exports (in part because of the Suez crisis), and an increase in automobile production. But industrial production failed to rise any further after the beginning of 1957; the economy entered into what we have called a turning-point zone, and a cumulative contraction developed in the second half of the year. The turning point came in July.

A number of deflationary forces were already at work in the first half of the year. Manufacturers' new orders for durable goods were declining, both because of disappointing sales of consumer durables and because a number of industries were beginning to cut back their investment programs. The latter were being curtailed chiefly because some excess capacity was beginning to emerge in many lines as sales leveled off or began even to decline. Tight money and declining profit margins may also have played a contributing role. On top of this, the

---

postwar cycles. A widely cited study of the rise in prices during 1955–1957 is Charles L. Schultze, *Recent Inflation in the United States*, Study Paper No. 1 in Joint Economic Committee, *Study of Employment, Growth, and Price Levels* (Washington, D.C., GPO, 1959). Schultze ascribes the general rise in prices to demand pressures in the capital-goods and related industries, with the resulting rise in prices and wages then spilling over into other sectors of the economy through a "cost-push" process.

decline in residential building, which was largely the result of tight credit, continued.

## THE RECESSION OF 1957–1958

The recession that followed was notable in a number of respects.[18] It was one of the briefest contractions of the last century, lasting only nine months, until April, 1958. Yet though brief, the decline was very rapid, and in terms of the decline in GNP and industrial production it was the most severe of the recessions that have occurred since World War II. There was a significant decline in long-term investment, yet a major depression did not develop. Prices continued to rise during the contraction in business activity, in marked contrast to their previous recession behavior. The recession was felt in a number of other countries, either as an actual decline in output or as a marked retardation in the rapid growth that had been under way for some years.

Once the downswing had begun it spread quickly in typical cumulative fashion. As output declined, so did employment and incomes. Retail sales fell off, particularly for durable goods. There was a sharp decline in inventory investment, and the decline in plant and equipment expenditures accelerated. Fears that this recession might turn out to be a serious one spread. Yet even as concern mounted in the spring of 1958, recovery suddenly took hold and a new upswing began.

The factors making for quick recovery included the effective working of the automatic stabilizers, special factors leading to an increase in farm incomes, the cyclical insensitivity of sectors that have steadily become more important, increased federal spending, the favorable behavior of housebuilding, and the autonomous supports provided by the continued rise in state and local government expenditures and by the relative stability of some important types of long-term investment. The result of these factors was that incomes and consumer expenditures were well maintained; the necessary inventory adjustment took place quickly, and output began to recover from the spring of 1958.

The automatic stabilizers operated powerfully, and again the most powerful stabilizer of all was corporate profits (Table 5.2). Whereas GNP declined by $11.6 billion between the third quarter of 1957 and the first quarter of 1958, $9.5 billion of this drop was absorbed by

18 In addition to the other sources cited in the preceding and following pages, see H. D. Osborne, "National Income and Product—a Review of the 1957–58 Decline and Recovery," *Survey of Current Business* (November, 1958): 9–17. See also G. H. Moore, "The 1957–58 Business Contraction: New Model or Old," *American Economic Review 49* (May, 1959): 292–308.

the decline in corporate profits, while dividends scarcely declined at all. In addition, transfer payments (particularly unemployment compensation) rose by more than $2.5 billion and personal taxes fell by $1 billion. The result was that disposable income did not fall at all, and neither did consumer expenditures.

Residential building again acted somewhat as an automatic stabilizer, although not so promptly as in 1954. Housebuilding remained relatively stable during the recession and then, from about April on, began to expand rapidly. As credit conditions eased, mortgage funds became much more readily available; in addition, the government liberalized the terms for borrowing on guaranteed and insured (FHA and VA) mortgages.[19]

This favorable short-run behavior of residential building was possible only because the underlying demand for housing remained strong owing to the continued upward trend in new families and in incomes, the migration to the suburbs, an increasing amount of demolition resulting from freeway construction and urban redevelopment, and a resurgence of apartment-house construction in the cities.

Business expenditures on plant and equipment declined by about $8 billion, or 22 percent, during the recession. The decline was heavily concentrated in manufacturing, where fixed investment fell by about one-third.[20] Investment held up fairly well in the public-utility and "commercial and other" sectors.[21] The investment boom of 1955–1957 had caused some impairment of investment opportunities, particularly in manufacturing but also in other sectors. As a result business fixed investment lagged in the recovery of 1958–1959 and failed to match its 1957 high in 1960, the next cyclical peak. Nevertheless, public-utility and commercial investment provided strong support during the downswing, and this support contributed to the mildness of the recession and permitted other forces making for recovery to take hold.[22]

Federal government expenditures, which had remained fairly constant during 1957, increased significantly after the beginning of 1958.

---

[19] Interest rates fell rapidly in late 1957 and early 1958 as credit restraint was followed by monetary ease. The Federal Reserve authorities were slower to act, however, than they had been in 1953. Their first positive steps to ease the pressure on bank reserves did not come until October–November, 1957, several months after business had already turned down.

[20] There were also large relative declines in mining, railroads, and nonrail transportation, but the amounts involved were much smaller than in manufacturing.

[21] Cf. *Economic Report of the President,* January, 1960, p. 190.

[22] The total of public utility and "commercial and other" expenditures on plant and equipment declined by only about 7.5 percent and recovered more promptly than manufacturing investment.

Defense expenditures rose after reaching a low point in the fourth quarter of 1957, and an acceleration in the placing of new defense orders, even before money was actually spent, provided a further stimulus. In addition, there was a sharp increase in nondefense expenditures, chiefly to purchase farm commodities under the farm support program. Also, the steady rise in expenditures of state and local governments accelerated in the second half of 1958, stimulated in part by easier credit conditions that facilitated the sale of bonds.

Thus what looked as if it might become the first serious depression of the postwar period quickly developed into what was essentially a minor recession. There was a significant decline in private long-term investment, especially in manufacturing, but the decline was largely in producer durables rather than construction. Although total private long-term investment was declining, a substantial part was offset by the rise in government expenditures, both federal and state and local. The fact that there was not a complete offset plus the sharp decline in inventory investment and in net exports account for the decline in aggregate demand (Table 5.2). The automatic stabilizers, aided by the special circumstances that led to an increase in farm incomes, kept disposable income and consumer expenditures from falling significantly.

## WEAK EXPANSION AND RETARDED GROWTH, 1958–1961

### A Disappointing Recovery

After April, 1958 the economy began to expand again. The ensuing upswing reached its peak in May, 1960, to be followed by a brief and mild downswing that ended in February, 1961. The cyclical expansion of 1958–1960 proved to be disappointing. It was relatively brief—the shortest of the entire postwar period—and ended when the unemployment rate was still as high as 5 percent. Indeed, on an annual average basis unemployment remained above 5 percent for seven successive years, from 1958 through 1964. This was a period in which the American economy failed to achieve its potential by a considerable margin.[23]

Inventory liquidation ended in the second quarter of 1958, marking the end of the 1957–1958 downswing. The early stages of the new expansion were aided by a significant increase in federal government expenditures through 1958 as well as by a continued rise in state and

[23] Developments during 1958–1961 can be followed in the *Economic Report of the President* for those years and in the annual review issues of the *Survey of Current Business*. See also the useful collection of charts in any recent issue of *Business Conditions Digest*.

local government spending. Business fixed investment lagged somewhat as the recovery got under way.

Expansion continued in fairly steady fashion through the second quarter of 1959. The second half of the year was strongly affected by a protracted steel strike (from July to November), which led to a significant decline in output, not only of steel but also of fabricated metal products and automobiles. Inventory investment increased sharply in the second quarter as business firms stocked up in advance of the strike, declined during the strike, and increased again after November as depleted inventories were built up again. The restocking continued through the first quarter of 1960, and the ensuing decline in inventory investment helped bring the expansion in total output to an end. In constant prices, total GNP fell in the third quarter of 1959, recovered the loss in the fourth quarter, and spurted ahead in the first quarter of 1960 to a peak that was barely maintained in the second quarter. The peak in industrial production came in January, but expansion in other sectors deferred the turning point in general economic activity until May, when a new recession began.

Residential building followed its usual cyclical pattern, rising strongly in the first half of the upswing to a peak in the second quarter of 1959. In the next year it fell by over $3 billion as it responded in typical fashion to tightening credit conditions.[24]

While expenditures on business plant and equipment moved up with total output during 1958–1960, the expansion was not a strong one, and there were various indications that some lines of business were still suffering from excess capacity built up during the investment boom of 1955–1957. Capacity utilization in manufacturing, for example, averaged only about 80 percent in 1959–1960, much below utilization rates achieved in 1955–1957.[25] In constant prices, nonresidential fixed investment did not quite return to its 1957 high. Plant and equipment expenditures at the peak in 1960 were significantly below their 1957 highs in manufacturing, railroads, and the public-utility industry. These deficiencies were only partially offset by net gains in other transportation (aircraft) and particularly in the "commercial and other" sector. In short, between 1957 and 1959 business fixed investment did not do its

[24] The peak in residential building in the second quarter of 1959, if taken in current prices, was a new high for the postwar period, although in constant prices it was slightly exceeded by the figures for the first half of 1955. In constant prices, the level of residential building reached in 1955 and 1959 was barely equaled in 1963 and not significantly exceeded until 1971.

[25] Capacity utilization data for manufacturing are presented in the appendix tables in any recent *Economic Report of the President.*

share to generate increased aggregate demand in line with the growth in potential output. And this deficiency was exacerbated by the behavior of the federal budget.

Federal expenditures on new goods and services, after rising during the 1957–1958 recession, declined steadily from the fourth quarter of 1958 to the first quarter of 1960. This decline was not offset by a rise in transfer payments, although interest payments on the federal debt increased. With declining expenditures and rapidly rising tax receipts, the budget shifted from a $12 billion deficit in the second quarter of 1958 to a $7 billion surplus in the first quarter of 1960.[26] Tax receipts rose rapidly as business improved because of the sensitivity of corporate and personal income taxes; in addition, social security taxes were increased by about $2 billion in January, 1960, further adding to the budgetary surplus in the national income and product accounts. State and local government expenditures, on the other hand, continued their fairly steady and seemingly inexorable upward trend.

While we expect a significant improvement in the federal budget during a cyclical upswing, as tax receipts rise faster than government spending, the expansion in the private sector was not sufficiently vigorous to offset the strong retarding influence from the federal budget in 1959–1960. In terms that began to be used widely only in the early 1960s, tax rates were sufficiently high, given the level of federal expenditures, so that the "full-employment surplus" in the federal budget was about $15 billion. This represented a sharp increase compared to the several preceding years and was clearly deflationary, particularly in view of the failure of private investment to expand any more rapidly than it did.[27]

In short, the failure of the economy to achieve full employment in 1960 before sliding into another recession was due primarily to the

26 U.S. Department of Commerce, *The National Income and Product Accounts of the United States*, 1929–1965, pp. 52–53.

27 The figure cited for the full-employment surplus is from the Federal Reserve Bank of St. Louis *Review* (June, 1967): 10. For a new set of estimates of the full-employment surplus between 1955 and 1969, which gives a slightly lower figure for 1960, see Arthur M. Okun and Nancy H. Teeters, "The Full Employment Surplus Revisited," in Arthur M. Okun and George L. Perry, eds., *Brookings Papers on Economic Activity*, 1970:1 (Washington, D. C., Brookings, 1970), pp. 104–105. In these authors' words, "The full employment surplus is an estimate of what the federal surplus would be if the economy were operating along the path of its potential gross national product (GNP). It is thus not affected by fluctuations in economic activity that shrink or swell the revenue base relative to that associated with the path of potential growth [i.e., at full employment]" (*ibid.*, p. 78). For the origins of the concept, see *ibid.*, pp. 78–79, and Herbert Stein, *The Fiscal Revolution in America* (Chicago, University of Chicago Press, 1969), pp. 364–366.

combination of a deflationary federal budget and some deterioration in underlying private investment opportunities that held back the expansion in capital expenditures. Given these elements of weakness, the expansion was further impeded by the Federal Reserve's restrictive credit policy in 1959 and the early months of 1960.[28]

As we have already noted, inventory investment began to decline after the first quarter of 1960, when the heavy restocking that followed the end of the steel strike in November, 1959 had been accomplished. The decline in inventory accumulation was heavily concentrated in metal products and durable goods, and the sharp drop in inventory investment led to a decline in output in these sectors. The flattening out and subsequent decline in output in turn reacted unfavorably on plans for further investment; as we have already noted, capacity was more than ample for the levels of manufacturing output reached in 1960.

Thus it is not too much of a simplification to say that the 1960 downturn resulted from a sharp decline in inventory investment superimposed on a weakening situation with respect to business long-term investment and a federal budget that was generating a high and rising full-employment surplus. To this should be added the steady decline in residential building after mid-1959 and the attendant decline in sales of household appliances and furniture.[29]

The pronounced rise in prices in the mid-fifties abated significantly during 1958–1960. Indeed, the Wholesale Price Index moved horizontally during the upswing, although industrial prices increased moderately at first. Wages continued their uninterrupted rise. With some retardation in the rise in labor productivity after mid-1959, the resulting rise in unit labor costs put a squeeze on profits in the second half of the expansion. Consumer prices continued to increase moderately throughout the upswing and the ensuing recession. As usual, the most rapid rise was in the price of services.

## The Emerging Balance-of-Payments Problem

Let us now turn to a new problem that began to plague the American economy during the cycle of 1958–1961 and was to become worse during the decade that followed. Beginning in 1958, the American balance of payments suffered a serious deterioration. The problem was not in the merchandise balance of trade, although this suffered a

[28] We shall refer to Federal Reserve policy again in the final section of this chapter.

[29] In response to easier credit conditions, residential building started to rise after the beginning of 1961.

temporary decline in 1957–1959 following the upsurge at the time of the Suez crisis.[30] The difficulty lay with the invisible items in the balance of payments—primarily the rapid increase in American long-term investments aboard. Also beginning in the mid-fifties with the stabilization of the world's currencies and the general relaxation of restrictive regulations, short-term capital movements again began to play an important role in the demand for and supply of national currencies, including the dollar.[31]

In fact the United States had run a modest deficit in its balance of payments from the beginning of the 1950s, but the size of the deficit increased sharply in 1958 and continued at the higher level in 1959–1960. Private capital exports had increased significantly as early as 1956, but the deterioration in the balance of payments in 1958–1959 was due primarily to a sharp but temporary decline in the merchandise balance of trade; the large deficit in 1960 was associated with a sudden and large increase in the outflow of short-term capital.

In effect, because of American private investment abroad, government foreign aid and loans, and military spending overseas, the United States was supplying more dollars to the rest of the world than the latter needed to purchase the American surplus of exports over imports. This situation became worse in the late 1950s. American deficits in the early and mid-fifties permitted other countries to build up their depleted holdings of gold and dollars. This was the period of the so-called "dollar shortage." The process was completed by the late 1950s, and the steadily growing supply of dollars began to press on the market. This increasing supply of dollars had two effects. Foreign governments began to convert some of their surplus dollars into gold.[32] And short-term capital movements became important as investors moved their funds back and forth among countries in response to differentials in interest rates and expectations as to changes in foreign exchange

30 The balance of trade did deteriorate seriously in the second half of the 1960s (see pp. 179–181).

31 See the sections on the balance of payments in the annual review issues of the *Survey of Current Business* and in the *Economic Report of the President* for the relevant years. With respect to the latter, the balance-of-payments problem was first emphasized in the January, 1960 *Economic Report*. Beginning in the early sixties, the American balance-of-payments problem was the subject of frequent hearings before and reports by congressional committees. See, for example, *U.S. Payments Policies Consistent with Domestic Objectives of Maximum Employment and Growth*, Report of the Subcommittee on International Exchange and Payments of the Joint Economic Committee, 87th Cong., 2d sess. (Washington, D.C., GPO, 1962).

32 Between 1950 and 1957 the American gold stock remained approximately constant. During the next four years it declined by about $6 billion.

rates. In 1960–1961 the United States experienced its first net outward flow of short-term capital in the postwar period. Others were to follow.[33]

## The Downswing

The business contraction from May, 1960 to February, 1961 was mild and brief. In current prices GNP hardly declined at all (see Table 5.3); in constant prices the decline was about 1.5 percent. Unemployment rose from about 5 to 7 percent. Consumer prices continued to rise during the downswing, as did the price deflator for total GNP, but wholesale prices moved horizontally.

As Table 5.3 suggests, we have here the usual features of a minor recession with which we have become familiar. Consumer expenditures did not decline; they actually rose. Business fixed investment fell only about 6 percent; the chief deflationary force at work during the downswing was the decline in inventory investment. There was, however, a greater decline in residential building than in the previous postwar recessions, and despite easier credit conditions there was no significant upturn in building before the general recovery began. Federal and state and local government expenditures on goods and services rose moderately, although the increase in federal spending in 1960 represented little more than some speeding up in expenditures already authorized.

Again the most powerful stabilizer at work was the decline in corporate profits while dividends remained unchanged. There was also a significant increase in government transfer payments. Since personal income did not fall, there was no decline in personal income tax receipts.

Beginning early in 1961, federal government expenditures began to rise rapidly, and the increase in transfer payments continued through the first half of the year. The federal budget moved from surplus into deficit in the fourth quarter of 1960; the deficit reached about $5 billion in the first quarter of 1961. This represented a swing of about $12 billion within a year. The Kennedy administration, which assumed office in January, 1961, took a number of steps to speed up spending under existing programs.

[33] For a useful survey of the deterioration in the American balance of payments in the late 1950s, see Walter S. Salant *et al., The United States Balance of Payments in 1968* (Washington, D.C., Brookings, 1963), esp. chap. 1. See also Hal B. Lary, *Problems of the United States as World Trader and Banker* (New York, National Bureau of Economic Research, 1963), and *Economic Report of the President,* January, 1962, chap. 3.

**Table 5.3** Components of Gross National Product for Selected Calendar Quarters, 1958–1961 (Seasonally adjusted annual rates; in billions of dollars)

|  | First Quarter, 1958 | Second Quarter, 1960 | First Quarter, 1961 |
|---|---|---|---|
| Consumption expenditures | 284.5 | 326.3 | 328.4 |
| Durables | 37.9 | 46.1 | 41.9 |
| Nondurables | 137.8 | 152.0 | 154.1 |
| Services | 108.9 | 128.1 | 132.4 |
| Gross private domestic investment | 57.3 | 76.0 | 64.3 |
| Nonresidential construction | 17.3 | 17.9 | 18.4 |
| Producer durables | 25.7 | 31.2 | 27.6 |
| Residential construction | 19.7 | 23.1 | 21.7 |
| Change in inventories | −5.4 | 3.9 | −3.5 |
| Net exports | 2.6 | 3.5 | 6.6 |
| Government expenditures[a] | 90.2 | 98.8 | 104.3 |
| Federal | 51.3 | 53.0 | 55.4 |
| State and local | 38.9 | 45.9 | 49.0 |
| Gross national product | 434.7 | 504.7 | 503.6 |
| National income | 357.9 | 417.1 | 412.2 |
| Less: Corporate profits | 36.4 | 51.6 | 45.0 |
| Other deductions[b] | 15.2 | 20.7 | 20.9 |
| Plus: Government transfer payments | 22.7 | 26.1 | 29.8 |
| Other additions[c] | 25.3 | 30.5 | 30.5 |
| Personal income | 354.2 | 401.3 | 406.6 |
| Less: Personal taxes | 42.0 | 50.8 | 51.8 |
| Disposable income | 312.2 | 350.4 | 354.8 |
| Personal saving[d] | 21.2 | 16.5 | 18.4 |

[a]On goods and services. Excludes transfer payments.

[b]Chiefly social security contributions.

[c]Includes government interest payments, corporation dividends, and business transfer payments.

[d]Personal saving in the national income accounts is less than the difference between disposable income and consumption expenditures. The discrepancy is accounted for by consumer interest and personal transfer payments to foreigners.

Source: U.S. Department of Commerce, *The National Income and Product Accounts of the United States, 1929–1965.*

Credit conditions eased during the downswing, but interest rates remained above the low levels reached in earlier postwar recessions (see Figure 6.4, page 158). The Federal Reserve began to relieve the tightness of credit in 1960 even before the downturn occurred, and during the downswing it took a number of steps—lowering the discount rate, purchasing government securities, reducing reserve requirements, and others—to make credit more readily available at lower cost.[34]

The Fed was hampered in its efforts to move toward an expansionary policy by the new strain on the balance of payments to which we have referred. Low short-term interest rates encouraged the outflow of short-term capital. To cope with this problem the Federal Reserve System shifted its open-market purchases of government securities toward the longer maturities, thus seeking to avoid a further decline in short-term rates but attempting also to keep long-term rates low in order to encourage private investment.

The turnaround in inventory investment together with expansionary monetary and fiscal policy—given no serious worsening in long-term investment opportunities—provided the basis for a new cyclical expansion, and recovery began. The new upswing, slow and halting at first, was to cover the remainder of the decade of the sixties—the longest expansion in American history (at least as far back as our records go).

But before we move on to the Kennedy years and the flowering of "New Economics," let us look back at the evolution of monetary and fiscal policy during the 1950s.

## STABILIZATION POLICY IN THE FIFTIES

During the eight years of the Eisenhower administration (1953–1960), growth and particularly price stability were more important goals than a high target for full employment, and toward the end of the decade restoring balance-of-payments equilibrium took on high priority also. Avoidance of substantial unemployment was, of course, a primary objective, and the government took seriously its obligations under the Employment Act of 1946. But, particularly in its second term, the Eisenhower administration emphasized price stability, growth, and

[34] The Federal Reserve authorities came to realize that they had tightened credit too soon and too much in 1958–1959 and began to adopt an easier policy a couple of months before the downturn. Cf. Friedman and Schwartz, *op. cit.*, p. 619. See also *Annual Report of the Board of Governors of the Federal Reserve System*, 1960.

(over the long run) a budgetary surplus to such an extent that it was prepared, as in 1959–1960, to settle for an unemployment rate in the neighborhood of 5 percent.[35]

Reducing inflation was probably the most important single objective. After the Korean war considerable emphasis was also placed on rapid growth, to be achieved particularly by tax incentives and a budgetary surplus. Nonetheless, some minimum full-employment target was a *sine qua non* for the pursuit of other objectives. The Eisenhower administration was no more prepared than the Democratic administrations that preceded and followed to accept unemployment levels even half as high as those that had prevailed during most of the 1930s.

When we turn to the instruments rather than the goals of macroeconomic policy, the most striking development was on the side of monetary rather than fiscal policy. As we have seen, the independence of the Federal Reserve System was restored by the Treasury–Federal Reserve Accord of 1951, and from then on the Fed pursued an active contracyclical policy. That "money does matter" was increasingly recognized from the beginning of the 1950s on, and the Fed acted on this assumption.

The Board of Governors of the Federal Reserve System was also aware of its responsibilities under the Employment Act, but it conceived of its job in the short run primarily in contracyclical terms, to "lean against the wind." This meant monetary restraint during cyclical expansions, even if (as in 1959) unemployment was still moderately high, and a policy of credit ease during business recessions. Over periods longer than the cycle, the Fed also accepted the responsibility of ensuring a rate of increase in the money supply adequate for the needs of economic growth.[36]

In pursuing its contracyclical policy the Fed made some mistakes. For example, it was late in adopting an easy-credit policy after the downturn in 1957. Its most serious error, however, was probably its restrictive credit policy in 1959, which may indeed have been more restrictive than it intended.[37] This added to the deflationary pressure exerted by the unduly large full-employment budgetary surplus in 1959–

35 Cf. Stein, *op. cit.*, chaps. 13–14; Bach, *op. cit.*, pp. 99 ff. It is interesting in this connection to examine the last few *Economic Reports* of the Eisenhower administration. Quantification of the full-employment target in terms of a national unemployment rate of 4 percent did not occur until the beginning of the Kennedy administration. See R. A. Gordon, *The Goal of Full Employment* (New York, Wiley, 1967), pp. 52–53.

36 Cf. Friedman and Schwartz, *op. cit.*, pp. 627 ff. For a review of monetary policy in the 1950s, see both this source and Bach, *op. cit.*

37 Friedman and Schwartz, *op. cit.*, p. 619.

1960, the combined effect being to hold back the expansion and to precipitate a new recession while unemployment was still at an unsatisfactorily high level.

This is not the place to review Federal Reserve policy during these years in detail. The Fed used its regained independence to cope with each cyclical phase as it occurred after the Korean war, employing the instruments that had been given to it by Congress. During the fifties it was more concerned with inflation than with full employment, but it nonetheless pursued a reasonably vigorous expansionary policy during recessions. The Board of Governors was not the partially paralyzed body that it had been during 1930–1933 or a slave of the Treasury, as it had been during World War II and the early postwar years.

The great advance in fiscal policy following World War II was acceptance of the argument that no attempt should be made to balance the federal budget during recessions. The automatic fiscal stabilizers were to be permitted to do their work, allowing tax receipts to fall and unemployment compensation and other transfer payments to rise when a recession occurred. But fiscal policy during the Eisenhower years did not go much beyond this. There was some modest speeding up of government spending under existing appropriations during recession, but that was about all.[38]

The Eisenhower administration made no use of discretionary tax changes, either to curb an inflationary boom (as in 1956–1957) or to cope with business recessions and rising unemployment.[39] There was a reduction in income tax rates at the beginning of 1954, and later in the year Congress took the initiative in reducing excise taxes. But the amount and timing of the cut in income taxes had been determined long before by Congress, and the reduction in excise taxes was entirely at the initiative of Congress.

The possible need of a tax cut during the recession in 1958 was seriously debated within the government, but no action was taken. Interestingly, then-Vice President Richard Nixon was in favor of reducing taxes to cope with the recession.[40]

There was one respect in which the federal government's fiscal activities played a destabilizing role, both in the 1950s and in the 1960s. This arose out of the wide swings in military expenditures. In

[38] On fiscal policy during the Eisenhower years, see Stein, *op. cit.*, chaps. 11–14, Holmans, *op. cit.*, and Wilfred Lewis, Jr., *Federal Fiscal Policy in the Postwar Recessions* (Washington, D.C., Brookings, 1962).

[39] We have already noted that in 1950, at the beginning of the Korean war, the Truman administration raised taxes substantially and very promptly.

[40] On this 1958 episode see Stein, *op. cit.*, chap. 13; Bach, *op. cit.*, p. 100.

the period covered in this chapter, the economy experienced the huge increase during the Korean war, the sharp cutback thereafter, and another large increase in 1956–1957. Similar large and destabilizing changes occurred in the following decade, particularly in connection with the escalation and subsequent decline of American military activities in Vietnam. Thus, as one observer has complained, federal spending has been the least stable of the major components of aggregate demand.

President Eisenhower and his advisers placed considerable emphasis on the contribution that fiscal policy could make to stimulating economic growth. This was to be done through changes in the tax structure to favor investment and through a budgetary surplus that would release private savings for private investment. During his second term the President put increasing emphasis on the need for a large surplus in the federal budget. Not only would this stimulate growth and maintain international confidence in the dollar, he believed, but even more important, a large budgetary surplus was essential to control inflation.[41] The result was the rapidly rising full-employment surplus in 1959–1960, which, as we have seen, contributed to the weakness of the expansion in those years and helped bring on recession before full employment was achieved.

Thus as the Kennedy administration took over in January, 1961 there was ample room for more active use of discretionary fiscal policy to "promote maximum employment, production, and purchasing power." This was the "continuing policy and responsibility" that had been assigned to the federal government by the Employment Act of 1946. With the advent of the Kennedy administration and its emphasis on the "New Economics," a more vigorous role was assigned to fiscal policy. Also, the goal of full employment was made more explicit and was pursued more actively after 1960 than it had been during the 1950s.

41 Cf. Stein, *op. cit.*, chap. 14.

# 6

# From the New Economics to Nixon's New Economic Policy

The dozen years between the inauguration of President Kennedy and the beginning of President Nixon's second term form a dramatic period in the history of American macroeconomic policy. The period began with the national unemployment rate around 7 percent, with prices relatively stable, and with a vigorous debate going on regarding the importance of "structural unemployment." The economy was then at the bottom of another mild recession; more serious, however, the preceding boom had been a weak one, the rate of growth had been retarded since the mid-1950s, and 1961 was to be the fourth successive year in which the annual unemployment rate was 5.5 percent or more.

## A BRIEF OVERVIEW

Then began the longest cyclical upswing on record—from February 1961 to November, 1969. After some hesitation the Kennedy administration embarked on a new and vigorous program of using discretionary fiscal policy to restore full employment, and by the end of 1965 the unemployment rate was down to the long-sought figure of 4 percent. "Full employment" had been achieved. The first half of the sixties marked the apparent triumph of the "New Economics," dramatized by the successful tax reduction in 1964. But then came the rapid buildup of military expenditures associated with the deepening American involvement in the Vietnam war, and the reputation of the New Economics was quickly tarnished by the failure of the Johnson administration to control an inflation that escalated during the late 1960s despite the belated imposition of a tax increase in 1968 and severe monetary restraint in 1966 and 1969.

Dramatic developments followed. The national unemployment rate rapidly increased—from 3.5 percent in December, 1969 to 6.1 percent in December, 1970—and remained stubbornly at about 6 percent all through 1971 and the early months of 1972, although a new cyclical expansion began at the end of 1970. Despite the substantial unemployment, inflation continued at an unacceptably high rate. And to make matters still worse, the American balance of payments, which had been under pressure throughout the preceding decade, deteriorated dramatically in 1970–1971.

The result was President Nixon's New Economic Policy announced in August, 1971—imposing a wage and price freeze followed by direct wage and price controls, providing an array of tax incentives to stimulate the economy, and suspending the convertibility of the dollar for the first time since 1934 (as well as temporarily imposing a surcharge on all dutiable imports). The wage and price controls in (relative) peacetime were unprecedented. One had to go back to the New Deal for comparable action with respect to the balance of payments. And the fiscal action, accompanied by large increases in government spending and an unprecedented peacetime federal deficit, rested on Keynesian thinking, despite the increased influence of "monetarist" economists. This was how a presumably conservative President ended his first term in the White House.

These are the years, from 1961 to 1972, that we shall now review. This period can be divided naturally into three subperiods. The first covers the years 1961–1965, marking the temporary triumph of the New Economics and the final achievement of full employment at the end of 1965. The second period includes the remainder of the 1960s, years dominated by a demand-pull inflation engendered by excess demand associated with the Vietnam war. There followed the painful years 1970–1972, marked by the combination of high unemployment, continued inflation, and a deteriorating balance of payments, culminating in the drastic measures of the New Economic Policy.

## NONINFLATIONARY EXPANSION, 1961–1965

### The Gradual Return to Full Employment[1]

Business recovery began only a month after President Kennedy assumed office in January, 1961, but the new administration could hardly take credit for the end of the downswing, except possibly as promises of vigorous action contributed to business and consumer confidence. Industrial production rose rapidly after February and by the end of 1961 had exceeded its previous peak in early 1960 (Figure 5.1, page 111). There was a sharp reversal in inventory investment. Housing investment began to expand also, at first slowly and then more

---

[1] Arthur Burns offers a useful and compact analysis of the expansion during 1961–1966 in *The Business Cycle in a Changing World* (New York, National Bureau of Economic Research, 1969), pp. 262–276.

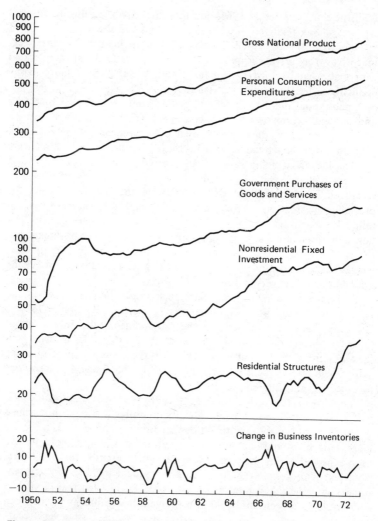

**Figure 6.1** Gross National Product and Components, 1950–1972 (billions of 1958 dollars)

(Source: *Business Conditions Digest,* January, 1973.)

rapidly as interest rates remained close to their recession lows and mortgage credit was readily available.

Of the main components of aggregate demand, the laggard was private business investment (Figure 6.1). Recovery here did not begin until the third quarter of 1961, and then the expansion during the next two years was relatively moderate. By 1962 the sluggish behavior of business investment caused the government to inaugurate special tax incentives for private capital spending in the form of accelerated depreciation and an investment tax credit. We shall have more to say about these fiscal stimuli a bit later.

A substantial increase in federal government expenditures on goods and services, combined with a continued (though retarded) rise in state and local spending, also provided a significant stimulus to the economy. The first fiscal actions by the Kennedy administration were on the side of spending rather than tax reductions. Between the first quarters of 1961 and 1962, federal spending on goods and services expanded by $6.5 billion, well over twice the increase during the preceding year. Considerably more than half this increase was in military expenditures, largely in connection with the Berlin crisis. The new administration also expanded some types of transfer payments, but the net increase there was smaller than during the preceding year, chiefly because unemployment compensation payments began to decline after business recovery began.

Unemployment did not reach its peak until May, 1961, when the national rate (seasonally adjusted) was 7.1 percent. By May, 1962 the figure had fallen to 5.5 percent, and it remained stubbornly at about this level through the rest of 1962 and all of 1963. Indeed, even with the stimulus of the tax cut in March, 1964 the unemployment rate was still as high as 5 percent in December, 1964. The magic 4 percent was not reached until the end of 1965.

The pace of recovery slowed significantly during 1962 and the first half of 1963 (see Table 6.1). The main problem was with business investment. Inventory investment declined during this period, while the increase in plant and equipment expenditures was less than might have been expected during the second year of a substantial business recovery. Total expenditures on new plant and equipment in 1962 (in constant prices) were less than they had been in 1957, although real GNP had risen some 17 percent in the interim.[2] Given the significant gap between actual and potential output that had existed for the past several years and the continuance of some excess capacity through the late fifties and early sixties, long-term business expectations were not optimistic enough to generate the level of private investment needed for full employment. At least this was the case given the level of other types

2 This statement refers to plant and equipment expenditures deflated by the implicit price deflator for nonresidential fixed investment, which includes more than plant and equipment.

**Table 6.1** Average Quarterly Change in Components of Aggregate Demand for Selected Subperiods, 1961–1965 (In billions of 1958 dollars)

| | I/1961–IV/1961 | IV/1961–II/1963 | I/1964 II/1963– | I/1964–IV/1965 |
|---|---|---|---|---|
| Gross national product | 9.70 | 5.72 | 8.37 | 9.36 |
| Consumer expenditures | 4.43 | 3.57 | 5.13 | 6.13 |
| Nonresidential fixed investment | 0.57 | 0.75 | 1.47 | 2.11 |
| Residential construction | 0.57 | 0.35 | 0.10 | −0.17 |
| Inventory investment | 2.97 | −0.11 | 0.00 | 0.83 |
| Net exports | −0.57 | 0.17 | 1.13 | −0.49 |
| Government purchases of goods and services | | | | |
| Federal | 1.23 | 0.52 | −0.17 | 0.16 |
| State and local | 0.53 | 0.45 | 0.77 | 0.97 |

Source: U.S. Department of Commerce, *1971 Business Statistics*, p. 4.

of nonconsumption expenditures (chiefly government spending on goods and services and residential building) and given the leakages in the form of gross savings and taxes that determined the ratio of consumer spending to GNP (i.e., the propensity to consume out of GNP). To put the matter another way, taxes and savings are "leakages" that hold consumption below the level of GNP. This gap must be filled by private investment and government spending. In 1962–1963 existing tax rates would have helped to generate a volume of leakages at full employment greater than the volume of investment and government spending that could have been expected.

A major effort was made in 1962 to provide stronger incentives to business investment. The Treasury Department liberalized its guidelines for determining depreciation allowances, thereby permitting corporations to show lower profits and thus incur smaller tax liabilities. And the Revenue Act of 1962 provided for an investment tax credit, permitting a deduction of 7 percent of the cost of new machinery and equipment from tax liabilities. The investment tax credit was to remain in effect through most of the 1960s.

Business investment responded to these tax incentives with a considerable lag. Plant and equipment expenditures were slightly less in the first half of 1963 than in the last two quarters of 1962. The long investment boom of the 1960s did not begin until the second half of 1963, by which time business expectations were presumably affected by the imminence of the large reduction in corporation and personal income taxes that was being debated in Congress, as well as by the tax incentives granted in 1962.

The rate of expansion accelerated in the second half of 1963 and speeded up still further after the large tax reduction passed by Congress early in 1964. The accelerating pace of the expansion can be followed in Table 6.1, which shows average quarterly changes in the main components of aggregate demand for selected intervals between the trough of the 1960–1961 recession and the final attainment of a 4 percent unemployment rate at the end of 1965—when the rapid acceleration of federal spending on the Vietnam war was just beginning.

The second column in Table 6.1 summarizes the nature of the retarded recovery during 1962 and the first half of 1963. Inventory investment turned slightly deflationary, the rise in residential building slowed down, and there was a significant decline in the rate of increase in federal government spending. Business fixed investment did not take up the slack.

It is clear from the third column of Table 6.1 that the expansion began to accelerate again in the second half of 1963, well before the stimulus from the 1964 tax cut took effect. Business fixed investment began to take off on a boom that was to continue through the rest of the decade; net exports added a further stimulus, and so did the accelerated rise in state and local government spending. Interestingly, federal spending on goods and services was not an expansionary influence in the months before the 1964 tax reduction.

The rise in GNP accelerated further after the first quarter of 1964, and it is generally accepted that the 1964 tax reduction was largely responsible for this.[3] Business fixed investment increased at a more rapid rate, partly because of the stronger tax incentives for business (including delayed effects of the tax concessions in 1962) and partly because of the stimulus of the accelerated rise in consumer spending. Inventory investment also provided a new, strong stimulus during 1964–1965. And consumer spending, by far the largest component of GNP, spurted ahead for two reasons: the direct effect of the reduction in personal income taxes, which raised the ratio of disposable income and of consumption to GNP, and the multiplier effects of the accelerated rise in business investment.

As we have noted, by December, 1965 the unemployment rate was down to 4 percent. The gap between actual and potential output had been closed. Discretionary fiscal policy, in the form of deliberate use

[3] Milton Friedman and other monetarists do not agree (see p. 152).

of tax reductions to stimulate the economy, had apparently brought the
economy back to full employment with only a very modest rise in
prices during the first half of the 1960s. This was the high point of the
"New Economics."

## Prices, Wages, and the Guideposts

The gradual return to full employment during 1961–1965 was accompanied by relative price stability. Wholesale prices remained stable during 1961–1964. Between 1960 and 1965 the Consumer Price Index
inched upward at an annual rate of about 1.3 percent; the rise in the
comprehensive GNP deflator was only slightly more (see Figure 6.2).
At the end of the decade, as they struggled to cope with inflation rates
of 5 and 6 percent per year, troubled policy makers looked back on the
early 1960s as a Utopian period of price stability.

This good price performance in the first half of the decade reflected
the behavior of wages and labor productivity (output per man-hour).
Average hourly compensation and output per man-hour together determine unit labor costs. For the private economy as a whole, the sum
of unit labor costs and a markup to cover overhead and profits determines the average price of output.[4] In the short run variations in the
markup over unit labor costs will reflect the changing relation between
demand and supply—as reflected, for example, in variations in the rate
of capacity utilization.[5]

The rise in labor productivity accelerated somewhat in the first half
of the sixties, but this was not true of wages. Indeed, the increase in
wages in the early 1960s was less than might have been expected from
the relationship between wage increases and the rate of unemployment
(and other variables) that had existed in earlier postwar years (this is
the famous relationship referred to as the Phillips curve). This was in
sharp contrast with the accelerating wage inflation that began in the
second half of the 1960s.

A frequently cited reason for the restrained behavior of wages in

[4] This is substantially the case for a relatively self-sufficient economy like that of
the United States. In more open economies like those of the United Kingdom or
the Netherlands import prices must also be taken into account.

[5] For an example of econometric research reflecting this approach to the study of
prices, see Otto Eckstein and Gary Fromm, "The Price Equation," *American
Economic Review 58* (December, 1968): 1159–1183; also Robert J. Gordon, "Inflation in Recession and Recovery," in *Brookings Papers on Economic Activity,*
1971:1, esp. pp. 126–130. A more complete survey of econometric research on
price determination is provided in *The Econometrics of Price Determination: Conference,* sponsored by the Board of Governors of the Federal Reserve System and
Social Science Research Council (Washington, D.C., Board of Governors, 1972).

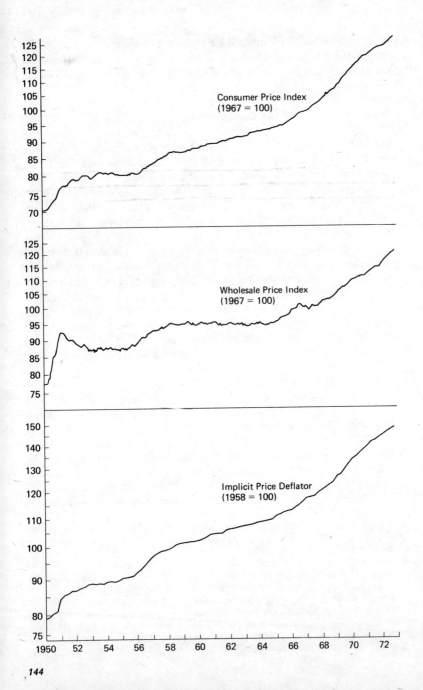

Consumer Price Index
(1967 = 100)

Wholesale Price Index
(1967 = 100)

Implicit Price Deflator
(1958 = 100)

the early 1960s is the set of wage-price guideposts promulgated by the Kennedy administration. These guideposts called for holding the increase in wages down to the long-run growth in average labor productivity in the private sector so that there need be no increase in prices on the average. Prices would rise in industries in which manhour output did not increase as fast as wages, but under the guideposts they should fall in industries in which productivity increased faster than wages. An essential aspect of the program was that, in industries with above-average increases in productivity, wages should rise only as fast as the guidepost—that is, the increase in output per man-hour for the entire private economy. This guidepost for wage increases was eventually set at 3.2 percent per year.[6]

The guideposts represented a form of macroeconomic policy frequently referred to as "incomes policies." Such policies seek in various ways, ranging from appeals for voluntary cooperation by labor and business to legally binding wage and price controls, to bring about wage and price behavior different from that which would result from the free play of market forces.[7]

The guideposts were without legal force and could not cope with the demand-pull inflation that erupted after 1965. They relied on "jawboning"—informal pressure applied by the White House both behind the scenes and publicly. The most dramatic example of successful jawboning occurred in 1962, when President Kennedy forced the United States Steel Corporation and other leading steel companies to withdraw an announced price increase. The price increase came shortly after the United Steelworkers had settled for a relatively modest increase in wages.

Economists are still debating what role, if any, the guideposts played in the restrained behavior of wages and prices in the first half of the

---

[6] For the original statement of the guideposts, see *Economic Report of the President*, January, 1962, pp. 185–190. The figure of 3.2 percent was not mentioned in the original statement of the guideposts but came to be used later. See, for example, *Economic Report of the President*, January, 1966, p. 92, and January, 1967, pp. 120 ff. A reasonably full history of the guideposts through 1966 is presented in John Sheahan, *The Wage-Price Guideposts* (Washington, D.C., Brookings, 1967).

[7] Lloyd Ulman and Robert Flanagan present a useful survey of European experience with incomes policies in *Wage Restraint: A Study of Incomes Policies in Western Europe* (Berkeley, University of California Press, 1971).

**Figure 6.2**   Selected Price Indexes, 1950–1972

(Source: *Business Conditions Digest*, March, 1972; May, 1972; January, 1973.)

1960s. A study by George Perry in 1967 gave the guideposts major credit.[8] More recent studies have raised serious questions as to how effective the guideposts really were and have suggested that other factors were primarily responsible for the moderate behavior of wages. The issue remains in doubt. Perhaps it is not far from the truth to say that the guideposts helped create an environment favorable to wage restraint but that the chief factors at work were the absence of inflationary expectations and a continued high level of unemployment.[9] These restraining influences disappeared after 1965.

Although, as we have seen, the rise in prices was moderate during the first half of the sixties, it is still true that prices rose somewhat faster than unit labor cost. Profit margins per unit of output increased, and, with an expanding volume of sales, total profits rose even faster. The early and mid-1960s were a profitable period for American business, and rising profits created a business climate favorable to the investment boom that got under way in late 1963. As we shall see, a squeeze on profits developed later in the decade.

While profit margins increased in the early and mid-sixties, average hourly compensation rose significantly faster than the Consumer Price Index. In manufacturing, for example, gross hourly earnings in real terms (that is, corrected for price changes) rose considerably faster during 1960–1965 than they did during 1965–1970. The same was true, though to a less marked extent, for the entire private nonfarm economy.

---

8 George L. Perry, "Wages and the Guideposts," *American Economic Review 57* (September, 1967): 897–904. A number of other studies published at about the same time, generally favorable to the guideposts, are cited in Sheahan, *op. cit.,* chap. 7.

9 For more recent econometric studies testing the restraining effect of the guideposts, see George L. Perry, "Changing Labor Markets and Inflation," in *Brookings Papers on Economic Activity,* 1970:3, pp. 425, 428; Robert J. Gordon, "The Recent Acceleration of Inflation and Its Lessons for the Future," *ibid.,* 1970:1, p. 17; and Otto Eckstein and Roger Brinner, *The Inflation Process in the United States,* prepared for the Joint Economic Committee of the U.S. Congress (Washington, D.C., GPO, 1972), pp. 15–17. Arthur Okun, the last chairman of the Council of Economic Advisers in the Johnson administration, comes to a similar conclusion: "It is impossible to tell just how much influence they [the guideposts] had in 1962–1965, but there is considerable evidence that they deserve some credit." *The Political Economy of Prosperity* (Washington, D.C., Brookings, 1970), p. 51. Two other and on the whole skeptical evaluations of the effectiveness of the guideposts are offered by Martin Estey and Thomas G. Moore in their papers in Phillip Cagan *et al., Economic Policy and Inflation in the United States* (Washington, D.C., American Enterprise Institute, 1972).

## TRIUMPH OF THE NEW ECONOMICS:
## FISCAL AND MONETARY POLICY TO 1965

### The New Economics

Use of the "New Economics" to bring the economy back to full employment represented more than the enactment of tax reductions to increase spending, output, and employment. Discretionary fiscal policy was the major tool used, but a range of new concepts and a new approach went with this more active use of fiscal policy.

In the words of Walter Heller, chairman of the Council of Economic Advisers under President Kennedy, the New Economics involved "not only new norms but new semantics for stabilization policy, especially in its fiscal aspects."[10] These new norms and concepts—new, at least, in the way they were used to influence policy—were chiefly the following.

*A new emphasis on and quantification of the goal of full employment* The Kennedy administration clearly attached greater importance to a low level of unemployment than its predecessor, and for the first time the goal of full employment was expressed officially in numerical terms. The "interim goal" was set at 4 percent. It was hoped that manpower and other programs would eventually permit the achievement of a still lower rate without unacceptable inflation.[11]

*The goals of full employment and of growth were tied together by emphasizing the related concepts of "potential output" and the "gap"* These are both concepts with which we are already familiar. Potential output is the output that can be produced at full employment; the gap is a measure of the output not produced when unemployment exceeds 4 percent. The rate of growth in potential output was estimated, and charts similar to Figure 6.3 were regularly published in the *Economic Report of the President* during the Kennedy and Johnson administrations.

*The main objective of macroeconomic policy was expressed in terms of "closing the gap"* Closing the gap meant returning to full employment and permitting the economy to grow along the path permitted by potential output.

*Emphasis on the "gap" meant a shift away from a countercyclical policy to one attempting to close the gap* Thus, even if the economy

---

[10] Walter W. Heller, *New Dimensions of Political Economy* (Cambridge, Mass., Harvard University Press, 1966), p. 64. See all of Chapter 2 of that volume.

[11] Cf. *Economic Report of the President,* January, 1962, pp. 46–48; R. A. Gordon, *The Goal of Full Employment* (New York, Wiley, 1967), pp. 52–55.

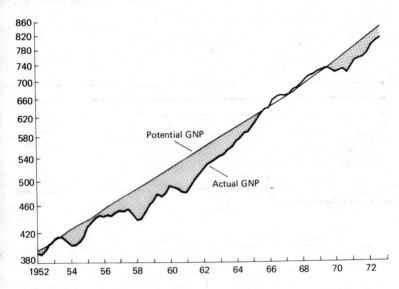

**Figure 6.3**  Potential and Actual GNP, 1952–1972 (billions of 1958 dollars)
(Source: *Business Conditions Digest*, January, 1973.)

were already expanding (as it was in 1962–1963), further stimulative action might be desirable in order to close the gap further and speed the return to full employment. This was in contrast to previous policies, as, for example, in 1959–1960. Then restrictive monetary and fiscal policies held back the expansion and eventually helped bring on a downturn when the unemployment rate was still above 5 percent. The Federal Reserve in particular had followed a policy during the 1950s of "leaning against the wind"—that is, tightening credit during a cyclical expansion even if unemployment was still above 4 percent and, in the terms of the New Economics, even if a substantial gap existed between potential and actual output. Arthur Burns, first chairman of the Council of Economic Advisers under President Eisenhower, has described this aspect of the New Economics as follows:

The central doctrine . . . is that the stage of the business cycle has little relevance to sound economic policy; that policy should be growth-oriented instead of cycle-oriented; that the vital matter is whether a gap exists between actual and potential output; that fiscal deficits and monetary tools need to be used to promote expansion when a gap exists; and that the stimuli should be sufficient to close the gap—provided significant inflationary pressures are not whipped up in the process.[12]

On the side of fiscal policy, three closely related concepts were emphasized.

*The full-employment (or high-employment) budget* What matters is not the current budgetary deficit but what the surplus or deficit would be at full employment—assuming existing government spending programs and taking into account the higher tax revenues that prevailing tax rates would yield at a full-employment level of income. The concept of a full-employment surplus was not a new one—it went back to discussions during World War II and an early postwar statement on fiscal policy by the Committee for Economic Development, a national organization of businessmen whose public statements on issues of national economic policy receive respectful attention.[13]

As we have already noted in Chapter 5, a high and rising full-employment surplus was a serious drag on the economy during 1959–1960, and it was still large in 1961–1963. The Kennedy administration argued that it would be difficult to return to full employment because of the large full-employment surplus. As private spending increased, tax receipts would rise much faster than government expenditures, thus acting as a drag on the economy. In order to reduce the full-employment surplus it was necessary to reduce tax rates, even though the current budget was still in deficit.[14]

In short, the economy had to cope with a *fiscal drag*. Indeed, such a drag is one aspect of the built-in flexibility of the tax system—rapidly rising tax revenues as output expands. During recessions, of course, we welcome the sensitivity of the tax system, since declining tax revenues tend to support after-tax income and spending.

Associated with the fiscal drag is the possibility of *fiscal dividends*.

[12] Quoted approvingly by Okun, *op. cit.*, p. 43. The original source is Arthur F. Burns and Paul A. Samuelson, *Full Employment, Guideposts, and Economic Stability* (Washington, D.C., American Enterprise Institute, 1967), pp. 31–32.

[13] For the early history of the full-employment budget concept, see Herbert Stein, *The Fiscal Revolution in America* (Chicago, University of Chicago Press, 1969), pp. 184–194, 220–232.

[14] The concept of the full-employment budget continued to be used by the Nixon administration. Thus in his budget message for fiscal 1973 President Nixon referred to "our goal of a balanced budget in a time of full employment" and urged Congress "to respect the full-employment spending guideline this year." Executive Office of the President, Office of Management and Budget, *The U.S. Budget in Brief* (Washington, D.C., GPO, 1972), p. 3.

Just as in a cyclical upswing rising incomes bring larger tax revenues and create a fiscal drag, so in the longer run the process of growth increases tax revenues at full employment and provides the opportunity for a fiscal dividend—in the form of either tax reductions or increases in government spending. The rise in the full-employment surplus over the years, as between 1958 and 1963, is a measure of the fiscal dividend still available—either to taxpayers or to the potential beneficiaries of further increases in government expenditures. In 1963, the Kennedy administration proposed to distribute a good part of the dividend in the form of a large-scale reduction in taxes. During 1961–1965, there were also substantial increases in expenditures.[15]

## Expansionary Fiscal Policy at Work

Tax reduction played no role in the initial program of the Kennedy administration when it assumed office in January, 1961. Fiscal stimulus was to be applied through a moderate increase in government expenditures, which would also help bring about desired economic reforms. Actually, unexpected foreign developments led to an upsurge in military expenditures on top of the planned increase in nondefense spending, and in 1961 Kennedy had to be dissuaded from proposing a tax *increase* to finance the increased military spending.[16]

From the beginning the Kennedy administration emphasized the problem of retarded growth of the American economy, not merely the need for cyclical recovery in the short run. Accelerating the rate of growth, in actual as well as potential output, called for a higher level of private investment. Hence the first tax concessions made were to

---

[15] Heller estimates that during 1961–1965 the federal government distributed $48 billion in fiscal dividends. Only one-third, or $16 billion, took the form of tax reductions. The remaining $32 billion went into rising expenditures and transfer payments. Of this, over one-third ($11 billion) financed an increase in military and space expenditures and only $3 billion was used for increased purchases of other goods and services. The remaining $18 billion represented increased transfer payments to persons, grants-in-aid to state and local governments, and interest on the federal debt. According to Heller's estimates, of the total of $48 billion, $34 billion represented growth in tax revenues at full employment and $14 billion consisted of the full-employment surplus already existing at the end of 1960. See Heller, *op. cit.*, p. 71.

[16] The details of fiscal policy during 1961–1965 can be followed in Stein, *op. cit.*; Heller, *op. cit.*; Okun, *op. cit.*; G. L. Bach, *Making Monetary and Fiscal Policy* (Washington, D.C., Brookings, 1971). See also "Federal Fiscal Policy in the 1960's," in *Federal Reserve Bulletin* (September, 1968). For a critical review of the New Economics and of fiscal policy in the sixties, see the paper "Fiscal Failure: Lessons of the Sixties" by Charles E. McClure, Jr., in Cagan *et al.*, *op. cit.*, pp. 7–87.

business—in the form of an investment tax credit and a change in Treasury regulations permitting accelerated depreciation of plant and equipment. Both went into effect in 1962. The investment tax credit, which permitted business firms to deduct 7 percent of their expenditures on new equipment from their income tax liability, was proposed in 1961 but was not approved by Congress until late in 1962.

Interestingly, the business community did not welcome the investment tax credit at first, and, as we have seen, the incentives to business investment introduced in 1962 operated only with a lag. Subsequent evaluations by economists vary in the amount of credit they give these tax incentives for stimulating investment from 1962 on. They certainly had some stimulating effect.[17] The investment tax credit was terminated at the peak of the inflationary boom in 1969 but was reinstated as part of President Nixon's New Economic Policy in 1971 in an effort to speed recovery after the 1970 recession.[18]

As the pace of recovery began to decelerate in the first half of 1962, bringing with it fears in Washington of a possible "Kennedy recession," and as another year passed with a persistently large gap between actual and potential output, President Kennedy became more receptive to proposals for a substantial tax reduction to reduce the depressing overhang of a large full-employment budgetary surplus. In June, 1962 the President announced his intention to propose a tax reduction to Congress. Actually, the proposal for a significant reduction in personal and corporate income taxes, combined with a substantial package of proposed tax reforms, was not submitted to Congress until January, 1963, and it was not until February, 1964 that the tax reduction bill (largely stripped of tax reform) was passed by Congress and signed by President Johnson.[19]

The Revenue Act of 1964 provided for a substantial reduction in

[17] See, for example, Gary Fromm, ed., *Tax Incentives and Capital Spending* (Washington, D.C., Brookings, 1971), and the paper by G. M. Brannon in Tax Institute of America, *Tax Incentives* (Lexington, Mass., Heath Lexington Books, 1971). Both sources contain numerous references to other relevant literature.

[18] The investment tax credit was temporarily suspended as inflationary pressures mounted in 1966 but was reinstated during the "minirecession" of 1967.

[19] For an interesting account of the debates that went on in and out of Congress and the educational efforts of the administration to sell the tax package, see Stein, *op. cit.*, chap. 17. In Arthur Okun's words, "The press served as the textbook for the biggest course in elementary macroeconomics ever presented" (*op. cit.*, p. 45). For a detailed analysis of the tax bill presented by President Kennedy and the legislation that actually resulted, see Joseph Pechman, "Individual Income Tax Provisions of the Revenue Act of 1964," *Journal of Finance 20* (May, 1965): 247–272.

tax rates on personal incomes and on corporate profits in two installments, the first and larger installment to take effect immediately and
the second to go into effect at the beginning of 1965. At 1964 income
levels the total package reduced tax liabilities by about $14 billion,
of which $11 billion represented tax relief for individuals and the
rest a decline in corporate tax liabilities. The reduction in personal
income taxes amounted to about 2.25 percent of personal income
before taxes; the cut in corporate taxes equaled about 4.5 percent
of corporate profits before taxes. Withholding rates on payrolls were
reduced immediately to reflect both installments of the reduction in
tax liabilities, and there was a corresponding immediate upsurge in
disposable incomes.

As we have already seen, the recovery in business investment and
in GNP had already begun to accelerate moderately in the second
half of 1963. The expansion speeded up more after the tax cut. A
further fiscal stimulus was applied in mid-1965 in the form of a large
reduction in federal excise taxes, to become effective in several stages
extending to 1969. In addition, social security benefits were liberalized
in the second half of 1965.

By the closing months of 1965, rising military expenditures associated with the escalating American involvement in Vietnam added
to the succession of fiscal stimuli during the two preceding years. In
December the national unemployment rate was down to 4 percent.
The rise in prices, which had been gratifyingly slow during 1961–1964,
was beginning to accelerate. At the beginning of 1966 the Council of
Economic Advisers worriedly concluded that the combined effect of
budgeted future expenditures "and tax laws now in effect would be
more stimulative than now seems appropriate for the year ahead."[20]
They were right.

Despite dissenting opinions from the monetarists, the 1964 tax reduction is generally given a major share of the credit for the accelerated expansion in 1964–1965 and for the return to full employment by the end of the latter year. It is difficult to estimate precisely
how strong the stimulus was and to separate the effects of the fiscal
stimulus from those of the accommodating monetary policy that accompanied the tax reduction.[21] An early estimate by Arthur Okun

[20] *Economic Report of the President,* January, 1966, p. 53.

[21] As would be expected, Milton Friedman has argued that it was the accommodating monetary policy of the Federal Reserve, with the accompanying accelerated expansion in the money supply, that was responsible for the speeding up of
the expansion, and not the tax cut. See Milton Friedman and Walter W. Heller,
*Monetary vs. Fiscal Policy: A Dialogue* (New York, Norton, 1969), pp. 55–57.

suggests that the 1964 tax cut added about $24 billion to GNP by the second quarter of 1965 and that the total increase eventually amounted to about $36 billion.[22] An accommodating monetary policy contributed significantly to this result.

Accelerated expansion in 1964–1965 brought in rapidly rising tax revenues while government expenditures rose more slowly, with the result that a moderate budgetary deficit in the first half of 1964 was converted into a modest surplus in the first half of 1965.[23] At the same time the *full-employment* budget shifted from a surplus of over $10 billion in the last quarter of 1963 to a slight deficit in the second half of 1965.[24] Thus the "fiscal drag" was eliminated. Indeed, because of the Vietnam war the full-employment budget was to show a large deficit during 1967 and the first half of 1968, until it was finally eliminated by the tax surcharge in the latter year. But that part of the story comes later.

## Monetary Policy

Economic expansion in the first half of the 1960s "reflected a unique partnership between fiscal and monetary policy."[25] Federal Reserve policy during these years was largely accommodative, permitting the money supply to grow in line with the rise in total spending. In the words of one observer, "monetary policy generally remained in the background."[26] The supply of money (adjusted demand deposits plus currency in circulation) expanded at a moderately, but irregularly, accelerating rate during 1961–1964, although there was a temporary interruption in the expansion during the retardation of recovery in 1962 (see Figure 6.4, page 158). Credit remained fairly easy, al-

[22] Arthur Okun, "Measuring the Impact of the 1964 Tax Reduction," in Walter W. Heller, *Perspectives on Economic Growth* (New York, Vintage Books, 1968), pp. 25–49. For other, and somewhat lower, estimates, see Lawrence R. Klein, "Econometric Analysis of the Tax Cut of 1964," in James S. Duesenberry *et al.*, eds., *The Brookings Model: Some Further Results* (Skokie, Ill., Rand McNally, 1969), pp. 458–472.

[23] This statement refers to the federal budget as it is presented in the national income and product accounts.

[24] Estimates of the full-employment surplus vary, depending on how the calculations are made. Arthur Okun and Nancy Teeters give a figure of $11.7 billion for the full-employment surplus in the fourth quarter of 1963. (See their paper "The Full Employment Surplus Revisited" in *Brookings Papers on Economic Activity*, 1970:1, pp. 104–105.) Another estimate puts it at about $14 billion. Both estimates show a full-employment deficit of $1-2 billion for the second half of 1965.

[25] Okun, *The Political Economy of Prosperity, op. cit.*, p. 53.

[26] Bach, *op. cit.*, p. 119.

though free reserves of member banks gradually declined and finally became negative in 1965.[27]

During 1961–1964 the Fed did not "lean against the wind," tightening credit and accelerating the rise in interest rates, as it had in earlier postwar expansions. It was sensitive to the level of unemployment and to the existence of the gap between actual and potential output. As long as prices remained relatively stable and there was no dramatic deterioration in the balance of payments, it was prepared to permit the expansion of bank reserves needed to support the rising level of output and spending. In the latter part of 1965, however, as the rise in prices started to accelerate and the big upsurge in military spending began, the Fed became concerned about the danger of inflation. In December, 1965, in a step opposed by President Johnson and his chief economic advisers, the Board of Governors approved an increase in the discount rate. This minor episode was a herald of much more restrictive action to come, which led to the "credit crunch" in the late summer and early fall of 1966.[28]

All through the 1960s the Fed had to concern itself with the worsened position of the American balance of payments.[29] As we shall see later, the Kennedy and Johnson administrations took a number of steps to reduce the excess supply of dollars flowing into foreign-exchange markets. On its side, the Federal Reserve System tried to alter the term structure of interest rates in order to restrain the outflow of short-term capital while at the same time keeping long-term interest rates low so as to stimulate private investment at home. This program was known as "Operation Twist." By planning its open-market operations so that it bought relatively more long-term securities, the Fed had some success in holding down long-term interest rates while rates on short-term securities rose (see Figure 6.4). The Treasury cooperated in this program by increasing the share of short-term maturities in its regular offerings of new government securities. The Federal Reserve also took steps to restrain the expansion of foreign loans and investments by American banks and other financial institutions.[30]

---

27 Free reserves are excess reserves minus borrowings from the Federal Reserve Banks.

28 For an account of the episode involving raising the discount rate in December, 1965, see Bach, *op. cit.*, pp. 120–126. For the Board's official review of developments in 1965 and the growing feeling of the need for restraint, see its *Fifty-Second Annual Report* for 1965.

29 See pp. 179–185.

30 For further discussion of monetary policy during 1961–1965, largely from a monetarist position, see Cagan, "Monetary Policy," in Cagan *et al.*, *op. cit.*, pp. 92–98.

## VIETNAM AND ACCELERATING INFLATION

The happy combination of rapidly expanding output, falling unemployment, and relative price stability ended in the latter part of 1965. In July President Johnson announced the beginning of expanded American involvement in Vietnam. Government expenditures began to rise rapidly while the expansionary effects of the fiscal stimuli applied in 1964–1965 were still being felt; business expectations improved still further, and the rise in business investment accelerated.

Thus, just as full employment was being reached, a new and powerful expansionary stimulus was injected into the economy. Total spending began to rise much more rapidly than output. The American economy entered a period of demand-pull inflation that persisted (except during the first half of 1967) until restrictive policies in 1969 helped bring on a new recession. Even then, inflation continued at an unacceptably high rate through 1970 and into 1971.

### Spending and Prices in 1965–1966

Federal government expenditures on goods and services increased relatively little between mid-1963 and the second quarter of 1965 (see Table 6.1). The accelerating expansion in economic activity was carried along by the rise in private spending, aided by tax reductions (and some increase in transfer payments) and by the steady upward trend in the expenditures of state and local governments.

All this changed radically after mid-1965. Military expenditures increased by over $3 billion at an annual rate (6.5 percent) in the last two quarters of 1965 and by $13 billion (25 percent) in 1966. The rapid rise in defense spending began to taper off gradually after the first quarter of 1967, reaching a plateau at the end of 1968. The peak came in the third quarter of 1969. All told, defense spending increased by about $30 billion, or by more than 60 percent, between the middle of 1965 and the end of 1968. During the same period total federal expenditures on goods and services rose by about $35 billion, or by 54 percent.[31]

This massive fiscal injection of course had its multiplier effects. However, these were partially offset in 1966 by several factors operating to hold back the rise in aggregate demand. Automobile sales, after a boom year in 1965, declined after the first quarter of 1966. More important, residential building, which had stopped rising after the end of 1963 (as it usually does when a cyclical expansion picks up speed and mortgage credit becomes more difficult to obtain), declined

---

[31] These figures are as reported in the national income and product accounts. See the appendix tables in the *Economic Report of the President*.

precipitously after the first quarter of 1966 as credit conditions tightened markedly. Home building was the chief sufferer in the "credit crunch" in the second half of 1966. In addition, net exports, which had reached a peak in 1964, began a decline that was to continue during the rest of the 1960s.

Largely offsetting these restraining influences was a very large increase in inventory investment brought on both by the need to build up stocks of materials and goods-in-process in defense industries and by a spurt of inventory accumulation in other sectors. The latter was occasioned particularly by newly generated inflationary expectations. After seven years of remarkable stability, wholesale prices began to rise rapidly from the beginning of 1965, even before the upsurge in military spending began, and the rise gathered momentum as the magnitude of the planned increase in government spending came to be recognized.

As we have seen, the national unemployment rate had fallen to 4 percent by December, 1965. During 1966 it declined further to 3.6 percent. As aggregate demand continued to expand, there was increasing pressure on available capacity (despite the additional plant and equipment resulting from the investment boom that was under way);[32] labor shortages were beginning to develop, and the rate of increase in wages began to accelerate. As typically happens in these circumstances, the rise in labor productivity began to diminish. As a result unit labor costs, which had been quite stable during the first half of the 1960s, began a rapid and accelerating rise that was to continue during the rest of the decade (with a brief pause during the "minirecession" of 1967).

All this had the expected effect on prices (see Figure 6.2). We have already noted that wholesale prices began to move upward rapidly early in 1965. The rise was particularly marked in farm products and processed foods, but it was also substantial in industrial commodities. The rise in the Consumer Price Index, which had been very modest during 1961–1965, accelerated rapidly after the beginning of 1966. Between December, 1965 and December, 1966, the CPI rose 3.4 percent. During 1960–1965 the average annual increase had been only 1.3 percent.

Largely because of the behavior of farm prices, the Wholesale Price Index moved more or less horizontally during the closing months of

---

[32] According to Federal Reserve data, the capacity utilization rate in manufacturing in 1966 was higher than it had been in any year since the Korean war, slightly exceeding the rate in the boom year of 1955. See, for example, *Economic Report of the President*, February, 1968, p. 252.

1966 and most of 1967. The rapid rise in wholesale prices resumed during 1968 and accelerated still further in 1969. The rate of increase in the Consumer Price Index slowed in the last quarter of 1966 and the first quarter of 1967 but then began to accelerate again.

## Monetary Policy and the Credit Crunch of 1966

Fiscal policy was not prepared to cope with the inflationary pressures unleashed at the end of 1965. The Council of Economic Advisers expressed concern in their annual report of January, 1966, but the President was not then ready to recommend a tax increase to Congress. Fiscal restraint was confined to the rescinding of reductions in excise taxes that had gone into effect, a speedup in corporate tax payments, the introduction of graduated income tax withholding (which accelerated tax receipts but did not alter taxpayers' total liabilities), and a moderate reduction in nondefense expenditures on goods and services. All this was on top of a substantial increase in social security taxes that went into effect at the beginning of the year. On the other side, however, the rise in defense spending in 1966 was badly underestimated, and the package of fiscal bits and pieces was inadequate to control the inflationary pressures released by the rapid rise in government spending and the accelerated advance in business investment.[33] Monetary policy had to step into the breach, and the responsibility for restraining the new inflationary forces fell on the shoulders of the Board of Governors of the Federal Reserve System.[34]

Early in 1966 the Federal Reserve began seriously to restrain the rate of increase in bank reserves and in the money supply. In the second quarter of the year, the expansion in the money supply was brought to a complete halt (see Figure 6.4). By midsummer commercial banks were no longer able to increase their loans and investments despite a demand for credit that was still rapidly expanding. Interest rates shot up dramatically to levels not experienced in nearly 50 years (but still well below those to be reached in 1969). The economy faced a situation in which a rapidly rising demand for bank credit (fed by expanding output and sales, inflationary expectations,

---

[33] In October, 1966, after the Federal Reserve's restrictive credit policy had already taken hold, the investment tax credit was suspended. It was reinstated in the spring of 1967, during the slowdown in the first half of the year.

[34] For a review of these policy developments in 1965–1966, see Okun, *The Political Economy of Prosperity, op. cit.,* pp. 62–82; Bach, *op. cit.,* pp. 120–132; and the *Economic Report of the President* and the *Annual Report* of the Board of Governors of the Federal Reserve System covering these years.

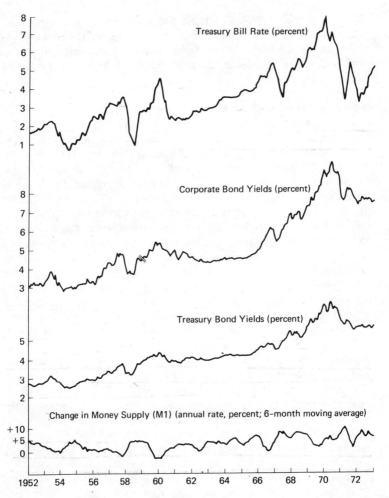

**Figure 6.4** Selected Interest Rates and Rate of Change in the Money Supply, 1952–1972

(Source: *Business Conditions Digest,* January, 1973.)

and fears that credit would get still tighter) faced a supply that was no longer increasing.

The greatest victims of the developing credit stringency were the housing industry and the financial institutions serving it, particularly the savings and loan associations. Private-housing starts (seasonally adjusted) fell by 40 percent between February and October, 1966, and the flow of funds into savings and loan associations virtually ceased as savers turned to assets yielding higher rates of return. While there was some evidence of overbuilding in particular areas, the drastic decline in home building was due primarily to the growing scarcity of mortgage credit.[35]

The increasing tightness of credit reached almost crisis proportions in late August and early September, 1966, and talk of a possible financial panic filled the air. At that stage the Federal Reserve stepped in, providing additional reserves to the banking system through open-market operations and assuring member banks that they were free to replenish their reserves by rediscounting at the Federal Reserve Banks if they confined themselves to meeting legitimate business demands for credit. By the end of September the situation had eased. The Fed continued to feed more reserves into the banking system in the closing months of the year, bank reserves and the money supply started to increase again, and interest rates began to decline. The credit crunch of 1966 was over.

Restrictive monetary policy in 1966 succeeded in curbing, albeit only temporarily, the inflationary pressures unleashed in the closing months of 1965. It also helped bring on the "minirecession" of 1967.

## Not Quite a Recession

In the first half of 1967, the economy paused briefly in the expansion that had been under way since 1961. GNP in constant prices was very slightly less in the first quarter than in the preceding three months. Since prices continued to rise, though at a slower rate, there was no decline at all in GNP measured in current prices. The sensitive index of industrial production reached a temporary peak in December, 1966 but declined only about 2.5 percent during the next six months, after which it began to rise again. The unemployment rate, which had been

[35] The Federal Reserve's controversial Regulation Q played an important role in diverting funds from savings and loan associations and, to a lesser extent, from mutual savings banks. Under Regulation Q the Federal Reserve controls the maximum interest rate that commercial banks may pay on time deposits. In December, 1965 the Fed substantially increased ceiling rates on time deposits. Commercial banks immediately began to offer higher interest rates on certificates of deposit (CDs), which for large investors are as liquid an asset as Treasury bills. The result was a large-scale diversion of funds to the commercial banks. Cf. Bach, *op. cit.,* p. 126, and the *Annual Report* of the Board of Governors of the Federal Reserve System for 1965 and 1966.

as low as 3.6 percent in November, 1966, crept up only to 4.1 percent in October, 1967. Business fixed investment fell very little, and residential construction began to increase rapidly after its collapse in 1966.

The major deflationary force at work in the 1967 "minirecession" was the sharp decline in inventory investment (Table 6.2). As we have seen, there was a sharp spurt in inventory accumulation in the latter part of 1966. In the fourth quarter business increased its inventories at an annual rate of about $20 billion. In constant prices, it was the highest rate of inventory investment since the first year of the Korean war. This was clearly an unsustainable rate of increase in inventories, particularly since final sales stopped increasing in the fourth quarter as residential building continued its decline and the rise in business fixed investment tapered off.[36]

During the next six months inventory investment fell about $15 billion (annual rate). Representing the largest half-year decline in such investment on record, this was a substantial deflationary shock for the economy to absorb. Under other circumstances a minor recession of not insignificant proportions could have developed. As it was, GNP in constant prices fell by only a trivial amount for one quarter and was higher in the second quarter of 1967 than in the last quarter of 1966. Measured in current prices, GNP continued to rise. The decline in inventory investment was offset by the accelerating rise in federal military outlays, the continued increase in state and local government expenditures, and an accelerated rise in consumer spending (see Figure 6.1).[37] Some recovery in residential building and improvement in the export surplus also helped. Disposable income and consumer spending were supported, as they typically are in recessions, by a decline in corporate profits while dividends were maintained, and by a rise in transfer payments.[38]

By the second half of 1967, the expansion was picking up steam again. The rise in aggregate demand accelerated, and so did the rise in prices. The economy thus entered the last two years of the longest cyclical expansion on record. During these two years, as inflationary pressures mounted, both fiscal and monetary policies were used in attempts to restrain the boom. By the end of 1969 these restrictive efforts had finally helped to bring on a recession.

---

[36] Final sales are GNP minus the net change in inventories—that is, the part of total GNP that does not go into inventory accumulation.

[37] See also Table 6.2.

[38] See Table 6.2.

**Table 6.2** Components of Gross National Product for Selected Calendar Quarters, 1966–1970 (Seasonally adjusted annual rates; in billions of dollars)

| | Fourth Quarter, 1966 | First Quarter, 1967 | Third Quarter, 1969 | Fourth Quarter, 1970 |
|---|---|---|---|---|
| Gross national product (constant dollars) | 668.1 | 666.6 | 729.2 | 718.0 |
| Implicit price deflator for GNP (1958 = 100) | 115.4 | 116.2 | 129.1 | 137.9 |
| GNP components in current prices: | | | | |
| Consumption expenditures | 474.5 | 480.7 | 583.7 | 626.5 |
| Durables | 71.9 | 69.8 | 90.6 | 87.5 |
| Nondurables | 209.1 | 213.1 | 247.3 | 271.3 |
| Services | 193.5 | 197.8 | 245.8 | 267.7 |
| Gross private domestic investment | 126.2 | 114.0 | 143.8 | 137.8 |
| Nonresidential construction | 28.2 | 29.0 | 35.4 | 36.3 |
| Producer durables | 56.0 | 53.9 | 64.8 | 62.1 |
| Residential construction | 22.1 | 21.6 | 33.0 | 33.6 |
| Change in inventories | 19.9 | 9.6 | 10.6 | 5.7 |
| Net exports | 4.9 | 5.5 | 2.6 | 2.8 |
| Government expenditures[a] | 165.2 | 174.2 | 211.6 | 222.6 |
| Federal | 82.1 | 87.7 | 99.3 | 95.0 |
| State and local | 83.0 | 86.5 | 112.3 | 127.6 |
| Gross national product (current prices) | 770.7 | 774.4 | 941.7 | 989.7 |
| National income | 637.3 | 638.5 | 774.6 | 804.1 |
| Less: Corporate profits | 83.7 | 78.3 | 79.8 | 66.9 |
| Other deductions[b] | 39.5 | 41.0 | 54.9 | 58.6 |
| Plus: Govt. transfer payments | 44.5 | 47.6 | 62.3 | 80.6 |
| Other additions[c] | 46.3 | 47.6 | 57.3 | 60.6 |
| Personal income | 605.0 | 614.2 | 759.6 | 819.8 |
| Less: Personal taxes | 79.4 | 80.8 | 116.4 | 115.8 |
| Disposable income | 525.6 | 533.4 | 643.2 | 704.0 |
| Personal saving[d] | 37.7 | 39.3 | 42.6 | 59.2 |

[a]On goods and services. Excludes transfer payments.

[b]Chiefly social security contributions.

[c]Includes government interest payments, corporation dividends, and business transfer payments.

[d]Personal saving in the national income accounts is less than the difference between disposable income and consumption expenditures. The discrepancy is accounted for by consumer interest and personal transfer payments to foreigners.

Source: *Survey of Current Business.*

## THE END OF THE BOOM

### The New Upsurge in Spending

Between the second quarter of 1967 and the third quarter of 1969, GNP in current prices rose at an annual rate of 8.5 percent.[39] Considerably less than half of this, 3.6 percent, represented growth in real output; the remainder, about 4.8 percent, reflected the increasingly rapid rise in prices. The end of the prolonged boom of the 1960s came in November, 1969; GNP in constant prices was slightly lower in the fourth quarter of that year than in the third. The ensuing recession was brief and relatively mild.

In the second half of 1967 and the first half of 1968—up to about the time the tax surcharge was passed by Congress—the chief stimulus to renewed expansion came from the continued rise in federal, state, and local government spending, the recovery in residential building, and the increase in inventory investment after the sharp decline in the first half of 1967. Business fixed investment was relatively slow to expand again after the 1967 minirecession. The rate of saving (as a percentage of disposable income), which had risen significantly at the end of 1966, remained high through the second quarter of 1968, and this had some restraining effect on the rise in consumer spending.

While the personal saving rate remained high through the second quarter of 1968, consumer spending expanded in line with the rise in disposable income. The expansion was particularly rapid in spending on durable goods. Beginning early in 1968 a sharp upsurge occurred in purchases of automobiles, making 1968 a record year for the automobile industry. This important component of consumer spending reached a new high in the second half of 1968 and even expanded slightly more in 1969, with the peak coming in the fourth quarter.[40]

The stimulus to the continued rapid rise in aggregate demand changed after the middle of 1968. The federal budget became a restraining influence, while private fixed investment took off on a new upsurge that lasted through all of 1969. Not only did Congress pass the 10 percent tax surcharge in June, 1968, but the rise in federal government expenditures on goods and services came to a virtual

[39] For further details on developments during these years, see the *Economic Report of the President* and the January issues of *Survey of Current Business* for the years in question; Cagan *et al.*, *op. cit.*, Okun, *The Political Economy of Prosperity*, *op. cit.*, chap. 3; and any recent issue of *Business Conditions Digest*.

[40] For consumer expenditures on durables other than automobiles, the peak came in the second quarter of 1969. (All of these statements refer to expenditures in current prices.)

halt. Although the peak in military spending did not come until the third quarter of 1969, there was little increase between mid-1968 and mid-1969, and the rise in nondefense expenditures on goods and services was brought to an almost complete stop.

In contrast, the expansion in business fixed investment accelerated sharply (see Figure 6.1, page 139). Even residential building continued to provide strong support to the expansion through the second quarter of 1969, despite the rapid rise in interest rates and growing monetary tightness in 1969. Residential building declined in the second half of 1969, but there was nothing like the collapse in housing construction that occurred during the credit crunch of 1966, even though interest rates soared to levels much higher than those reached in 1966 (see Figures 6.1 and 6.4, pages 139 and 158). Not only did the underlying demand for housing remain strong, but a number of financial reforms instituted by the federal government after the 1966 experience made the flow of mortgage funds less sensitive to general credit tightness than had previously been the case.[41]

Consumer spending continued to rise rapidly after mid-1968, despite the surcharge. The unexpectedly large increase in consumer expenditures in the face of a 10 percent increase in personal taxes was associated with a sharp drop in the rate of personal saving, from 7.6 percent in the second quarter of 1968 to 5.3 percent in the same quarter of 1969. Thereafter the savings rate increased again, and the rapid rise in spending on durable goods came to a halt. Indeed, in constant prices consumer expenditures on durable goods (including automobiles) declined slightly in the second half of 1969, and this behavior, in turn, was reflected in manufacturing output and business expectations.[42]

During the business pause in 1967, unemployment had risen only moderately, to 4.1 percent in October, after which it began to decline again. By the end of 1968 the national rate was down to 3.3 percent, and it averaged as low as 3.5 percent for the full year 1969. These figures, however, understate the tightness that had developed in the national labor market. Teenagers and women had become a significantly larger share of the labor force during the 1960s, with a

[41] For a summary of these measures, see *Economic Report of the President*, January, 1969, pp. 44–45.

[42] The Federal Reserve index of industrial production, seasonally adjusted, reached its peak in September, 1969. Production of automobiles also peaked then and declined 17.5 percent during the remainder of the year. In general, production of consumer durable goods reached a peak earlier, and declined more, during the remainder of 1969 than was the case for finished producer goods.

corresponding decline in the fraction of the work force accounted for by prime-age males. It is the latter group that has the lowest unemployment rates, and by 1968–1969 unemployment rates for men aged 25 to 64 had fallen even below the very low figures during the Korean war, when the national unemployment rate declined to 3 percent and below.[43]

This increasing pressure on the experienced work force had a number of consequences. The rate of increase in man-hour productivity slowed markedly as less experienced workers were drawn into employment and the inefficiencies associated with pressure on capacity developed in various industries. Equally important, the very low unemployment rates increased the upward pressure on wage rates, with a consequent rapid acceleration in the rise of unit labor costs and prices.

## Mounting Inflationary Pressures

The accelerating rise in prices during 1966–1969 can be traced in Figure 6.2 (page 144) and Table 6.3 (last three columns). The annual increase in the Consumer Price Index accelerated from 2.9 percent in 1967 to 5.4 percent in 1969, and the rise accelerated further in 1970 even after a new recession brought on rising unemployment and declining output. Similar acceleration occurred in the more comprehensive implicit price deflator for private nonfarm GNP. The rise in wholesale prices also accelerated, although not as markedly as in the other two price indexes mentioned.[44]

Wages rose at a rapid date during 1966–1969 (Table 6.3). The problem was not so much continued *acceleration* in the rate of increase in wages after 1966 as it was the persistently high rate at which hourly compensation continued to rise—at the same time that the rate of increase in productivity slowed down. Indeed, output per man-hour actually declined slightly in 1969. The result was a rapid acceleration in the rise in unit labor costs (column 3 of Table 6.3) and a consequent acceleration in the rise in prices.

Even so, prices did not rise as fast as labor costs per unit (compare column 3 with the remaining columns in Table 6.3), and profits were under some pressure from 1966 on. The share of profits in income

[43] Comparisons of unemployment rates for particular groups before and after 1967 are complicated by a change in the manner in which the data are collected that went into effect in that year. But the underlying trends described in the text still show up when appropriate adjustment is made for this change.

[44] The small increase in wholesale prices in 1967 shown in Table 6.3 was due primarily to a decline in farm prices.

**Table 6.3**  Annual Rates of Change in Output per Man-hour, Compensation, Unit Labor Costs, and Prices, 1966–1972

| Year or Quarter | Annual Rate of Change (percent) | | | | | |
|---|---|---|---|---|---|---|
| | Output per Man-hour[a] | Man-hour Compensation[a] | Unit Labor Costs[a] | Implicit Price Deflator | Consumer Price Index | Whole-sale Price Index |
| 1966 | 3.5 | 6.1 | 2.4 | 2.1 | 2.9 | 3.3 |
| 1967 | 1.6 | 5.7 | 4.0 | 3.3 | 2.9 | 0.2 |
| 1968 | 2.9 | 7.3 | 4.3 | 3.5 | 4.2 | 2.5 |
| 1969 | −0.2 | 7.0 | 7.2 | 4.4 | 5.4 | 3.9 |
| 1970 | 0.7 | 7.2 | 6.5 | 5.0 | 5.9 | 3.7 |
| 1971:1 | 7.4 | 9.1 | 1.5 | 4.5 | 3.1 | 5.5 |
| 2 | 3.2 | 7.5 | 4.2 | 4.0 | 4.4 | 4.7 |
| 3 | 2.5 | 5.2 | 2.5 | 2.7 | 4.0 | 3.2 |
| 4 | 4.7 | 4.9 | 0.3 | 0.1 | 2.3 | 0.3 |
| 1972:1 | 5.2 | 9.1 | 3.8 | 3.7 | 3.3 | 7.9 |
| 2 | 5.1 | 4.6 | −0.5 | 1.5 | 3.3 | 4.2 |
| 3 | 6.6 | 6.1 | −0.4 | 1.4 | 3.6 | 5.9 |
| 4 | 4.3 | 7.4 | 3.0 | 2.1 | 3.5 | 4.4 |

[a]For the private nonfarm economy.

Source: *Economic Report of the President*, January, 1973; U.S. Bureau of Labor Statistics, *Chartbook on Prices, Wages, and Productivity*, February, 1973.

originating in the corporate sector declined significantly during 1966–1969. In manufacturing alone, after-tax profits per dollar of sales declined from 5.6 cents in 1966 to 4.8 cents in 1969. Despite an increasing volume of business, the rate of return on stockholders' equity in the manufacturing sector also declined significantly between 1966 and 1969.[45]

The figures in Table 6.3 clearly indicate that the wage-price guideposts ceased to have any significant effect as demand pressures built up from 1966 on. On the side of wages, the guideposts were severely weakened by a large wage increase for airline machinists in 1966, and other large increases for both union and nonunion workers quickly followed. In the January, 1967 *Economic Report* the wage guidepost of 3.2 percent was abandoned, but during 1967–1968 the

[45] See the tables on corporate profits in the statistical appendix in any recent *Economic Report of the President*. See also Arthur M. Okun and George L. Perry, "Notes and Numbers on the Profits Squeeze," in *Brookings Papers on Economic Activity*, 1970:3, pp. 466–473.

Johnson administration continued a policy of exhortation and "jaw-boning" in an attempt to restrain wage and price increases in particular oligopolistic industries.[46]

The guideposts were officially interred by the Nixon administration after it took office in 1969. But two-and-a-half years later, the same administration imposed a freeze on wages and prices followed by a far-ranging system of wage and price controls.

One other aspect of the accelerating inflation during 1966–1969 needs to be mentioned here: the effect on price expectations. The continued acceleration in the rate of increase in prices naturally engendered expectations as to still further price increases, and these expectations affected both wage demands and the behavior of interest rates. Virtually all attempts to explain the rapid rise in wages during 1968–1971 assign an important role to the rise in prices.

With respect to interest rates economists distinguish between the *market* (or nominal) rate of interest and the *real* rate. The latter is the market rate adjusted for the expected rise in prices (decline in the purchasing power of the dollar) over the life of the security or the term of the loan. The sharp rise in interest rates during 1968–1969 to levels not reached in a century reflected not only a restrictive monetary policy in 1969 but also an increasing allowance made by lenders and borrowers for still further price increases expected in the future. Thus bond yields and mortgage interest rates of 9 percent or more in 1969 restrained business investment and home building less than would have been expected in a situation in which prices were rising much less rapidly.

### Fiscal and Monetary Restraint, 1968–1969

Although by the end of 1965 the Council of Economic Advisers felt that the inflationary potential of the economy called for a general increase in income taxes, the President believed that such action was politically impossible in 1966.[47] As a result fiscal restraint in 1966 was confined, in Arthur Okun's words, to a "bits-and-pieces revenue package" that had relatively little effect in restraining the continued rise in aggregate demand.[48] The failure to take decisive action was exacerbated by the fact that military spending rose much more rapidly in 1966 than the administration had foreseen.

---

[46] The end of the guideposts is described by Thomas G. Moore in his paper in Cagan *et al., op. cit.*, pp. 216–221. See also the *Economic Report of the President* for 1967–1969.

[47] Okun, *The Political Economy of Prosperity, op. cit.*, pp. 70–71.

[48] *Ibid.*, p. 70. See also p. 157.

The President made his first proposal for a general increase in income taxes in January, 1967. Then the proposal was for a surcharge of 6 percent—that is, an across-the-board 6 percent increase in the income tax liabilities of individuals and corporations. In August, 1967 the proposed increase was raised to 10 percent, and this request was renewed in January, 1968. The 10 percent surcharge was not passed by Congress, however, until late in June, 1968 (when it was accompanied by restraint on nonmilitary spending). For individuals, it was made retroactive to April 1; for corporations, to January 1, 1968. The tax increase was a temporary one, to expire at the end of June, 1969.[49] It was continued by the Nixon administation at the 10 percent rate through 1969, reduced to 5 percent at the beginning of 1970, and eliminated at the end of June, 1970; by then unemployment was rising rapidly.[50]

The 1968 surcharge represented a significant amount of fiscal restraint. The increase in tax rates, combined with the imposed limitation on federal expenditures, led to a very substantial swing in the full-employment budget—from a full-employment deficit of about $11 billion in the first half of 1968 to a surplus of about $10 billion in 1969.[51] Yet the discernible effect on consumer and business spending was disappointing small. As we have already noted, the rate of personal saving dropped sharply, and there was a rapid increase in spending on durable goods, particularly automobiles. Business also seemed to pay little attention to the increase in corporate income taxes. A new upsurge in business fixed investment began in the second half of 1968, *after* the surcharge was in effect.

What went wrong?[52] A widely accepted explanation centers on the *temporary* nature of the tax increase. Most recent theoretical and empirical work suggests that consumer spending depends much more

---

[49] For further details see *Economic Report of the President*, January, 1969, pp. 38–39; Arthur M. Okun, "The Personal Tax Surcharge and Consumer Demand, 1968–70," *Brookings Papers on Economic Activity*, 1971:1, pp. 169–170.

[50] Another act of fiscal restraint in 1968 (and again in 1969) was postponement of scheduled reductions in federal excise taxes.

[51] Okun and Teeters, *op. cit.*, p. 105. Another estimate, by the Federal Reserve Bank of St. Louis, suggests that the magnitude of the swing toward a restrictive full-employment budget may have been even larger than implied by the figures cited in the text.

[52] These words form the title of a paper by Robert Eisner on the failure of fiscal and monetary policy to restrain inflation in the late 1960s. See "What Went Wrong?" *Journal of Political Economy 79* (May–June, 1971): 629–641. This should be read in conjunction with his earlier, widely cited article, "Fiscal and Monetary Policy Reconsidered," *American Economic Review 59* (December, 1969): 897–905.

on permanent income (or expected future income) than it does on income currently being received. Yet the surcharge was a temporary measure, originally intended to last only one year. Thus, it is argued, consumers geared their spending to long-run expectations, proceeded to offset the tax increase by reducing their rate of personal saving, and continued to spend almost as if the surcharge had not been passed. And indeed, as we have seen, there was a sharp drop in the savings rate after the surcharge went into effect.[53]

The same argument can be extended to business investment. The increase in corporate income taxes was also temporary, and business firms geared their investment plans to (optimistic) expectations as to the longer-term future—reinforced by expectations as to continuing inflation, the felt need to substitute capital for labor as unit labor costs rose at an accelerating rate, and the sustained rise in consumer spending. In addition, there were special factors operating to generate a sustained investment boom in the public-utility and communications industries.[54]

Another reason cited for the apparent failure of restrictive fiscal policy in 1968 is the action of the monetary authorities in easing credit in the second half of the year, apparently in the mistaken belief that the tax increase and constraints on government spending were sufficient to do the job.

Further restrictive fiscal action was taken by the Nixon administration in 1969. Strong efforts were made to restrain the rise in government spending, the investment tax credit was terminated (in April), scheduled reductions in excise taxes were again postponed, and the 10 percent tax surcharge was extended to the end of the year. In

[53] This argument is more fully developed in the two articles by Robert Eisner cited in the preceding footnote. So far as consumer spending is concerned, this argument has been challenged by Arthur Okun. Using the consumption functions in four current econometric models, he found that consumer spending on nondurable goods and services and on durables other than automobiles behaved substantially as these models predicted, taking the surcharge into account. There was, however, no discernible effect on automobile purchases. He concludes that the evidence from these models "indicates that the surcharge curbed consumption nearly as much as was expected in the models, and that any shortcomings in its effectiveness have no evident connection to the permanent income hypothesis." Okun, "The Personal Tax Surcharge and Consumer Demand, 1968–70," *op. cit.,* p. 198.

[54] Cf. Lawrence R. Klein, "Empirical Evidence on Fiscal and Monetary Models," in James J. Diamond, ed., *Issues in Fiscal and Monetary Policy* (Chicago, Depaul University, 1971), p. 40.

addition, a scheduled increase in social security tax rates went into effect in January.[55]

Let us turn now to monetary policy. Federal Reserve action during 1968–1969 went through three phases: moderate tightening of credit from late 1967 to mid-1968 as Congress delayed action on the tax surcharge, an easier policy during the second half of 1968 once fiscal restraint was imposed, and then an increasingly restrictive monetary policy during 1969. Thus, as the boom accelerated in 1968, first monetary policy carried the primary responsibility for restraining inflation, and then the burden passed to fiscal policy. Not until 1969 were monetary and fiscal policy working in harness to bring the boom under control. The joint effort succeeded, but only in part. The rise in aggregate demand was restrained to such an extent that a new recession began at the end of the year. But this did not significantly retard the rise in prices and wages. The demand-pull inflation of 1968–1969 turned into the cost-push inflation of 1970–1971.

Late in 1967 the Federal Reserve authorities began to take restrictive action, which continued through the first half of 1968. The discount rate was raised in several steps, there was a modest increase in reserve requirements, and pressure was put on bank reserves through open-market operations. Interest rates rose significantly above the temporary lows in the first half of 1967 but nowhere near the levels to be reached in 1969.[56]

Credit conditions eased in the second half of 1968. There was a short-lived decline in interest rates, to be reversed before the end of the year; the discount rate was lowered slightly; the expansion in bank credit accelerated; and the Fed pursued an accommodative policy of supplying reserves to the banking system to support the expansion in bank credit. This policy is now recognized as having been a mistake.

This was realized by the Fed before the year ended. The new shift toward restraint began late in 1968 and increased in severity during 1969. Using the instruments of control available to it, the Federal Reserve System prevented any expansion in bank reserves during 1969

[55] See *Economic Report of the President,* February, 1970, pp. 30–33, and Mc-Clure in Cagan *et al., op. cit.,* pp. 58 ff.

[56] One student of this period, a monetarist in his approach, argues that Federal Reserve policy was in fact not restrictive from the end of 1967 to mid-1968, regardless of the behavior of interest rates or member-bank reserves, or statements by the Federal Open Market Committee. The reason is that there was only modest retardation in the rate of growth of the money supply. Cagan *et al., op. cit.,* p. 103. His review of monetary policy during the later 1960s appears on pp. 98 ff. of this source.

despite the mounting demands for bank credit.[57] Interest rates soared to levels not reached in a century; and the rate of increase in the money supply was sharply curtailed, from an annual rate of about 7.5 percent in the fourth quarter of 1968 to about 1.5 percent in the fourth quarter of 1969 (see Figure 6.4, page 158). In the latter part of 1969, as a result of this policy of increasing credit tightness, "bank liquidity was reduced to the lowest levels of the post-World-War-II period."[58]

Combined with a restrictive fiscal policy, extreme monetary tightness succeeded in bringing the boom to an end, and the 1970 recession began.[59] But the rate of inflation in wages and prices was surprisingly resistant to deflationary pressures. Restrictive macroeconomic policy was able to bring about a decline in output and a rise in unemployment, but it was unable to bring inflation down to an acceptable rate before the Nixon administration was forced to take more drastic measures.

## THE WORST OF THREE WORLDS: 1970–1971

### The Course of the Recession

The peak of the long boom of the 1960s came in November, 1969. The ensuing recession was brief and mild, the trough coming a year later in November, 1970. Unemployment rose from 3.5 percent in November–December, 1969 to 6.1 percent in December, 1970. (The national unemployment rate had climbed above 7 percent in the two preceding recessions.)[60]

[57] The steps taken by the Federal Reserve included raising the discount rate (twice), increasing reserve requirements, engaging in restrictive open-market operations, and refusing to raise ceiling interest rates on CDs so that time deposits flowed out of commercial banks into market securities bearing higher yields. Other restrictive steps were also taken, including imposing a reserve requirement on bank borrowings from the Eurodollar market.

[58] Board of Governors of the Federal Reserve System, *Annual Report*, 1969, p. 6. See also *Economic Report of the President*, February, 1970, pp. 33–39.

[59] Although restrictive monetary policy certainly contributed significantly to bringing on the recession, a government survey concluded that "the direct impact of monetary policy on business investment was relatively light and that it lagged in time." The same was true in 1966. The effects on residential building and on capital expenditures of state and local governments were more serious. See Henry Shavell and John T. Woodward, "The Impact of the 1969–70 Monetary Stringency on Business Investment," *Survey of Current Business* (December, 1971): 19–31, 40, where reference is also made to an earlier study of the impact of monetary tightness in 1966 on business investment.

[60] For more detailed treatment of developments during and following the recession of 1969–1970, see the *Economic Report of the President*, the *Annual Report*

Although the recession was mild, it was accompanied by seemingly intractable problems in terms of the major goals of macroeconomic policy. Although the unemployment rate barely went above 6 percent, it remained stubbornly at about this figure all through 1971 and the early months of 1972. And despite the high level of unemployment, there was only modest retardation in the rate of increase in wages and prices during 1970 and the first six months of 1971 (see Table 6.3). Just before President Nixon introduced his New Economic Policy in August, 1971, the goals of full employment and price stability still seemed very distant.[61] And accompanying these problems on the domestic side was a dramatic deterioration in the American balance of payments that finally forced the administration to suspend the convertibility of the dollar.

The main cause of the 1970 recession was a restrictive monetary and fiscal policy that brought the rise in aggregate demand (in real terms) to a halt and adversely affected business expectations. Thus 1969–1970 is an example of a "policy recession," a term used more in Western Europe than in the United States.

The peak in industrial production came in September, 1969. Business expenditures on plant and equipment in constant prices declined slightly after the third quarter of 1969 but began expanding again, although slowly, during the second and third quarters of 1970 before being adversely affected by the General Motors strike in the fourth quarter.[62] Some types of fixed investment were very resistant to deflationary forces—for example, in the electric-power, gas, and communications industries.

As Table 6.2 brings out (page 161, last two columns), the decline in aggregate demand in current prices was confined to consumer expenditures on durables, investment in producer durables and particularly in inventories, and federal expenditures on goods and services. The decline in inventory investment, as in all of the postwar recessions, was particularly important. In current prices, this component of investment

---

of the Board of Governors of the Federal Reserve System, and the January issues of the *Survey of Current Business* for the appropriate years.

[61] The rise in unemployment, of course, also meant a slower rate of growth. Between the third quarter of 1969 and the fourth quarter of 1971, the average rate of increase in real GNP was only 1.4 percent per year.

[62] We have deflated business expenditures on plant and equipment in current prices by the GNP deflator for nonresidential fixed investment. These figures for plant and equipment expenditures exclude certain outlays included in nonresidential fixed investment in the national income accounts—for example, investment in agriculture, the professions, and nonprofit institutions.

declined by about $10 billion between the third quarter of 1969 and the first quarter of 1970 and then recovered part of the loss during the next two quarters.

The decline in federal expenditures on goods and services shown in Table 6.2 reflected a substantial decline in military spending offset in part by a moderate rise in other federal outlays. The decline in military spending had a significant effect in increasing unemployment in defense-oriented industries and in some parts of the country, particularly California.

The decline in federal military expenditures on goods and services was considerably more than offset, in terms of the immediate effect on personal incomes, by the very large rise in government transfer payments shown in Table 6.2. This reflected chiefly a substantial increase in social security benefits but also included significant increases in unemployment compensation payments and veterans' benefits.

As can be seen in Table 6.2, GNP *in current prices* rose by nearly $50 billion during the recession, although there was a modest decline in GNP in constant prices. The rise in disposable income was significantly greater than the increase in GNP. The reason for this is contained in three lines in the lower half of Table 6.2. First, as in previous recessions, corporate profits declined significantly while dividend payments were maintained. The second reason is the large increase in government transfer payments to which we have already referred. And finally, the tax surcharge was reduced to 5 percent at the beginning of 1970 and eliminated at the end of June. As a result personal taxes declined slightly during the recession despite the substantial increase in personal income before taxes.

Consumer spending, however, rose significantly less during the recession than did disposable income, with the result that there was a large increase in personal saving. The personal savings rate increased sharply from about 6.5 percent in the second half of 1969 to over 8 percent in the second half of 1970 and remained at an abnormally high level during 1971, the peak coming in the second quarter of that year.

This unusual behavior of savings has not yet been adequately explained. The typical explanation runs in terms of the increasing feeling of uncertainty among consumers generated by the behavior of both unemployment and prices. Fear of losing their jobs, it is argued, led consumers to be conservative in their spending, and so did fear of further rapid inflation. (One might think that expectation of further inflation would lead people to anticipate future needs and increase their spending relative to their income, particularly on durable goods.)

Whatever the reason, personal saving in 1970 was greater than would have been predicted from the past behavior of the savings rate.[63]

After declining for two quarters GNP in constant prices rose modestly during the second and third quarters of 1970, recovering about half the loss of the preceding half-year. A new and somewhat sharper decline occurred in the fourth quarter, largely as a result of the prolonged General Motors strike. It is quite probable that there would have been a further increase in real GNP in the last three months of 1970 had it not been for the strike, in which case we should have dated the trough of the recession earlier than November, 1970.[64]

## Recovery Begins

In any event recovery began as soon as the strike was over. Real GNP and industrial production increased rapidly in the first quarter of 1971, after which the pace of recovery slackened. Employment increased, but no faster than the labor force, so that unemployment remained stubbornly at about 6 percent all through 1971. Labor productivity had increased markedly in 1970 and continued to increase at a rapid rate in 1971 and 1972.[65] As a result of the accelerated rise in productivity, the rate of increase in unit labor costs decelerated significantly in 1970–1971.[66] The rate of inflation in prices showed some

[63] The relationship between inflation and consumer spending and saving is explored in some detail in F. Thomas Juster and Paul Wachtel, "Inflation and the Consumer," in *Brookings Papers on Economic Activity*, 1972:1, pp. 71–114. The authors find that the effect on personal saving depends to a considerable extent on whether the inflation is anticipated. They conclude tentatively that "a primary effect of unanticipated inflation is to reduce spendng and increase saving . . ." (p. 106).

[64] The evidence here does not all point the same way. Industrial production moved more or less horizontally during the first eight months of 1970, and a number of other cyclical indicators showed little decline or actually rose somewhat during part or all of the half-year preceding the strike. But some other significant measures did not behave this well—manufacturing employment, for example, and particularly total unemployment. The unemployment rate rose steadily throughout the year, from 3.5 percent in November and December, 1969 to 5.1 percent in August, 1970 and to a peak of 6.1 percent in December. The rapid rise in the unemployment rate was due not only to a moderate decline in total employment but also to an unusually rapid rise in the civilian labor force (including about 400,000 returning veterans).

[65] The rise in output per man-hour in 1970 was temporarily interrupted in the fourth quarter by the direct and indirect effects of the General Motors strike.

[66] The marked deceleration in the rise of unit labor costs in 1970 and the first half of 1971 was not fully reflected in the behavior of prices because of a marked acceleration in the rise in nonlabor charges per unit of output. The latter include depreciation, indirect business taxes, interest payments, and before-tax profits. See,

deceleration in the months before the price-wage freeze in August, 1971, but the picture was very mixed.[67] As for wages, there was only the slightest evidence of any slowing in their rate of increase before the freeze, despite the continuing high level of unemployment.

The pace of recovery during the last three quarters of 1971 was disappointingly slow, particularly in light of overly optimistic expectations expressed by the administration at the beginning of the year. In constant prices, business fixed investment rose relatively slowly; inventory investment averaged less during the year than in 1970; because of the continued winding down of the Vietnam war, federal expenditures declined significantly between 1970 and 1971, although the decline was reversed after the middle of the latter year; and there was a sharp and alarming decline in the net export surplus. The strongest supports to the recovery were a vigorous housing boom that developed after mid-1970, the continued rise in the expenditures of state and local governments, and a steady although not particularly rapid expansion in consumer expenditures. Consumer spending was held back by the abnormally high and rising rate of personal saving, which reached the unusual figure of 8.6 percent in the second quarter of 1971. It then declined through the rest of the year and into 1972, providing an additional stimulus to the rise in consumer spending.

The housing boom that began began in the second half of 1970 reached an unprecedented level in 1971, and the volume of residential construction increased still further in 1972. By now we are familiar with the typical cyclical behavior of residential construction—the tendency to decline as money becomes tight in the late stages of a boom followed by a rapid rise during the subsequent business recession and early stages of business recovery as credit becomes easy and mortgage funds again become readily available. In 1971 this usual cyclical behavior was strongly reinforced by an underlying shortage of housing resulting from curtailed building in 1966–1967 and 1969, and unusually strong demand generated by a high level of household formation, a strong replacement demand, and a variety of forms of government aid to the housing market.

---

for example, the national income accounts as presented in the *Survey of Current Business.*

[67] See Table 6.3, p. 165, for the story told by different price indexes. Deceleration in the rate of inflation shows up most clearly in the Consumer Price Index for commodities less food and in various versions of the GNP deflator. The rise in the Wholesale Price Index for industrial commodities actually accelerated in the spring and summer of 1971.

## Monetary and Fiscal Policy, 1970–1973

The Federal Reserve's restrictive credit policy began to ease early in 1970 as it became increasingly evident that a new recession had begun. Nonetheless, throughout the year the Fed continued to be concerned about inflation and the disequilibrium in the American balance of payments.[68] After virtually stopping the expansion of the money supply in the second half of 1969, the monetary authorities took action early in 1970 to relieve the pressure on the banking system. The stock of money increased at an annual rate of nearly 6 percent in the first half of the year and at a rate of nearly 5 percent in the second half.[69] The administration, which was reluctant to embark on a very expansive fiscal policy, would have preferred an even easier monetary policy.

Federal Reserve policy in the spring and summer of 1970 was particularly concerned with a developing "liquidity squeeze" as the demand for funds in the capital markets threatened to outrun the available supply. A number of factors were involved. Many firms entered 1970 facing the need to reduce short-term debt and to build up liquid assets. The way to do this was through the sale of long-term bonds or stock issues, but many companies had postponed doing this in 1969 because of the unprecedentedly high interest rates. In 1970 there was a very large increase in corporate bond issues, state and local governments increased their demands on the capital market, and as the federal budget moved from surplus into deficit the demand for funds by the federal government was added to the others.

This increasing tightness in long-term capital markets in the first half of the year was exacerbated by a sharp drop in stock prices, the financial difficulties of a growing number of firms, and finally the bankruptcy of the Penn Central Railroad in June. The Federal Reserve authorities actively intervened—through open-market operations and in other ways—to make funds readily available to the banking system, and the incipient crisis quickly passed.

Short-term interest rates began to decline early in 1970 but rose again in the spring as the credit squeeze developed. Long-term interest rates, however, did not reach their peak until midyear. In the second half of the year, all interest rates declined; short-term rates fell much more than long-term ones (see Figure 6.4).

[68] See the *Annual Report* of the Board of Governors of the Federal Reserve System for 1970, particularly the reasons given for the Board's policy actions during the year.

[69] Early in 1970 the Federal Open Market Committee began to pay much more attention to the stock of money as an intermediate target variable than it had in the past. Cf. John H. Kareken, "FOMC Policy: 1970 and Beyond," in *Brookings Papers on Economic Activity*, 1970:3, pp. 475–476.

The monetary authorities continued to maintain an expansionary policy in 1971, although there was some slight tightening in the second quarter. The money supply was permitted to grow at a rate of about 10 percent in the first half of the year. Interest rates began to move up again after March. Long-term rates reflected the continued heavy demand for funds from business and state and local governments, the unpredecented level of residential building, and the increasing deficit of the federal government.[70] Short-term rates responded not only to domestic demands for short-term funds but also to the developing international financial crisis. And affecting all financial markets were renewed fears that inflation was not being brought under control.

All this changed radically once President Nixon's New Economic Policy was announced in August. Interest rates, particularly short-term ones, declined markedly, and at the end of the year they were below the levels reached at the end of 1970. The Federal Reserve authorities took steps to ease credit further in the closing months of 1971. Nonetheless, the increase in the money supply was at a much lower rate in the second half of 1971 than in the first half, though for the year as a whole the money stock grew at a comfortable rate of slightly more than 6 percent. For a variety of reasons the public's demand for cash weakened after the New Economic Policy was announced.

Credit remained easy in 1972. The money supply expanded more than it had in the second half of 1971 as the pace of business recovery began to accelerate. Short-term interest rates began to rise with the expanding demand for credit but remained well below the levels of 1969–1970. There was little increase in long-term rates. After the temporary solution of the balance-of-payments crisis in the closing months of 1971, and with the rate of inflation restrained by wage and price controls, the Fed could concentrate on expediting the business recovery during 1972. The money supply grew at a rate of more than 8 percent during the year. By the beginning of 1973, however, with the business recovery accelerating and wage and price controls relaxed, the Federal Reserve authorities were beginning to move cautiously toward a more restrictive credit policy.[71] Monetary policy became

---

[70] The Federal Reserve sought to moderate the rise in long-term rates by shifting its open-market purchases toward longer-term government securities, repeating the "Operation Twist" in which it had engaged in the 1960s (see p. 154). For monetary developments in 1971, see the *Annual Report* of the Board of Governors for that year.

[71] There is a brief review of monetary policy in 1972 in *Economic Report of the President*, January, 1973, pp. 45–46. See also the *Annual Report* for 1972 of the Board of Governors of the Federal Reserve System.

still more restrictive as the rate of inflation accelerated in the spring of 1973.

Let us turn now to fiscal policy. During 1970 the Nixon administration relied more on monetary than on fiscal action to bring the recession to an end and to expedite recovery. It underestimated the severity and length of the recession, believing it would be even milder than it actually was; it was opposed to "fine tuning" through frequent fiscal action; and it was committed to holding down federal government spending.[72]

Nonetheless, as typically happens during recession, the current federal budget moved from surplus to deficit. Tax revenues declined, reflecting the retarded growth of personal income, the fall in corporate profits, the reduction and then termination of the surcharge, and the impact of several tax reform measures. Total federal spending on goods and services was reduced; a significant drop in military spending considerably more than offset a modest rise in other expenditures. There was, however, a substantial increase in transfer payments—chiefly in social security benefits, unemployment compensation, and veterans' benefits. The full-employment budget remained in surplus all through 1970, although the amount of the surplus declined by about $5 billion between 1969 and 1970.

At the beginning of 1970 the administration emphasized the need to maintain a surplus in the *current* federal budget. As this proved impossible, it shifted its emphasis to keeping the *full-employment* budget in surplus or at least in balance.

As we have seen, the pace of recovery in 1971 slowed after the first quarter of rebound following the General Motors strike. Nonetheless, the federal government remained cautious about taking any vigorous fiscal action before the New Economic Policy was announced in August. Some modest tax relief was contained in provisions of the 1969 Tax Reform Act that went into effect in 1971, and liberalized depreciation rules were proposed to improve incentives to business investment, but on the other hand social security contributions were increased again. Federal expenditures on goods and services showed little net increase in the first three quarters of 1971, a continued decline in military spending offsetting more than half of the increase in other expenditures. As in 1970, however, there were large increases in transfer payments (once more chiefly in the form of larger social

---

[72] Arthur Okun offers a critical review of fiscal as well as monetary policy during 1970–1971 in "Political Economy: Some Lessons of Recent Experience," *Journal of Money, Credit, and Banking* 4 (February, 1972): 23–39.

security benefits and unemployment and veterans' compensation); grants-in-aid to state and local governments also increased significantly.

The current federal deficit rose to about $22 billion in 1971, the largest annual deficit in the postwar period and considerably larger than the administration had estimated at the beginning of the year.[73] The current deficit continued at a high level during 1972. The full-employment budget moved from a small surplus in 1971 to a moderate deficit in 1972.[74]

To summarize, fiscal policy in 1971 before the New Economic Policy was announced was moderately expansionary, but to a considerable degree this resulted from scheduled increases in spending, from congressional initiative, and from the built-in needs of particular programs. Until the summer of 1971 the administration continued to rely heavily on monetary policy and optimistic expectations regarding the speed of recovery.

The President's New Economic Policy as finally approved by Congress provided for additional fiscal stimulus, chiefly through a modest reduction in personal income taxes, reinstatement of the investment tax credit, and removal of the excise tax on automobiles. In addition, a proposed increase in social security taxes was postponed for a year. It has been estimated that these changes reduced tax revenues in 1972 by more than $7 billion.[75] As the economy ended its second year of recovery, in November, 1972, it was benefiting from a significant amount of stimulus, but the President was by then seeking to reduce the deficit that had developed in the full-employment budget.[76] These efforts at fiscal restraint continued into 1973.

[73] As a percentage of GNP, however, the deficit in 1971 was no greater than the $10.2 billion figure for 1958, when GNP was less than half that in 1971. The figure for the deficit cited here refers to the federal budget as reported in the national income and product accounts. The "unified budget" showed an even larger deficit. For a reconciliation of these two versions of the budget, see *Economic Report of the President,* January, 1973, p. 270.

[74] The full-employment deficit would have been considerably larger in 1972 had it not been for some $9 billion in overwithholding of personal income taxes. To some degree consumers offset the overwithholding by reducing their rate of saving. If the overwithheld taxes are not included in full-employment receipts, the expansionary shift in the full-employment budget in 1972 was quite substantial. Cf. *Economic Report of the President,* January, 1973, pp. 40–41.

[75] Cf. Charles Schulze *et al., Setting National Priorities: The 1973 Budget* (Washington, D.C., Brookings, 1972), p. 5. The fiscal measures proposed in the New Economic Policy are discussed on pp. 189–190.

[76] Fiscal policy in 1972 is reviewed in *Economic Report of the President,* January, 1973, pp. 40–45.

## FROM BAD TO WORSE: THE DETERIORATING BALANCE OF PAYMENTS

As we saw in Chapter 5, the balance of payments began to concern the American authorities at the end of the 1950s. The situation became more serious in the 1960s, particularly after 1964, and finally reached crisis proportions in 1970–1971 in response to growing evidence that the dollar was overvalued in terms of other currencies. The climax came in August, 1971, when the dollar's link to gold was broken as part of President Nixon's New Economic Policy.[77]

Major changes in the American balance of payments from 1960 to 1972 are summarized in Table 6.4. It is worth spending some time not only on the figures shown there but also on the way in which they are presented. Each of the subtotals in the table, referring to various kinds of "balances," summarizes an important aspect of this country's transactions with the rest of the world.

From the 1890s on, merchandise exports from the United States had regularly exceeded its imports. This merchandise trade balance from 1960 on is shown in the first line of Table 6.4. After a temporary slump in 1957–1958, American exports rose rapidly during 1959–1960, while imports declined during the 1960–1961 recession. During the early sixties the merchandise trade balance remained at a high level, reaching a peak in 1964. This large trade balance or export surplus, supplemented by a rapidly growing amount of income from past American investments in the rest of the world (line 3), provided the United States with the foreign currencies needed to meet the large payments it had to make abroad (apart from any foreign investment by American firms). American net purchases of foreign services—both military transactions and civilian payments for travel, transportation, insurance, and the like (lines 2 and 4)—required less than the proceeds of investment income throughout the years covered in Table 6.4, so that the balance on goods and services combined (line 5) was regularly larger than the merchandise trade balance taken alone. But as is brought out in Table 6.4, the balance on goods and services declined after 1964, dramatically so in 1971, as the merchandise balance of trade deteriorated and finally in 1971 became negative for the first time in this century. This deterioration resulted from an accelerated rise in

[77] Balance-of-payments developments in the 1960s and early 1970s can be conveniently followed in the *Economic Reports of the President,* particularly for recent years, and in the quarterly presentations of the balance-of-payments accounts in the *Survey of Current Business.* See also Council on International Economic Policy, Office of the President, *The United States in the Changing World Economy* (the "Peterson Report"), 2 vols. (Washington, D.C., GPO, 1972).

**Table 6.4** Summary of U.S. Balance of Payments, 1960–1972 (In billions of dollars)

| | 1960–1964 Average | 1965–1969 Average | 1970 | 1971 | 1972[a] |
|---|---|---|---|---|---|
| 1. Merchandise trade balance | 5.4 | 2.8 | 2.1 | -2.7 | -7.0 |
| 2. Military transactions, net | -2.4 | -2.9 | -3.4 | -2.9 | -3.6 |
| 3. Investment income, net | 3.9 | 5.8 | 6.2 | 8.0 | 7.4 |
| 4. Balance on other services | -1.0 | -1.2 | -1.4 | -1.7 | -1.8 |
| 5. Balance on goods and services | 5.9 | 4.4 | 3.6 | 0.7 | -4.9 |
| 6. Remittances, pensions, and other transfers | -0.7 | -1.1 | -1.4 | -1.5 | **-3.7** |
| 7. U.S. government grants | -1.8 | -1.8 | -1.7 | -2.0 | |
| 8. Balance on current account | 3.3 | 1.5 | 0.4 | -2.8 | -8.7 |
| 9. Long-term capital flows, net | -4.0 | -3.6 | -3.5 | -6.5 | -1.6 |
| 10. Balance on current account and long-term capital ("basic balance") | -0.7 | -2.2 | -3.0 | -9.3 | -10.2 |
| 11. Nonliquid short-term private capital flows, net | -1.1 | -0.2 | -0.5 | -2.4 | -0.6 |
| 12. Allocation of Special Drawing Rights | — | — | 0.9 | 0.7 | 0.7 |
| 13. Errors and omissions, net | -1.0 | -1.0 | -1.1 | -11.0 | -3.0 |
| 14. Net liquidity balance | -2.8 | -3.4 | -3.8 | -22.0 | -13.1 |
| 15. Liquid private capital flows, net | 0.7 | 3.4 | -6.0 | -7.8 | 1.5 |
| 16. Official reserve transactions balance | -2.2 | 0.0 | -9.8 | -29.8 | -11.6 |

[a] First quarters at annual rate.

Source: *Economic Report of the President*, January, 1972, p. 150; *ibid.,* January, 1973, pp. 293–294; *Survey of Current Business* (December, 1972): 34, 41.

imports, while the upward trend in exports was tending to decelerate. The apparent reason for these developments was a decline in the United States' competitive position in world trade. One answer to this problem was to make American exports cheaper—and foreign imports into the United States more expensive—by lowering the value of the dollar in terms of other currencies.[78]

A significant part of the positive balance on goods and services is used to finance the substantial demand for foreign currencies resulting from private remittances, pension payments, foreign grants by the federal government, and other transfer payments (lines 6 and 7). Deducting these transfers, we obtain the balance on current account (line 8), which declined steadily after 1964 and became negative in 1971. Thus by the latter year the normal current transactions of the American economy with the rest of the world were generating an excess supply of dollars—or, to say the same thing, an excess demand for foreign currencies. And the trend was clearly toward still further deterioration in the balance on current account.

But it was by maintaining a positive balance on current account that the United States had obtained most of the foreign currencies required for the large net outflow of long-term capital to other countries—to invest in everything from oil wells in the Middle East to new factories in the rapidly expanding economies of Western Europe, and also including foreign loans by the American government.[79] As can be seen in the table, the outflow of long-term capital from the United States reached record levels in 1971, increasing still further the supply of dollars flooding foreign-exchange markets.

If we add long-term capital flows to the balance on current account, we obtain what is probably the most important single balance shown in

[78] See, for example, *The United States in the Changing World Economy, op. cit.; Survey of Current Business* (March, 1972): 38–39; *Economic Report of the President,* January, 1972, pp. 149–153; William H. Branson and Helen B. Junz, "Trends in U.S. Trade and Comparative Advantage," *Brookings Papers on Economic Activity,* 1971:2, pp. 285–338; Organization for Economic Co-operation and Development, *Economic Outlook,* no. 10 (December, 1971): 8 ff. Other measures in addition to devaluation were also desired, particularly reduction of trade barriers against American exports.

[79] Throughout Table 6.4 the data refer to *net* balances. Thus the capital flow figures represent the excess of American investments abroad over foreign investments in the United States. In 1968 foreign private long-term investment in the United States—attracted by a booming stock market and high long-term interest rates—exceeded American private long-term investment abroad. The latter was restrained to some extent by a variety of restrictions by the American government on private long-term capital outflows.

Table 6.4 (line 10). This is increasingly being referred to as the "basic balance." It is basic in the sense that it measures the excess supply of (or demand for) dollars resulting from the longer-term trading and financial relationships between the American economy and the rest of the world—before any account is taken of volatile short-term capital flows or special financial transactions between the American government and foreign central banks and treasuries.[80]

A modest deficit in this basic balance was expected. Indeed, it provided a supply of dollars to other countries with which to finance the rapid expansion in world trade. The dollar, after all, was *the* international currency, and it has been an international means of payment accepted by traders and financial institutions in all countries.[81] But as the basic balance turned more and more unfavorable during the 1960s, international confidence in the dollar was impaired, and speculative flows of short-term capital into and out of the United States and other countries began to play an increasingly important role in the international balance of payments.

The negative amounts for the "basic balance" in line 10 of Table 6.4 represent a growing supply of dollars available either to private holders or to foreign governments. To this supply of dollars was added a direct outflow of short-term capital (lines 11 and 13). "Errors and omissions" reflect the unrecorded flow of short-term capital abroad—as, for example, when bank deposits in the United States are transferred abroad to benefit from higher foreign interest rates or in anticipation of an upward revaluation of one or another foreign currency. The startling increase in "errors and omissions" in 1971 reflects the massive flight of short-term capital out of the United States as confidence in the dollar deteriorated dramatically and as the international financial community

---

80 A caution is in order, however. Fluctuations in private long-term capital flows in 1971–1972 led a member of the staff of the U.S. Department of Commerce to warn that there are difficulties in "assuming that long-term capital flows necessarily reflect fundamental factors. In fact, such flows appear to be heavily influenced by changes in near-term expectations that induce temporary movements of funds and change the timing of long-term investments." *Survey of Current Business* (September, 1972): 25.

81 The role of the American deficit in providing liquid assets to the rest of the world through "international financial intermediation" has been emphasized by a number of writers. See, for example, the paper by Walter Salant in Fritz Machlup *et al.*, eds., *International Mobility and Movement of Capital* (New York, National Bureau of Economic Research, 1972). This paper contains a useful bibliography. See also Emile Despres, Charles P. Kindleberger, and Walter Salant, "The Dollar and World Liquidity: A Minority View," *The Economist* (London), February 5, 1966, reprinted as Brookings Institution Reprint No. 115.

came increasingly to believe that the dollar would have to be devalued.[82]

This brings us to the "net liquidity balance" in line 14, which became increasingly unfavorable in the 1960s. The huge increase in this negative balance in 1971 truly reflected a "flight from the dollar." In this year alone, short-term claims in the United States increased by $22 billion, or by more than twice the country's entire gold stock.

The final two lines of Table 6.4 convert the change in total short-term liabilities to the change in liabilities, liquid and nonliquid, due to foreign monetary institutions. To the extent that, on net balance, private foreign holders of liquid dollar claims transfer them to their central banks, as they did on a large scale in 1970 and 1971, the official reserve transactions balance will show a larger negative item than the net liquidity balance. In fact, foreign governments and central banks were flooded with an additional $30 billion or so in 1971 (line 16 of Table 6.4). About $2.3 billion of this was converted into gold and other international reserve assets previously held by the U.S. government. The remainder, about $27.5 billion, represented the net increase in dollar holdings, chiefly in liquid form, of foreign treasuries and central banks.[83]

Confidence in the dollar had been deteriorating in the late 1960s and increasingly so in 1970. <u>It collapsed completely in 1971</u>. Only the willingness of foreign governments to hold the mounting tide of dollars prevented the final crisis from occurring sooner than it finally did—in August, 1971.[84]

[82] We shall mention only in passing the Special Drawing Rights in line 12 of Table 6.4. These are a new form of international currency issued by the International Monetary Fund since 1970 and represent a positive item in the American balance of payments, since they can be used to meet payments due to other countries.

[83] These figures are from the *Survey of Current Business* (December, 1972): 41. It should be noted also that the figures in Table 6.4 are *net* balances, representing the difference between plus and minus items in the balance of payments. Thus the large negative items for 1970–1971 in line 15 for liquid private capital flows represent to a considerable extent the reduction of liquid assets held in the United States by foreign financial institutions and also the repayment of Eurodollar borrowings by American banks. In contrast, net liquid private capital flows had been a large positive item in 1969, more than offsetting the negative liquidity balance. This reflected primarily large-scale borrowing of Eurodollars by American banks during a period of marked credit stringency in the United States. In short, while short-term capital was still flowing out of the United States in 1969, part was being borrowed back by American financial institutions. This offsetting return flow was not repeated in 1970–1971.

[84] For an evaluation of the American balance-of-payments problem made just before official action in August, 1971, see *Action Now to Strengthen the U.S.*

All through the decade of the 1960s, the American government sought to curb the outflow of dollars through a variety of direct controls. It required that the proceeds of aid to underdeveloped countries be spent in the United States, even if the goods could be purchased more cheaply elsewhere. Similarly, American military purchases had to be made in this country as long as domestic prices were no more than 50 percent greater than the cost of foreign supplies. In other programs, also, a "buy American" policy was promoted. The duty-free allowance for returning American tourists was reduced. Beginning in 1963, an "interest equalization tax" was levied on the purchase of foreign securities (except Canadian). First voluntary and then compulsory controls were imposed on direct investment abroad by American firms. And the Federal Reserve System imposed restrictions on the foreign lending of American commercial banks in addition to taking other restrictive steps. Further, a variety of financial expedients were developed, such as negotiating prepayment of foreign debts due the U.S. government, sale of special government securities to foreign monetary authorities to absorb some of their liquid dollar assets, and short-term borrowings by the Federal Reserve System of other currencies from foreign central banks under so-called "swap arrangements."[85] All this was on top of restrictive monetary policy, particularly in 1966 and 1969, to curb inflation and (it was hoped) also to reduce the strain on the American balance of payments.

Balance-of-payments problems were not confined to the United States, of course. The United Kingdom experienced chronic balance-of-payments difficulties after World War II. France devalued her currency in 1967 and again in 1969. During the 1960s it became increasingly apparent that the German mark and the Japanese yen were undervalued. Indeed the mark had to be revalued upward in 1969, and in May, 1971 upward pressure on the mark became so strong that the German authorities allowed the mark to float upward. Similar action, either allowing their currencies to float upward or else raising their par values, was taken by several other European countries. Japan, however, despite her large and rapidly increasing balance-of-payments surplus, clung stubbornly to a value for the yen that was clearly too

---

*Dollar,* Report of the Subcommittee on International Exchange and Payments of the Joint Economic Committee, U.S. Congress (Washington, D.C., GPO, 1971). See also earlier reports of and hearings before this subcommittee.

[85] Most of these actions can be followed in the *Economic Report of the President.* For incomplete summaries see *Economic Report of the President,* February, 1971, pp. 143 ff., and Lawrence Krause, *Sequel to Bretton Woods,* Brookings Institution Staff Paper (1971), pp. 28–29.

low. By 1971 it was becoming increasingly evident, particularly to American officials, that a general realignment of currency values was required.

There were other international monetary problems that also called for action, particularly with respect to the future role of the dollar as the major international currency, providing adequate international liquidity for a rapidly expanding world trading system, the need for a more flexible system of adjusting currency parities to balance-of-payments disequilibriums, and so on. In brief, the international monetary and financial system set up at the end of World War II needed to be overhauled.[86]

The action of the U.S. government in suspending the gold value of the dollar in August, 1971 began the process. But even after new parities were established at the end of the year, a long period of international bargaining lay ahead before agreement would be reached on a new monetary system for the world.[87] Indeed, the new parities established in December, 1971 endured for only a little over a year before the dollar had to be devalued again.

## THE NEW ECONOMIC POLICY

On August 15, 1971 President Nixon startled the country with the dramatic announcement of his New Economic Policy.[88] We have already reviewed the developments that led to this unprecedented action: a continuing high level of unemployment, an unacceptable rate

[86] There is a considerable literature on the need for reforming the world monetary system. See, for example, William Fellner *et al., Maintaining and Restoring Balance in International Payments* (Princeton, N. J., Princeton University Press, 1966); George N. Halm, ed., *Approaches to Greater Flexibility of Exchange Rates: The Bürgenstock Papers* (Princeton, N. J., Princeton University Press, 1970); Fritz Machlup, *Remaking the International Monetary System* (Baltimore, Johns Hopkins Press, 1968); Lawrence H. Officer and Thomas D. Willett, eds., *The International Monetary System* (Englewood Cliffs, N. J., Prentice-Hall, 1969); Robert Triffin, *Our International Monetary System* (New York, Random House, 1968).

[87] As a start, a committee of representatives of 20 countries, the "Committee of 20," was set up in September, 1972 under the auspices of the International Monetary Fund, to begin discussions looking toward reform of the international monetary system. See, for example, *IMF Survey* (October 9, 1972). The situation at the end of 1972 with respect to the range of issues surveyed in this section is reviewed in the *Economic Report of the President,* January, 1973, chap. 5 and pp. 160–174.

[88] As one commentator put it, "In the compass of twenty minutes on television, [the President] did almost everything he had said he would not do, and almost everything that, supposedly, his previous economic policies had been designed to avoid." Tom Wicker, in the *New York Times,* August 17, 1971.

of inflation that stubbornly resisted efforts to bring it under control by conventional means, and the startling deterioration in the American balance of payments. Of these, it was particularly the last that forced the President to act when he did.

The New Economic Policy fell into three parts, corresponding to the three major problems of inflation, unemployment, and balance-of-payments disequilibrium. To cope with the first, the federal government imposed a 90-day freeze on prices, wages, and rents, to be followed by a "Phase II" during which there would be a mandatory system of controls, the details to be worked out during "Phase I," the period of the freeze. To stimulate the economy, the administration proposed a set of fiscal stimuli in the form of a package of tax reductions. And to deal with the balance-of-payments problem, the President suspended the convertibility of the dollar and imposed a temporary 10 percent surcharge on dutiable imports.[89]

## Coping with the Balance of Payments

By suspending convertibility into gold or other international reserves, the administration sought to lower the value of the dollar in terms of other currencies. It was hoped that by making exports cheaper to other countries and imports more expensive to Americans this would significantly improve the merchandise trade balance.

In addition, the administration imposed a tariff surcharge of 10 percent—in effect, an additional tax of 10 percent on merchandise imports.[90] This measure, which represented a reversal of American efforts to reduce barriers to world trade, was intended to be temporary. In effect it was a bargaining weapon to help induce other countries to accept American proposals with respect to reducing this country's balance-of-payments deficit. Certain other steps were also taken: Foreign aid was reduced, and the new investment tax credit proposed in the fiscal package was not to apply to imported machinery and equipment as long as the imports surcharge was in effect.

The dollar immediately began to fall in foreign-exchange markets. At the same time American officials plunged into a series of negotiations with representatives of other countries, particularly with its partners in the "Group of 10" leading industrial nations. The United States

---

[89] These measures are described in the *Economic Report of the President,* January, 1972. For more detailed discussion and evaluation see *The President's New Economic Program,* Hearings before the Joint Economic Committee, 92nd Cong., 1st sess. (Washington, D.C., GPO, 1971).

[90] Certain categories of imports were exempt. In all, the surcharge affected about half of total American imports.

had a number of demands: a lower value for the dollar in terms of the currencies of its important international competitors, removal of discriminatory barriers against American exports, a larger contribution by other countries to American military expenditures abroad (for example, in support of the NATO alliance), and working toward a new international monetary system that would depend less heavily on the dollar and would provide a more flexible system of currency parities that could adjust to balance-of-payments disequilibriums more easily than had been the case under the Bretton Woods system.

By the end of the year, negotiations had gone far enough for the signing of an international agreement at the Smithsonian Museum in Washington (hence the "Smithsonian Agreement").[91] A new set of parities was established among the "Group of 10" that resulted in devaluation of the dollar by varying amounts with respect to different currencies. To put it the other way, other currencies were revalued upward. The two largest revaluations were those of the Japanese yen and the German mark.

There were some other major provisions. One widened the "band" within which a currency might fluctuate—from a range of 1 percent on either side of parity to one of plus or minus 2¼ percent. In addition, the United States agreed to raise the price of gold from $35 to $38 an ounce, a move that required and eventually received congressional approval. This was largely a meaningless gesture, particularly since the Smithsonian Agreement did not provide that the United States should again make the dollar convertible into gold.

As an important *quid pro quo*, the United States removed the 10 percent surcharge on dutiable imports and made imported machinery and equipment eligible for the renewed investment tax credit (which was a part of the fiscal package included in the New Economic Policy).

Lowering the value of the dollar did not improve the merchandise trade balance during 1972. Indeed, the excess of imports over exports in the year following the Smithsonian Agreement was more than double what it had been in 1971, largely but not entirely because the accelerating recovery in the United States increased the demand for foreign goods (see Table 6.4). This development was not altogether unexpected. Apart from the effect of improved business conditions in the United States, devaluation could be expected to affect exports and imports only with a significant lag. Indeed, the initial effect is to worsen the balance of payments because more dollars than before have to be

[91] For further details and comment on the agreement, see the *New York Times*, December 20, 1971. One article of interpretive comment in this issue bore the title "The Dollar As Kingpin Is Dead."

spent to pay for the same physical amount of imports. Ultimately, the effect would depend on (1) the extent to which the devaluation was passed through in the form of a corresponding change in prices paid by foreign purchasers of American exports and American purchasers of foreign goods, and (2) the price elasticity of demand for exports and imports.[92]

Some estimates suggested that over a period of two to three years devaluation would improve the merchandise balance of trade, compared to what it would be without devaluation, by some $7-9 billion. Other estimates were less optimistic.

The Smithsonian Agreement did tend to some extent to restore international confidence in the dollar, but the improvement was only temporary. By January, 1973 international confidence in the dollar was again deteriorating; a massive new flight from the dollar began, and in February the dollar was again devalued.[93] Still the pressure on the dollar continued, and by the end of March all the countries of the European Common Market and Japan had given up trying to maintain fixed parities with the dollar, which was now allowed to float, more or less freely, in foreign exchange markets. During the spring and summer of 1973 the dollar continued to depreciate.

[92] Thus if American exporters raised their prices in dollars as the dollar became cheaper in terms of foreign currencies, there might not be much decline in prices of American exports in terms of foreign currencies. Similarly, if foreign exporters reduced their prices as their currencies became more expensive in dollar terms, the dollar price of the imports would not increase in proportion to the devaluation of the dollar. Even if prices paid by foreign and domestic buyers were fully to reflect the devaluation, the effect on exports and imports would depend on the price elasticity of demand. Thus a considerable fraction of American imports consists of tropical food products (like coffee and sugar), oil, and basic materials, the demand for which is relatively inelastic. Higher prices for these items through devaluation of the dollar is likely to *increase* the dollar value of imports. It should be mentioned here that elasticity of supply also enters the picture. If, for example, American firms can produce more to sell abroad only at rising costs, the dollar prices of the exports will rise, offsetting some of the effect of devaluation. For an extensive analysis of the effects of devaluation on the balance of trade, see William H. Branson, "The Trade Effects of the 1971 Currency Realignments" and the ensuing discussion, particularly by Lawrence Klein, in *Brookings Papers on Economic Activity,* 1972:1, pp. 15–69. See also *Economic Report of the President,* January, 1973, pp. 115–116.

[93] The new devaluation took the form of a further increase in the price of gold by 10 percent. The values of other currencies changed by varying amounts with respect to the dollar. Some countries, like the United Kingdom and Canada, already had floating exchange rates. The Japanese yen, which was still undervalued after the Smithsonian Agreement, was now allowed to float upward, and a new parity was not immediately set.

## Fiscal Stimuli

The fiscal package proposed by the President was somewhat modified by Congress. What finally emerged in the Revenue Act of 1971 (passed in December) was reinstatement of the investment tax credit at the former rate of 7 percent, removal of the excise tax on automobiles and light trucks, and a set of tax changes that had the effect of moderately reducing personal income taxes, particularly on lower incomes. Congress also made somewhat less liberal the provisions for accelerated depreciation that the administration had put into effect earlier in the year and provided for tax concessions to special subsidiaries of American corporations set up to promote export sales.[94]

In presenting its original fiscal proposals in August, 1971, the administration sought to emphasize that it intended to reduce expenditures to match the decline in revenues, at least for fiscal year 1972. Reducing expenditures was hardly appropriate for a fiscal package that "was primarily motivated by the desire to stimulate at once a more rapid expansion of the economy."[95] Or, to use the stronger words of one economist, this was "economic nonsense."[96] Reducing expenditures in line with tax receipts would, of course, provide no stimulus to the economy. In fact, however, most of the proposals for reducing federal spending were largely window dressing, putting off until fiscal 1973 revenue-sharing proposals that were certain not to be passed by Congress in fiscal 1972. The proposal to defer a federal salary increase was not accepted by Congress.

As already noted, these fiscal measures reduced tax revenues in 1972 by something over $7 billion, a not inconsiderable stimulus.[97] Combined with the effect of increased spending programs (including transfers to persons and grants-in-aid to state and local governments), the

---

[94] See *Economic Report of the President*, January, 1972, pp. 69–72; *New York Times*, December 3, 1971. The chief ways in which Congress modified the President's original proposals were the following: A permanent investment tax credit of 7 percent was substituted for a 10 percent credit the first year and 5 percent thereafter. The excise tax was eliminated for light trucks as well as for passenger cars. Personal income taxes were reduced somewhat more than originally proposed, particularly for low-income groups. The proposed tax concession to export sales companies was cut. Congress disapproved the Treasury's particularly liberal treatment of depreciation during the first year. Finally, the President's proposal that a scheduled salary increase for federal employees be deferred for six months was overruled.

[95] *Economic Report of the President*, January, 1972, p. 69.

[96] Charles Schultze, in *The President's New Economic Program*, Hearings before the Joint Economic Committee, Part 1, p. 43.

[97] See p. 178. This estimate includes the effect of a one-year postponement of a scheduled increase in social security taxes.

result was to move the full-employment budget into a moderate deficit in 1972.[98] As President Nixon moved into his second term in 1973, he was striving mightily to hold down government spending and to move the full-employment budget back to a modest surplus. By then the vigor of the recovery, which had moved into its third year, was strong enough to suggest that a full-employment deficit was no longer desirable —particularly given the continued threat of inflation as wage and price controls were relaxed.

## Wage and Price Controls

The part of the New Economic Policy that most directly affected Americans was the imposition of wage and price controls. Such action was unprecedented in (relative) peacetime. All wages, prices (except those of raw agricultural products), and rents were frozen for a period of 90 days (Phase I). The freeze was followed by a far-reaching system of wage and price controls (Phase II) administered by a Price Commission and a Pay Board, both of which reported to a Cost of Living Council. Earlier, forced into action by escalating wage increases in the construction industry, the President had established a Construction Industry Stabilization Committee to deal with wages in the building trades.[99]

Phase II lasted from November, 1971 to January, 1973, when it was succeeded by a quasivoluntary Phase III. Most of the detailed control machinery was then abandoned, and the Pay Board and Price Commission went out of existence. The Cost of Living Council remained to supervise the new program of voluntary cooperation by labor and business, but with power to take action against wage and price increases considered excessive. Mandatory controls were continued in three problem areas, however. These were the food, health, and construction industries.[100]

[98] See p. 178 of this book and Nancy H. Teeters, "The 1973 Federal Budget," *Brookings Papers on Economic Activity*, 1972:1, p. 224. The statement above refers to the federal budget as measured in the national income accounts.

[99] For a detailed description of these controls and of the organizational structure designed to implement them, see Executive Office of the President, Cost of Living Council, *Economic Stabilization Program Quarterly Report* covering the period August 15 to December 31, 1971. Later developments can be followed in subsequent *Quarterly Reports* of the Cost of Living Council. For briefer descriptions see the appropriate sections of the *Economic Report of the President* for January, 1972 and January, 1973.

[100] See the *New York Times* and the *Wall Street Journal*, January 12, 1973, and *Economic Report of the President*, January, 1973, pp. 78–82.

There is little doubt that the wage and price freeze during Phase I sharply curtailed the rate of inflation (see Table 6.3). There is more argument about the effectiveness of the controls during Phase II. After a temporary upsurge in wages and prices immediately following the freeze, the rate of inflation decelerated again but remained higher than the goals set by the administration.

These goals were a rate of increase in the Consumer Price Index of 2 to 3 percent and a rate of increase in wages of 5.5 percent.[101] These were linked together by the assumption that the trend rate of increase in labor productivity was about 3 percent per year. Thus the rationale underlying controls during Phase II was about as follows: Hold wage increases to a rate of about 5.5 percent. Permit firms to pass on cost increases in their prices but put limits on their profit margins. The resulting price increases, it was hoped, would not exceed 2.5 percent on the average.[102]

It is clear that there was retardation in the rate of wage and price increases during Phase II, which continued until just before President Nixon's second term began in January, 1973. The retardation was more marked in retail than in wholesale prices. Among the comprehensive price indexes to which reference is usually made, the deceleration in inflation shows up most clearly in the price deflator for private GNP, although some deceleration in both this index and the CPI was already evident before controls were introduced. Among the standard price indexes, least retardation was evident in the Wholesale Price Index. Most troublesome of all were food prices. At both the wholesale and retail levels, the rise in food prices was actually accelerating in the closing months of 1972, and the situation became even worse in the early months of 1973.

[101] The ceiling on hourly compensation was actually about 6.2 percent. In addition to the permitted 5.5 percent increase in straight wages, an additional 0.7 percent was permitted for increases in fringe benefits.

[102] Cf. Barry Bosworth, "Phase II: The U.S. Experiment with an Incomes Policy," *Brookings Papers on Economic Activity,* 1972:2, p. 355. The reader should refer to this and the sources cited earlier as to how, in fact, price controls were administered. Overall profit margins for particular firms were limited to an average of the two highest of the three fiscal years preceding the freeze. It should be mentioned also that all firms were divided into three "tiers." Only the largest firms had to secure approval in advance for price increases. A second group had to report increases after the event, and these increases might be modified. The third tier of small firms did not have to report price increases, but their records were subject to inspection. A similar three-tier system held for approval of wage increases. In addition, very small firms and workers receiving relatively low wages were eventually exempted from controls.

Phase II controls clearly had some retarding effect on wage increases, more so on union than on nonunion wages. The controls were most successful in reducing to manageable proportions the spectacular wage increases that had been occurring in the construction industry.

Economists will undoubtedly debate for a long time as to how much of the retardation in wages and prices was actually due to the controls and how much to underlying economic conditions—the continued high level of unemployment during 1971–1972, the continuation of excess capacity in many sectors, the accelerated rise in productivity, and the lagged effect on inflationary expectations resulting from the ending of the boom in 1969. It is probably true that the main restraint came "from the changed environment in which price and wage decisions are made,"[103] rather than from specific decisions limiting particular wage and price increases. Indeed it was the chief purpose of the controls to change the environment of inflationary expectations that had built up after 1965, and in this the controls had considerable but, as it turned out, temporary success. Relaxation of controls in January, 1973 unleashed new inflationary forces and created a new wave of inflationary expectations. The sharp spurt in prices after Phase III began in January eventually forced the administration to impose a new price freeze in June, 1973, followed by a Phase IV in July.

In any event the American experience with inflation during 1971–1972 was much better than that of Europe or Japan.[104] And the slower rise in prices in the United States than in other leading industrial nations held out some hope for improvement in this country's balance of payments beyond what might be expected merely from the devaluation of the dollar in 1971 and 1973.

## PHASE IV AND BEYOND

As President Nixon began his second term, the economy was in the midst of a vigorous recovery which soon turned into an inflationary boom. The unemployment rate had fallen to 5 percent, and (hopefully) it could be expected to fall still further as output and employment continued to expand. By January, 1973, the retardation in the rate of increase in wages and prices during the preceding two years had been enough to encourage the administration largely to dismantle the system

---

[103] Bosworth, *op. cit.,* p. 375.
[104] Cf. Organization for Economic Co-operation and Development, *Economic Outlook* (December, 1972): 15–22.

of wage and price controls built up during Phase II. In retrospect, this was clearly a mistake. The balance of payments was still creating serious problems, but there was some basis for hoping for improvement in the merchandise balance of trade, and negotiations were continuing toward international monetary reform. Still, the dollar had to be devalued again in the first month of the President's second term, and shortly thereafter, as the dollar came under renewed pressure, a number of countries let their currencies float upward.

As the economic boom accelerated in the first half of 1973, increasing concern began to be felt in and out of Washington. Aggregate demand was rising at a rate that clearly could not be sustained, and the rise in prices was threatening again to get out of hand. In the first quarter of 1973, the GNP in current prices rose at an annual rate of more than 14 percent, of which a fraction over 6 percent represented an increase in prices. While the meteoric rise in food prices was the chief culprit, the increase in nonfood prices also accelerated sharply. Although unemployment remained stubbornly at about 5 percent through the early months of 1973, tightness in particular labor markets was again developing. Increasingly, the evidence pointed to the need for more restrictive fiscal (as well as monetary) action—for example, by withdrawing or reducing the investment tax credit or the imposition of a new tax surcharge. Such restrictive action would also presumably have helped the American balance of payments. Yet the administration also had to pay attention to the fact that unemployment had not declined more than it had. A possible answer to this dilemma lay in combining more restrictive fiscal and monetary action with enlarged manpower and public-service employment programs, but this did not seem to be the direction in which the administration wished to move.

The rise in prices accelerated still further in the second quarter of 1973, and pressure on the administration to take strong action became irresistible. As a result a new price freeze, to last no more than 60 days, was imposed in June. Clearly Phase III had been a failure, and the administration needed time to plan a more effective set of controls.

Plans for Phase IV were announced in July. Food prices (except for beef) were unfrozen immediately, and arrangements were made for a return to detailed price controls when the freeze ended in August. Broadly speaking, Phase IV represented a return to the price-control system of Phase II, with, if anything, somewhat more stringent standards. The same ceiling on wage increases imposed in Phase II was continued in Phase IV. At the time that Phase IV was announced, the President expressed the hope that all controls could be removed by the end of 1973, but this statement was greeted with considerable skepticism, even within the administration.[105]

---

[105] *Wall Street Journal,* July 23, 1973. These last two paragraphs were written at the end of July, 1973.

# 7

# Retrospect and Prospect

## A LOOK AT THE RECORD

The preceding chapters have spelled out the American record of economic instability and growth during the last half-century or more. Clearly our ability to achieve some of our macroeconomic goals has improved. The record with respect to cyclical instability has been much better since World War II than it was during the 1930s or at the beginning of the 1920s, and we are not likely to experience again the catastrophic unemployment that prevailed during the decade of the Great Depression.

Our record with respect to growth has also been better in the last three decades than it was during the interwar period, although there was a troublesome period of retarded growth from the mid-fifties to the early 1960s. A question that remains unanswered is: What precise role did government policy play in fostering the more rapid rate of growth after World War II. It is worth remembering that accelerated growth after the war occurred in spite of the heritage of New Deal reforms that were anathema to many businessmen. And, one might add, the rate of growth slowed during the years of the Eisenhower administration, when government policy was aimed particularly at stimulating growth (and maintaining price stability) even though unemployment was permitted to remain at an uncomfortably high level during the closing years of the 1950s.

One conclusion, reinforced by European and Japanese experience, is that an important condition for rapid growth is the maintenance of a high level of employment—of full employment.[1]

[1] It is well to remember in this connection the distinction between actual and potential output. The growth of actual output will be held back by rising unemployment. Retarded growth in actual output, associated as it is likely to be with relatively slow growth in private investment, can in turn hold back the growth in potential output. It is also important to remember the distinction between *total* output and ouput *per capita*. Retardation in the rate of growth in population, particularly that of working age, will retard the rate of growth in total output even if there is no deceleration in the rate of increase in output per person employed. The most thorough study of the sources of economic growth has been made by

But as not only the United States but also other countries have learned all too well in the last generation, the price of full employment is a significant amount of inflation. Indeed, at least in part as a lagged effect of very low unemployment rates during the late 1960s, the United States had to undergo during the early 1970s both excessive unemployment and an unacceptable rate of inflation. The rate of inflation has been even more marked in most of Western Europe.

It is clear that we have a long way to go to achieve anything even approximating the goal of price stability. Two challenging questions face us as we move further into the 1970s. First, under the threat of chronic inflation, shall we lower our sights with respect to the goal of full employment—and if so, by how much? And second, what direct steps shall we take to achieve greater price stability? As part of this question we need to ask: Are we prepared to move toward a more or less permanent incomes policy, with more interference with the free operation of labor and commodity markets than we were accustomed to in peacetime before 1971? The Nixon administration's response to this last question as it began its second term seemed to be in the negative.

Thus our record is a mixed one with respect to achievement of the three *domestic* goals of macroeconomic policy. As far as the fourth macroeconomic goal is concerned—maintaining balance-of-payments equilibrium at a fixed gold value of the dollar—our story ends in complete failure, but there is some hope for the future. Twice within a year-and-a-half the American government was forced to devalue the dollar in the face of massive disequilibrium in the American balance of payments. As our story ends, the future of the dollar is still uncertain. Uncertain also is the sort of international monetary system that will eventually replace the one set up in Bretton Woods at the end of World War II. What does seem highly probable is that the world will move toward a system of international payments in which the dollar will play a much smaller role as an international means of payment than it did before 1971.

## THE CHANGED ROLE OF GOVERNMENT

If there is one major theme that emerges from the preceding chapters, it is the radical change in the role played by the federal government between the first decade of the period we have covered and the last. The shift toward greater government responsibility for promoting

---

Edward Denison. See his *Why Growth Rates Differ* (Washington, D.C., Brookings, 1967) and his new study to be published by the Brookings Institution.

economic stability and growth began in the 1930s and was dramatized by the passage of the Employment Act in 1946. This trend accelerated during the 1960s, particularly during the ascendancy of the New Economics. Nor was the trend really reversed by the Nixon administration. It was under this presumably conservative administration, after all, that wage and price controls were introduced in relative peacetime for the first time in American history.

The great contrast between the federal government's role in maintaining employment before and after the mid-1930s is well illustrated by two events reviewed in Chapters 2 and 3. These episodes involved the two worst depressions since World War I. In 1921, in the face of widespread unemployment, President Harding could say: "There has been vast unemployment before and there will be again. . . . I would have little enthusiasm for any proposed remedy which seeks either palliation or tonic from the Public Treasury."[2] Could any President say that today in the face of large-scale unemployment and remain in office? And in 1932, with the national unemployment rate approaching 25 percent, President Hoover sought and obtained a large tax increase in a vain attempt to balance the budget.[3] During the same period the Federal Reserve authorities seemed paralyzed (except when the gold standard appeared to be threatened) while the Depression deepened and public confidence in the banking system collapsed.

We may contrast such perverse action and paralysis not merely with government policies during the Kennedy and Johnson administrations but also with the New Economic Policy of President Nixon. Even during the relatively passive Eisenhower administration, the possible need for a tax reduction in 1958 was actively debated by the President's advisers, the Federal Reserve authorities pursued an active policy of "leaning against the wind," and the objectives of the Employment Act were not forgotten, even if a rigorous interpretation of the full-employment goal seemed to take second place to the goal of price stability.

Apart from the change in public attitudes that made the government more willing to intervene in order to promote economic stability and growth, we must take account of the enormously increased intervention of the federal government in the economy that has occurred since 1929. Expansion of the government's role did not end with the New Deal. Federal government spending—including transfer payments, grants-in-aid, and interest payments—as reported in the national in-

[2] See p. 21.
[3] See p. 55.

come accounts represented about 2.5 percent of GNP in 1929. This percentage had risen to 9.9 in 1939 and had nearly doubled to 18.5 by 1960. It had risen to about 21 percent in 1972, or more than eight times the corresponding figure for 1929.[4]

Thus the level of national income has come increasingly to depend on the behavior of government spending, and such spending does not show the cyclical fluctuations typical of private spending, particularly business investment. But government spending (on goods and services rather than transfer payments) has been a major destabilizing influence during and after wars—from World War II through Korea to Vietnam.

Related to the vastly increased level of federal spending is the rise in tax receipts to finance this spending. In the United States, with a relatively progressive tax system at the federal level, tax revenues are sensitive to changes in the national income in both the short run and the long run. In the short run the sensitivity of tax receipts to changing business conditions provides us with a welcome automatic stabilizer, at least during recessions. During recovery from a recession, however, this stabilizer may be a retarding influence, making it difficult to return to full employment. This was the case in the early 1960s before the tax reduction in 1964. While rising tax revenues, at unchanging tax rates, may on occasion retard recovery if the full-employment budget is in substantial surplus (as was the case in the early sixties), a progressive tax system by itself, without increased tax rates, cannot control an inflationary boom fed by both rising government expenditures and a boom in private investment. The Johnson administration learned this lesson during 1966–1968. Indeed, the sequel to this episode, involving the tax surcharge in 1968, left economists debating the effectiveness of discretionary fiscal policy as a means of controlling an inflationary boom, particularly if it is not supported by a strongly restrictive monetary policy.

Another indication of the increased importance of the federal budget can be found in the emphasis that has come to be placed on the full-employment budgetary surplus or deficit. Although the full-employment budget concept goes back to World War II, it began to provide a guide to policy during the 1960s and continued to be emphasized by the Nixon administration.

---

4 Federal expenditures on goods and services today make up less than half the total budget, the remainder consisting of transfer payments to persons, grants-in-aid to state and local governments, interest payments, and net subsidiaries. Between 1960 and 1972 federal expenditures on goods and services (including defense) increased by a bit over $50 billion, but the other categories of spending (essentially transfers) rose by about $100 billion.

## EVOLUTION OF THE MACROECONOMIC GOALS

As we have seen, even the New Deal in the 1930s had no precise notion of full employment as a goal of macroeconomic policy. The Employment Act did not come until 1946, and even then Congress was careful not to use the term *full employment*.[5]

How much unemployment is consistent with full employment? Neither the Truman nor the Eisenhower administration offered a precise answer to this question. Between 1946 and 1961 official policy seemed tacitly to accept an employment target in the neighborhood of 4 percent, but the target was not made explicit. Actually, a range rather than a single figure seemed to serve as a target—a range from about 4 percent to an upper limit in the neighborhood of 5 percent.

Where in this range successive administrations were prepared to settle depended on two sets of considerations. One was the set of value judgments held by each administration—that is, how much additional unemployment they were prepared to accept in order to achieve a given decline in the rate of increase in prices and vice versa. The other was their conception of the underlying trade-off between inflation and unemployment. How much faster, in fact, would prices rise if unemployment were reduced by, say, 1 percent. And how much of which policy instruments was required to achieve this result?[6]

As we have seen, the employment goal became more explicit—and a higher target was set—in the Kennedy administration than had been the case before. An "interim" target of 4 percent was established, with the hope that eventually a still lower rate could be achieved through manpower and related programs that would reduce the amount of frictional and structural unemployment and improve the employment opportunities available to the less skilled and the underprivileged portions of the labor force. In contrast, during 1959–1960 the Eisenhower administration seemed to be prepared to settle for

[5] The term had been used in the original Full Employment Bill introduced by Senator Murray in 1945. For the legislative history of the Employment Act, see Stephen K. Bailey, *Congress Makes a Law* (New York, Columbia University Press, 1950). See also R. A. Gordon, *The Goal of Full Employment* (New York, Wiley, 1967), pp. 45–49.

[6] The instruments as well as the goals of economic policy entered into these considerations. How much of an increase in government expenditures or a reduction in taxes would be required to achieve a given result, and how much discomfort did the resulting budgetary deficit cause the policy maker? For a fuller discussion of this range of issues as they affected the employment goal in the United States in the first 20 years after the Employment Act, see Gordon, *op. cit.*, pp. 52–55.

an unemployment rate of 5 percent or more, in good part because of the emphasis it placed on price stability and fiscal conservatism.

The New Economics, at least as it was practiced during 1961–1964, also attached considerable importance to the goal of price stability. The differences were that (1) it was not prepared to use the conventional tools of macroeconomic policy to achieve price stability if this meant an unemployment rate significantly above 4 percent and (2) it was prepared to use other tools, even if they might interfere to some extent with the free play of market forces, in order to reconcile the goals of full employment and price stability. The result was the wage-price guideposts.

During 1966–1968, the Johnson administration showed its increasing concern with the accelerating rate of inflation. By 1968, it was quite prepared to see unemployment rise moderately from its then very low level in order to retard significantly the unacceptably high rate of inflation. By then, however (and this was also true under President Nixon), interpretation of the goal of price stability was being relaxed. To halve a 5–6 percent rate of price increase would probably have been considered quite acceptable. Five years later, in 1973, President Nixon's target for "price stability" was set forth as a rate of increase in the Consumer Price Index of 2.5 percent by the end of the year.

Theoretically it was always possible after World War II to achieve a zero rate of increase in the Consumer Price Index. It could have been done by using a highly restrictive monetary and fiscal policy to bring about massive unemployment. This was a cost that no president from Truman to Nixon ever seriously considered—because it was a price that the American people obviously were not willing to pay.

In 1971, with unemployment remaining stubbornly at about 6 percent after the 1970 recession, the Nixon administration seemed to retreat from a strict interpretation of the full-employment goal. One official briefly referred to the 4 percent target as a myth. Members of the Council of Economic Advisers began increasingly to refer to a target in the neighborhood of 4.5 percent (or possibly higher). In the January, 1973 *Economic Report of the President,* the Council judiciously reviewed the evolution of the employment target since the beginning of the 1960s, emphasized that conditions had changed (both with respect to the composition of the labor force and because of the aftereffects of the inflation during 1966–1971), and concluded that it would be preferable to think of the employment and price objectives "not in terms of a single value but as a range of values."[7]

[7] *Economic Report of the President,* January, 1973, p. 72. See all of the accompanying discussion, pp. 71–74.

The unemployment target for the end of 1973 was set at about 4.5 percent. A lower rate might or might not be possible after that, depending on the circumstances—above all, the accompanying rate of inflation. What is important, the Council added, is not any particular number but the achievement of a situation "in which persons who want work and seek it realistically on reasonable terms can find employment."[8] Obviously this definition of full employment is subject to a wide range of interpretations.[9]

In lowering its sights as to what overall unemployment rate corresponded to full employment, the Nixon administration emphasized the changing composition of the labor force. The share of the labor force composed of women and youth had been growing rapidly. Yet unemployment rates for these groups, particularly teenagers, are significantly higher than for adult males. As a result, if the unemployment rates for each age-sex group experienced in the mid-1950s had also prevailed in the early 1970s, the national unemployment rate would have been significantly higher in the later period than in the earlier.[10] To reduce the national rate to 4 percent in the 1970s through an expansive monetary and fiscal policy implied forcing down unemployment rates for adult male workers so low as to exacerbate the upward pressures on wages that were already at work.

All this is to suggest that "structural unemployment," which does not respond readily to an increase in aggregate demand, is more important today than it was 15 or 20 years ago. The trouble is that the *composition* of the supply of labor has changed; at prevailing wage rates there is an oversupply of labor relative to demand in particular age-sex groups. At the end of the 1950s and the beginning of the 1960s, when the unemployment rate remained stubbornly above 5 percent for seven years, there was also a spirited debate regarding the importance of structural unemployment. Then the argument had to do with the composition of the *demand* for labor rather than the supply. It was alleged that automation and the shift toward white-collar

---

8 *Ibid.*, p. 74.

9 Paradoxically, while the Nixon administration abandoned the 4 percent figure with respect to the employment goal, it continued to define the full-employment budget in terms of what the budget would be if the unemployment rate were as low as 4 percent, with the resulting high level of tax receipts. This might be considered a case of having one's cake and eating it too.

10 See *Economic Report of the President,* January, 1972, pp. 113–116. The estimate is made there that if the same age-sex unemployment rates had existed in 1971 as in 1956, the changed composition of the labor force in the intervening years would have raised the national unemployment rate from the 1956 figure of 4.1 percent to 4.5 percent.

occupations requiring more education were moving the demand for labor away from the unskilled and least educated. Subsequent research did not tend to substantiate this argument, and expansion of aggregate demand reduced the national unemployment rate to 4 percent by the end of the 1965.[11]

Increased sensitivity to the higher unemployment rates prevailing among the unskilled and the least educated, among blacks and other minority groups, in urban ghettos, and in depressed rural areas led to a great expansion in manpower training programs in the 1960s and in efforts to improve the placement and counseling activities of the federal-state Employment Service. These efforts had mixed results, and some disillusionment with these programs was apparent in the early 1970s. Paradoxically, while it cited these structural problems as a reason for being willing to settle for a higher unemployment rate as it moved into its second term, the Nixon administration reduced its efforts in the area of manpower and related policies and attempted to shift more of the responsibility to state and local governments.

With respect to the goal of economic growth, it cannot be said that any great change in emphasis has occurred in the last 20 years or so. The goal continues to be recognized and cited, but only to a limited extent have specific measures been aimed at stimulating growth of potential output. Perhaps the greatest advance here occurred during the Kennedy years, when the concepts of potential output and of the "gap" became part of official thinking. As we have already noted, essential to a satisfactory rate of growth is the maintenance of employment at a high level. The goals of full employment and rapid growth are closely related.[12]

We can conclude this section with a few words about balance-of-payments equilibrium. This goal remained essentially unchanged from 1934 to 1971. It was to retain a fixed parity for the dollar in terms of gold, which in turn required avoiding excessive deflcits in the American balance of payments. The situation changed dramatically in 1971, and the United States was forced to devalue the dollar twice in a period of 18 months. In the future as in the past, the United States will seek to maintain approximate equilibrium in its balance of pay-

11 Cf. Gordon, *op. cit., passim.*

12 It was also during the Kennedy administration that the investment tax credit was introduced—a measure that presumably stimulates growth to the extent that it raises the level and rate of growth of investment above what they would otherwise be. At the same time provisions for accelerated depreciation provided a further stimulus to investment. The investment tax credit and accelerated depreciation were also important elements in the Nixon administration's fiscal program in 1971.

ments, but it is hoped that this will be done within a revised international monetary system that will permit more flexible parities, will require countries with persistent balance-of-payments surpluses to revalue their currencies upward, and will substitute some new international means of payment for the dollar.

Indeed, in recent years an increasing number of economists have come to ask: Why fixed parities at all? Why not let currency values, including the value of the dollar, respond continuously to changing demand and supply conditions as they are reflected in each country's balance of payments? The suggestion is enough to make some central bankers shudder, but this hardly seems a good reason for dismissing the proposal out of hand. Canada has had a floating dollar for some time; the British pound was allowed to float beginning in June, 1972; and other countries have allowed their currencies to float for varying periods.

There is one respect in which virtually all countries have changed their attitudes toward balance-of-payments equilibrium as a macroeconomic goal since the 1930s. Today no government is prepared to accept massive unemployment in order to protect its balance of payments at a fixed external value for its currency. This is in contrast to, for example, the behavior of the Federal Reserve authorities in 1931, when they tightened credit to stop an outflow of gold in the face of massive unemployment. In 1971 the Nixon administration was not willing to undertake a deflationary monetary and fiscal policy at home, in the face of an unemployment rate as high as 6 percent, in order to maintain the external value of the dollar.

## THE INSTRUMENTS OF POLICY

### Fiscal Policy

After the 1930s, in good part as a result of the Keynesian revolution, fiscal policy took on new importance as the United States and other countries sought to maintain a high and stable level of employment. After World War II it was taken for granted that no attempt should be made to balance the federal budget during recessions. Instead the automatic stabilizers should be allowed to have their full effect.

Nonetheless, the United States was relatively slow to adopt an active *discretionary* fiscal policy to cope with either economic downswings or inflationary booms. The timing of the tax reductions that helped ameliorate the recessions in 1948–1949 and 1953–1954 was largely accidental.[13] Until the 1960s fiscal stimulus in recessions was

13 See pp. 106 and 135.

largely confined to reliance on the automatic stabilizers and some acceleration of spending under already existing programs. And with respect to controlling an inflationary boom, as in the mid-1950s, primary reliance was placed on monetary policy (once the Federal Reserve System regained its independence).

As we saw in Chapter 6, discretionary fiscal policy began to play a much more important role in the 1960s. New emphasis was placed on tax reductions as the most important way of stimulating the economy. Thus between 1962 and 1965 the economy received a succession of stimuli from the investment tax credit and accelerated depreciation, the widely heralded reduction in personal and corporate income taxes in 1964–1965, and a reduction in excise taxes. At the same time the full-employment budget was officially adopted as a guide to policy.

The accelerating inflation after 1965 pointed up some of the weaknesses in fiscal policy, at least as it was being practiced in the American setting. Under the American Constitution only Congress can change taxes. Inevitably, therefore, there are delays before tax rates can be altered, either upward or downward. The delay in obtaining the tax increase in 1968 is a good example. Fiscal restraint would almost certainly have been more effective if the surcharge had gone into effect in mid-1966 instead of mid-1968.

An equally, perhaps more important lesson is that fiscal policy must have the strong support of monetary policy. Along with the delay in getting the tax increase after 1965, the worst blunder of American stabilization policy in the 1960s occurred when the Federal Reserve took its foot off the brakes in the second half of 1968 after the surcharge went into effect. In 1969 a combination of restrictive fiscal and monetary policies brought the boom to an end, although it did not succeed in reducing inflation to an acceptable rate.

This brings us to another limitation of fiscal and monetary policy. They operate on the level of aggregate demand, on total spending on goods and services. To control inflation fiscal restraint seeks to reduce aggregate demand relative to aggregate supply. For this to have an effect on the rate of increase in prices, the inflation must be of the demand-pull type. If, as in 1970–1971, the economy is suffering from a cost-push inflation, neither fiscal nor monetary policy can do the job—at least not without so restricting demand as to bring about a completely unacceptable increase in unemployment.

We may have learned one other lesson from the failure of the 1968 tax surcharge to restrain the rise in spending any more than it apparently did. The rationale underlying the use of discretionary fiscal policy rests on the existence of stable spending functions for the different types of consumption and investment in a Keynesian type of economic model. In particular, for fiscal policy to be effective there needs to be a stable, predictable response of consumer spending to a change in disposable income in the short run. The behavior of both consumer spending (particularly for automobiles) and business investment in 1968 surprised the experts both in and out of government.[14]

As we saw in Chapter 6, an expansionary fiscal policy did not at first play a significant role in the Nixon administration's program to cope with the high unemployment that resulted from the 1970 recession. But fiscal stimuli were an important part of the New Economic Policy announced in 1971. In addition, the President's statements and the reports of the Council of Economic Advisers placed increasing stress on the full-employment budget. In 1973, as the economy expanded rapidly, this emphasis took the form of insisting that the rise in federal spending be restrained so that, with increasing tax revenues as the economy continued to expand, the full-employment budget could be brought back into balance after the deficit experienced in 1972.

A new emphasis on fiscal policy was suggested in the January, 1973 *Economic Report of the President*. There the Council of Economic Advisers asked "whether the future conduct of fiscal policy could be improved if Congress were to develop expeditious procedures for temporary, limited changes in the level of particular taxes." It added that "experience has shown that the proper conduct of macroeconomic policy may sometimes call for a prompt and effective shift in the overall balance between the flow of Federal receipts and expenditures. Temporary and prompt changes in tax rates, which do not alter the basic structure of taxes, may provide an efficient way of accomplishing such required shifts."[15] It remained to be seen whether Congress would be any more sympathetic to this suggestion than to similar ones made by Presidents Kennedy and Johnson.[16] But obviously discretionary fiscal policy had come a long way from Eisenhower to Nixon.

## Monetary Policy

Let us look back now at the development of monetary policy. As we have seen, the Federal Reserve System regained its independence from the Treasury in the Accord of 1951. It was at about the same time

---

[14] See pp. 167–168.

[15] *Economic Report of the President,* January, 1973, pp. 75–76.

[16] In the *Economic Report of the President,* January, 1962, pp. 17–19, and January, 1965, p. 11.

that the role of money received new emphasis in macroeconomic analysis.[17] Moreover, during the next 20 years the influence of the "monetarists" under the leadership of Milton Friedman steadily increased. The debate between the monetarists and the Keynesians from the mid-fifties on was not about whether "money matters" but about whether "*only* money matters."

From the end of the Korean War through the remainder of the 1950s, the Fed used the conventional instruments of monetary policy in a contracyclical manner, to "lean against the wind" even if this sometimes meant helping to bring on a recession when unemployment was still uncomfortably high. During the first half of the 1960s, as fiscal policy moved to the forefront, monetary policy was accommodative but remained in the background. As fiscal policy demonstrated its inability to cope with mounting inflationary pressures after 1965, restrictive monetary policy had to step into the breach, notably in 1966 and 1969. In 1970 and the first half of 1971, the Nixon administration relied heavily on monetary policy to speed recovery. It was then that the growing influence of the monetarists experienced something of a setback. Extremely tight credit and a virtual halt in the increase in the money supply did not noticeably retard the rise in prices in 1969. Monetary ease in 1970–1971 did not promptly bring about rapid economic recovery.[18] If expansionary monetary policy was effective, it seemed to be so only with a distressingly long lag.

Monetary policy has both advantages and disadvantages compared to fiscal policy. The "inside lag" is much shorter. That is, the lag in getting something done is much briefer than it is in the case of discretionary fiscal policy. Once the need for action is recognized, very prompt action can follow in the form of open-market operations or changes in the discount rate or in reserve requirements.

But monetary policy also operates under some serious disadvantages. First of all, it is not clear what the *immediate* target of monetary policy should be. Open-market purchases or sales or changes in the discount rate do not immediately and in a perfectly predictable way affect the supply of money. The first effects are on interest rates and bank reserves. Effects on the money supply follow, with a variable

17 In a volume published in 1951, Howard Ellis aptly entitled his paper "The Rediscovery of Money." See *Money, Trade, and Economic Growth: In Honor of John Henry Williams* (New York, Macmillan, 1951).

18 Paradoxically, the pace of recovery accelerated after the third quarter of 1971, in the face of a marked decline in the rate of increase in the money supply in the second half of the year.

lag and with not altogether predictable results, at least in the short run. And the question still remains open, at least among all but the most confirmed monetarists: Through what channels and with what lags do changes in the money supply affect spending, prices, and output?

The Federal Reserve System has gone through considerable soul searching in recent years as it has sought appropriate proximate targets to guide it. The ultimate targets are the same macroeconomic goals that guide fiscal policy. But to achieve these goals should it seek first to influence bank reserves, short-term interest rates, or what? Traditionally the Federal Open Market Committee has emphasized indicators of ease or tightness in the money market—for example, very short-term interest rates and the level of free reserves of member banks. In recent years more attention has been paid to the monetary aggregates—both the money stock and some variant of bank reserves. As we noted in Chapter 6 (page 175), in 1970 the Fed began to pay more attention to changes in the stock of money. More recently it has been particularly responsive to one variant of bank reserves—reserves against private nonbank deposits (RPDs).

But the troublesome questions here still remain unsettled. On what intermediate targets should the monetary authorities concentrate, and through what channels and with what lags do changes in these intermediate target variables affect the ultimate target variables of employment, the rate of change in prices, and the balance of payments? The monetary authorities in this and other countries are still searching for the answers.[19]

## Other Policy Instruments

Is there any reason why we should pursue our macroeconomic goals with the help of only the conventional instruments of monetary and fiscal policy? The argument for doing so is that this involves the minimum interference with "the free play of market forces." But is that always and necessarily an advantage, particularly in a world of highly imperfect competition in both commodity and labor markets?

We have chosen to interfere with the free play of market forces in a wide range of microeconomic areas—agriculture, the environment, minimum-wage laws, industrial safety, social security, education, medi-

---

[19] For an evaluation of the evolution of Federal Reserve policy and suggestions for improvement, see G. L. Bach, *Making Monetary and Fiscal Policy* (Washington, D.C., Brookings, 1971). It is also illuminating to read the minutes of the Federal Open Market Committee in recent issues of the *Federal Reserve Bulletin*.

cal care, and so on. Why not in the field of macroeconomic policy if doing so will bring us closer to our policy targets?

Merely to ask this question is enough to make many readers bristle. But we have already made a start in this direction. Might it not be wise to take stock before emergencies arise and to prepare in advance a battery of possibly useful tools that can be put to work as needed?

During the 1960s and early 1970s, the federal government intervened extensively in this country's economic relations with the rest of the world in an effort to reduce the balance-of-payments deficit.[20] In the early and mid-sixties, the guideposts sought to influence wage and price behavior; in 1971–1972 we had a comprehensive system of wage and price controls. During the Korean war (as well as World War II), consumer credit controls restricted expenditures on automobiles and other consumer durable goods. Might it have been desirable to have had such controls available in 1968 or 1973, when a spurt in spending on automobiles added to inflationary pressures? It might be remembered also that the investment tax credit and accelerated depreciation, though they are instruments of fiscal policy, operate to affect particular types of decisions by businessmen—just as consumer credit controls are an instrument of monetary policy that affect particular spending decisions by consumers. Other fiscal and monetary instruments can be used to influence particular types of spending decisions.

There are indeed a wide variety of direct and indirect controls that have been used by various countries at different times.[21] For the most part such controls were used early in the postwar period, but some are in use in different countries today. Incomes policies to influence wage and price behavior have been resorted to repeatedly by one country or another during the postwar years, increasingly as the inflationary threat became more serious. Should we have a permanent incomes policy that can be eased or tightened as conditions seem to warrant?

It would go far beyond the intended scope of this historical survey to propose an arsenal of policy instruments that might aid us in achieving our macroeconomic goals, even if they did interfere with the way our imperfect market system normally operates. But perhaps enough has been said to raise some questions in the reader's mind and to stimulate him to look for answers. This is a search which needs to begin, as should consideration of all questions regarding government policy, with explicit recognition of one's own value judgments—one's social-welfare function—which determine how much of one desirable

---

[20] See p. 184.
[21] Cf. E. S. Kirschen *et al., Economic Policy in Our Time,* vol. I (Skokie, Ill., Rand McNally, 1964), especially chap. 5.

objective one is prepared to sacrifice in order to obtain a bit more of another, given the policy instruments to be used.

## A FINAL COMMENT

The two major goals of macroeconomic policy to most Americans remain what they have been through the last generation: a high level of employment and a reasonable degree of price stability. We attach greater importance to price stability than do the citizens of most other advanced countries, as is suggested by the higher rates of inflation these other countries have experienced through most of the postwar period.[22] Balance-of-payments equilibrium at a fixed value of the dollar in terms of gold is more of a constraint than a positive goal, a constraint that we are prepared to modify if it requires too much sacrifice of the goal of high employment. This proved to be the case in 1971 and 1973.

It is probably not too rash to predict that during the rest of the 1970s inflation will continue to be more of a threat than it was from 1953 to 1965—the interval between Korea and Vietnam. How shall we cope with this problem, and what sort of trade-off shall we seek between our conflicting goals of full employment and price stability? The answer lies in the future. Of one thing, however, we can be reasonably certain: This dilemma will not go away. The functioning of the economy will not suddenly change of its own accord so that we can have full employment and price stability at the same time without some form of government intervention.

A major question for the future is how we shall interpret the goal of full employment. Even in 1969, with an overall unemployment rate as low as 3.5 percent, the unemployment rate for blacks was 6.4 percent; for teenagers it was 12.2 percent; for black teenagers, it was over 20 percent. In the urban ghettos the rates for minority groups, particularly minority youth, were even higher than these figures suggest. Early in 1973, with the national unemployment rate at about 5 percent, the unemployment rates for the groups mentioned were, of course, significantly higher than they were in 1969.[23]

All this suggests that the time has come to redefine the goal of full employment—to express this goal in *structural* as well as aggregative terms. Is it enough (again, given our value judgments) to settle for a

[22] Germany has traditionally placed a high priority on price stability, but its attachment to this goal seems to have weakened in the last few years.

[23] In the last three months of 1972, the unemployment rate for black teenagers was no less than 36 percent, or nearly seven times the national unemployment rate of 5.3 percent. See *Employment and Earnings* (January, 1973): 157–158.

national unemployment rate of 4 or 4.5 percent if this means unemployment rates of 8 or 9 percent for blacks, 12 to 15 percent for teenagers, and 25 percent or more for black teenagers? To ask the question in this way is to suggest the answer.

Redefining the full-employment goal in structural terms calls for approximate employment targets for specific sectors of the labor force when classified by age, sex, and color (and perhaps other dimensions as well).[24] And to achieve these specific targets requires a much enlarged and improved set of governmental manpower programs, including inducements for private employers to hire and train the disadvantaged, and a program of public-service employment in which the government would be authorized to serve as the employer of last resort. These are controversial suggestions, and they do not represent the direction in which the federal government is now moving.

We shall continue to seek balance-of-payments equilibrium, but the conditions under which we pursue this goal are likely to change as a new system of international monetary relations gradually evolves. More flexible parities and some substitute for the dollar as the primary international means of payment will almost certainly be elements of that new monetary system. It is to be hoped that the American government can reach an agreement with other nations on presently debated issues of international financial and trading relationships without resorting to retaliatory trade restrictions in the form of higher tariffs and wider use of import quotas.

In the middle and late 1960s, a question frequently asked was: Is the business cycle obsolete? One does not hear the question asked any more. The business cycle is still with us, particularly in the United States, although in other countries business recessions since the 1950s have taken the form chiefly of temporary retardations in the rate of growth of total output rather than absolute declines. Such retardations in growth, however, can still mean periods of rising unemployment, falling profits, and other symptoms that we associate with business recessions.

And the problem of inflation is still very much with us—apparently increasingly so. The rate of change in prices and the level of unemployment are, from a policy (and welfare) point of view, our two most important measures of economic instability. The economy continues to grow—the trend in potential output is steadily upward—but economic instability remains a major problem that we have not yet solved.

24 Cf. Gordon, *op. cit.*, chap. 7.

# Index of Authors

# Index of Subjects